# THE HIDDEN PATHWAYS
## OF
# GERMANIC MYTHOLOGY

On the Neglected, Demonized, Repulsed, and
Repressed Archetypical Representations
of Original Germanic Culture

By
PAUL WASSMANN

CHIRON PUBLICATIONS • ASHEVILLE, NORTH CAROLINA

www.ChironPublications.com

Interior and cover design by Danijela Mijailovic
Printed primarily in the United States of America

ISBN 978-1-63051-712-0 paperback
ISBN 978-1-63051-713-7 hardcover
ISBN 978-1-63051-714-4 electronic
ISBN 978-1-63051-715-1 limited edition paperback

Library of Congress Cataloging-in-Publication Data
Names: Wassmann, P. (Paul), author.
Title: The hidden pathways of Germanic mythology : on the neglected, demonized, repulsed and repressed archetypical representations of original Germanic culture / by Paul Wassmann.
Description: Asheville, N.C. : Chiron Publications, [2019] | Includes bibliographical references and index. | Summary: "In the context of the Indo-European cultures, this book offers an overview of the hidden pathways of Germanic Mythology, focusing upon the Germanic Word View, the creation of the world, the Dawn of Gods and the psychological role of some of the most significant gods and goddesses"— Provided by publisher.
Identifiers: LCCN 2019020294 | ISBN 9781630517137 (hardcover) | ISBN 9781630517120 (paperback) | ISBN 9781630517151 (limited edition paperback) | ISBN 9781630517144 (electronic)
Subjects: LCSH: Mythology, Germanic. | Germanic peoples—Folklore. | Civilization, Germanic.
Classification: LCC BL860 .W37 2019 | DDC 293/.13—dc23
LC record available at https://lccn.loc.gov/2019020294

The cover shows *Vinternatt i Rondane* (*Winternight in the Mountains*) by Harald Sohlberg (1869-1935; National Gallery of Norway, Oslo). Copyright: National Gallery of Norway, Oslo.

Dedicated to Rigmor

# Table of Contents

Nøkken (neck) by Theodor Kittelsen (1857-1914; National Gallery of Norway, Oslo). Germanic religion and mythology comprise complex beliefs about the gods and the nature of the cosmos. One of the shape-shifting water spirits that was observed in wild, isolated nature is the neck (or nicor, nixie or nokken). During the mysterious dusk of the Nordic summer night when the fixed borders between reality, imagination and hallucination are whisked out, a neck scarcely lift himself from the profundity. Hardly breaking the surface, the neck with fluorescent eyes embodies how unconscious knowledge from the watery depth of our soul surfaces and infiltrates our open, light and airy consciousness. The suspicious, swelling and gentle surfacing represents challenges and vulnerabilities that may bring us out of our comfort zone. Each permeation, soft as it may be, produces ever widening circles that propagate throughout our psyche. Copyright: National Gallery of Norway, Oslo.

# Preface

*In the mythus a superhuman intelligence uses the unconscious thoughts and dreams of men as its hieroglyphics to address men unborn. In the history of the human mind, these glowing and ruddy fables precede the noonday thoughts of men, as Aurora the sun's rays.*

H. D. Thoureau

*In a Europe which leaves the old nationalism behind the old legends of Arthus, Siegfried or Charlemagne could become symbols of a history that all people share.*

E. Jacobsen

This book addresses a dangerous shortcoming in European culture and education: the ostracizing of major sectors of its mainstream mythologem background. A mythologem signifies an original pattern, fundamental, basic, recurrent theme or motif. The mythologemes are the basic stories that have the archetype at the "core"[1]. The archetypes are constant "parts of the world" in the unconscious and they are not individually acquired but exist a priori and are included in the structure of the psyche. Following mainly the work of Carl Gustav Jung (1874-1961)[2], but also Mircea Eliade[3] (1907-1986) and Joseph Campbell[4]

---

[1] https://de.wikipedia.org/wiki/Mythologem.
[2] Also called analytical psychology, it is a school of psychotherapy. It emphasizes the importance of the individual psyche and the personal quest for wholeness. Important concepts

(1904-1987), the term archetype means here a collectively inherited unconscious idea, pattern of thought, image, etc., that is universally present in the psyche of individuals and ethnic or cultural groups. There exists an evolutionary line of archetype inheritance that reaches from the archetypes over the mythologems to mythology and present-day culture. One may speculate to find the original mythology of today's Indo-European people when their various groups dominated, the mythologemes with the proto Indo-Europeans and the original archetypes back in Africa, prior to the emigration during the middle of the last Ice Age (see 2.2). At the bottom of all humans rests the base of humanity that we inherited in Africa.

In Europe (and other continents that are impacted by European immigration), we frequently face a restrictive, traditional focus upon Greek, Roman, and Christian culture, mythology, and humanistic education ideals. These guiding ideals exclude—culturally speaking—the bulk of European archetypal heritage, which only to a limited degree is based upon Greek and Roman culture (see chapter 1). The lack of adequate, all-inclusive cultural and archetypical caretaking in Europe supports incongruence between the potential and realized cultural niches. As we will see (chapter 9), this paves the ground for a range of cultural and political complications. During periods when subdued and bayed-up cultural energies accumulate in archetypical riverbeds that are concealed by the dominating cultural vegetation (see chapter 10), the lacking congruence results in unrest and even tragedy.

In order to address its generic goal, the book uses one of the most strongly suppressed European mythologies, the Germanic one, as the example to illustrate Europe's vital challenge. Every person wishes to be seen and valued for what he/she is and can contribute. Thus we have to develop an interest for all groups, cultures, and nations that surround

---

in Jung's system are individuation, symbols, the personal unconscious, the collective unconscious, archetypes, complexes, the persona, the id, ego, and super-ego, the shadow, the anima and animus, and the self. Analytical psychology is distinct from psychoanalysis, which is a psychotherapeutic system created by Sigmund Freud. For a recent overview, see Papadopoulos, R.K. (2012).

[3] Eliade, M. (1957); Eliade, M. (1961); Eliade, M. (1968); Eliade, M. (1963).

[4] Campbell, J. (1949); Campbell, J. (1974); Campbell, J. (1988).

us, irrespective of the opinion and attitude of mainstream culture. The book shows that numerous historic challenges derive from the ignorance and rejection of the culture of the alleged uncivilized and barbarians (e.g., chapter 7). What the world needs the most is a road map to peace that, based upon understanding and tolerance, includes all of humanity, including the plethora of inadequately respected mythologies (see chapter 10). This road can only be trodden through an all-including attitude where the archetypical culture of the entire world is opened up for and addressed.

The book elucidates the consequences of neglect, demonization, repulsion, and repression of archetypal representations of one sector of the European civilization, the original Germanic culture. The author is neither a specialist in Germanic mythology nor anthropology, religious science, or psychology, but a natural scientist (marine ecology). It is thus a mythology amateur (French amateur = lover of) that steps forward to illuminate the subdued significance of Germanic mythology. A few lines seem required to illustrate the author's qualifications to deal with the subject.

Born in the early 1950s in the Ruhr region (Federal Republic of Germany), the largest heavy-industry region of Europe, the author was exposed to an environment that was a far cry from wild nature. He was raised in the northern regions of the town Essen, characterized by coal mines, coke plants, and factories. Miners and heavy-industry workers dominated his childhood. In those days the environmental stress upon a population of basically nonprosperous immigrants from all over Germany and Poland was considerable. It is told that Kaiser Wilhelm II strictly opposed the foundation of a university in the Ruhr region, the reason being that this was a region where "proles" should work and not deal with culture. During the times of the author's upbringing the residents of the Ruhr region held some of the lowest cultural ranks in the Federal Republic of Germany. The probability to experience Germanic gods roaming through wild nature was inconceivable.

For many reasons, the author left for northern Norway, where he has been living for more than 40 years. He resides and works 600 kilometers north of the Arctic Circle in a boreal climate (supporting agriculture and one of the world's most important fisheries), but Arctic light conditions (over the course of the year the sun is two months above and below the horizon). Only 0.05 percent of the human population resides in the Arctic region. They do not live within the technical virtuality that characterizes big towns. Storms, snow, and avalanches can isolate in winter. Electricity may disappear. Delays in transportation for hours (or days) happen, but despite all challenges, life is characterized by surprising regularity and flexibility. Life can, though, be demanding when somebody needs acute medical treatment in hospitals and the weather is not on the side of the patient. In the very north of Europe, inhabitants are thus much less inclined to the most common psychological disorder of our times: technological hubris (here an extreme or dangerous overconfidence that brings downfall). And thus, people in the very north are closer to the power of nature, which the technology of big towns seduces us to forget. In the northern outskirts of Europe, a far more realistic attitude to nature prospers: People know and experience that nature is powerful and dominating men's existence. In more central sections of Europe this attitude - base for a sustainable development - is suppressed by technology hubris.

The Norwegian term *natur* means basically untouched nature, wilderness. And breathtaking, forceful, and at times dangerous, nature is indeed part of daily life in the High North. Germanic mythology is a nature religion, in which the natural world is an embodiment of divinity, sacredness. or spiritual power[5]. Nature is a significant element in Norwegian views on culture, and this has long traditions in Norse texts, such as the Edda[6]. The particular attitude to nature in the north helps locals to come closer to the original mythology that history, technological hubris, and culture arrogance has made us forget. Scandinavia is far from Rome: The original Germanic civilization survived parallel to and under the surface of Christian culture.

The author has a background in biodynamic agriculture[7]. Combined with northern Norway's powerful nature, the author takes note of the

---

[5] Wolfram, H. (1995); Maier, B. (2003); Nemenyi, G.v. (2004); Pötzl, N.F. & Saltzwedel, J. (2013).
[6] Witoszek, N. (1998).
[7] Initially developed in the 1920s, it was the first of the organic agriculture movements,

genius loci (spirit of a place). The reality of his daily life in the High North—in the middle of high-tech science—brings the author closer to nature (and Germanic mythology) than his original heavy-industry home in central Europe. Further, parts of the northern Norwegian population are Sami, indigenous Finno-Ugric people inhabiting the Arctic area of Sápmi[8]. Before Christianization in the early 19th century, the Sami had a polytheistic religion based upon shamanism. Combined with a strong atavistic Norse tradition, their attitudes, beliefs, and practices have an influence upon the residents of Europe's High North. Northerners visit their excellent physicians when they get sick, but when relatives and friends turn ill, they also involve faith healers. This practice is difficult to explain, but it is a form of "Christian shamanism." Healers include people's suffering into their prayers, and one may even find faith healers associated with hospitals. The shamanistic tradition, which the Europeans inherited when their forefathers moved from central Asia into Europe (see 2.2), is also reflected in atavistic capacities such as the common ability to stop bleeding (through "white" incantation)[9]. Shamanistic elements are thus still part of the background of the commons in the High North. And thus, nature religion such as the Norse mythology in which shamanism plays a vital role, is more easily accessible in the north than in central Europe.

The author got his father's childhood copy of Germanic heroic stories (*Germanische Götter und Heldensagen*) when he was young[10]. He got his own copy in a less völkisch language when he was 13 years old[11]. At age 14, the author met the charismatic Norwegian Dan Lindholm, author of one of the best German prose version of the Edda[12]. At 19 years old, he bought a copy of the poetic Edda (see 3.3). During his first sojourn in Norway, he bought a copy of Snorri Sturluson's famous book

---

treating soil fertility, plant growth, and livestock care as ecologically interrelated tasks, emphasizing spiritual perspectives.

[8] Today encompassing parts of far northern Norway, Sweden, Finland and the Kola Peninsula of Russia.

[9] e.g. Tjelle, I. (2015).

[10] Weitbrecht, R. (no year).

[11] Eigel, K. (1953).

[12] Lindholm, D. (1965).

*Kongesagaer*[13]. During a visit to the C.G. Jung Institute in Küsnacht, Switzerland, in 1983, the author read *Germanische Mythologie, zwischen Verdrängung und Verfälschung* by M. Burri[14]. It opened the author's eyes not only to the neglect, demonization, repulsion, and repression of archetypal representations, but also to the forgery of an important segment of European culture: the original culture of the Germanic people (see 7.4). Later the author was also strongly influenced by *The well of remembrance*[15] by R. Metzner, *Jung's Wandering Archetype*[16] by C,B. Dohe, *Iron Age Myth and Materiality*[17] by L. Heddeager, *The Tree of Salvation*[18] by G. Ronald Murphy, and *Norse Revival*[19] by S. von Schnurbein. Gradually, an entire plethora of books dealing with Norse and Germanic mythology accumulated and incited the mythology amateur behind this book[20].

The author's qualifications are thus based upon a.) the archaic world and powerful nature of northern Norway and the Arctic, b.) a connection to shamanistic tradition that is essential to the original Germanic culture, c.) a lifelong interest in Germanic mythology, d) frequent lectures at the C.G. Jung Institute in Küsnacht, and e) a thorough interest in psychodynamic tradition. Finally, the author wishes to mention that remnants of personal Germanic culture woke up after he, over the years abroad, started to clean the Augean stables of German history, supported by the peace of distant Norway. This effort lifted the generic curse that recent heritage imposes upon sections of German culture.

To be a specialist often implies not only exact knowledge, but also taking care about details, testing hypotheses, and to trouble the intellect

[13] Sturlason, S. (1970).
[14] Burri, M. (1982).
[15] Metzner, R. (1994).
[16] Dohe, C.B. (2016).
[17] Hedeager, L. (2011).
[18] Murphy, G.R. (2013).
[19] Schnurbein, S. v. (2018).
[20] Davidson, H.R.E. (1964); Egerkrans, J. (2016); Engelmann, E. (1889); Golther, W. (1895); Engelmann, E. (1895); Enoksen, L.M. (2008); Gimbutas, M. (1982); Hasenfratz, H.-P. (1992); Hedeager, L. (2011); Herrmann, P. (1898); Herrmann, P. (1903); Jacoby, E. (2011); Nemenyi, G.v. (2003); New Larousse Encyclopedia of Mythology (1959); Simek, R. (1998); Simek, R. (2004); Simek, R. (2006); Steinsland, G. (2005); Wagner, W. (1901).

with a multitude of objections. This frequently results in nonspecialist readers losing both overview and attentiveness. The love for exactness and precision supports often tribal language that prevents reaching out to interested but nonacademic circles. Few scientists are blessed with the capacity of conceptualization and synthetization; even fewer enjoy the support of a genuine language that reaches the common peoples. To reach out in manners not easily provided to the average specialist, amateurs can apply more freedom, beyond the demands for details and the practice of tribal language. The obvious challenges for the amateur are lack of depth and precision or even misunderstanding. In order to bring together widespread material into a new context, the author has applied a lot of literature and used the web vigorously. The book enters a terra incognita by combining renowned literature (such as on Germanic mythology) and information from widely different fields (such as analytical psychology). References are provided throughout the book, but to ease readability, citations are listed as numbered notes. The applied literature is listed at the end of the book.

Writing is an act of discourse power, endowed with the privilege of interpretation and attribution. Like every author, this privilege of discourse power was applied. But if the Germanic tribes and their impact upon European culture are viewed as a blessing or a curse is a dilemma that cannot be resolved once and for all. However, the author is convinced about John 8:32: "Then you will know the truth, and the truth will set you free." Raising suppressed material from the unconscious and enhancing the consciousness regarding the original cultures of mainstream Europe can result in healing, psychic growth, increased freedom, and autonomy. Each window of the soul that is opened provides the existence with a new frame. Framing is an underevaluated, coordinating activity for human development. It is a precondition for understanding, because without it we lose ourselves in the expanse of continuous reality. Inside each mental frame we detect reality and understand connections and constructs. The more frames that are applied and windows opened, the more enhanced wholeness can be achieved, which is the ultimate goal of the present book.

Needless to say, the author is responsible of any mistake that may have occurred.

# Acknowledgements

The first person who connected me in earnest to my Germanic heritage was my charismatic teacher Robert Zimmer. His facilitation of the comedic poem *Þrymskviða* (*How Thor Got Back His Hammer*) in alliterative verses for children and the introduction to his friend Dan Lindholm[21] paved the road for my first and influential contact with Germanic mythology. On the background of the ethnic mix and powerful nature of the remote fjord Gullesfjorden in Troms county, my father-in-law, Rolf Moelv, introduced me with significant empathy and enthusiasm to the lore of supernatural features and hair-raising accounts of northern Norway. Through him I got some of the supernatural background of northern Norway under my skin.

Feeding the soul and opening unknown doors and windows are part of the delightful strategy of the C.G. Jung Institute (www.junginstitut.ch/english/) and ISAPZURICH (www.isapzurich.com/). Practically every year since 1983, I listened to some lectures at the C.G. Jung Institute. They turned into a veritable source of inspiration. Thanks go to Monika Steinmann Dubs for recommending me to get invited to teach Germanic mythology in Zürich. These lectures and the Ergriffenheit[22] they created turned into the direct cause for writing this book. The local base for my Zürich visits was the home of my close friend Mathias Zopfi and his

---

[21] Lindholm, D. (1965).
[22] Dohe, C.B. (2011); See also an exhibition of paintings illustrating the term (https://www.kunstmuseumluzern.ch/en/exhibitions/ergriffenheit-works-from-the-collection-from-hodler-to-henning/).

family. Their marvelous and all-embracing hospitality turned into indispensable support for my journey through Jung's universe. Conversations with the composer Lasse Thoresen opened new perspectives of the role Germanic mythology had in Norway. The author thanks Ørjan Garfjell and in particular Rudi Caeyers for support and design of some of the figures.

My sincere appreciation to Chiron Publications and their team: Rob Mikulak for his copy editing and Danijela Mijailovic for her design of the interior and cover.

In Norse mythology, a fylgja is a female spirit that accompanies a person in connection with its fate and fortune, similar to the Christian guardian angel that is assigned to protect and guide our lives. All the way from childhood into adulthood, I had a vivid connection to this inner female entity. She not only accompanies me. With somnambulistic confidence, I was able to select decisive directions at the crossroads of life thanks to the fylgja.

The original Germanic mythology is a nature religion. The experience of a powerful nature, the proximity of wilderness, the multiethnic setting and the notion of an archaic spirituality enabled me to investigate Germanic mythology through the base of my district home and the northernmost university of the world (UiT—The Arctic University of Norway[23]). Without the distance to my home country of Germany and the solid base in the High North, this book would not have become a reality.

Over a span of more than 50 years, Rigmor Moelv has been my partner and fellow combatant in cultural matters. Without her introduction to and company through northern Norway, her vivid engagement inside the psychodynamic tradition and her patience to endure the struggle of elaborating and developing constructs and face unanswerable questions regarding our joint Germanic backgrounds, this book would not have seen the day of light. Under the impact of guilt and a feeling of responsibility for the sins of the fathers the pale light of

---

[23] https://en.uit.no/startsida.

collective Germanic remembrance at the horizon of memory seemingly disappeared for the generations of post-World War II Germany. Rigmor helped understand and remove the undeserved curse and heavy burden that recent German history had placed upon the author's shoulders. I thank her for a veritable fascinating, challenging, and inspiring companionship that made me find the roots that had been obscured by my ancestors' faults, the maltreatment of time and the suppression, demonization and repression by a cultural elite. With utmost pleasure and strong commitment this book is dedicated to Rigmor Moelv.

Tromsø
20 May 2019

*Natteglød* (*Evening Glow*) by Harald Sohlberg (1869-1935; National Gallery of Norway, Oslo). The sun of the golden age, the holy time of the beginning, radiates into the present from far behind the horizon of our memory. We experience the intensity of the dusk time and we have to imagine the sunshine of the Great Time, the source of our mythology and mythologems. Copyright: National Gallery of Norway, Oslo.

# 1. Prologue

*Whether we listen with aloof amusement to the dreamlike mumbo jumbo of some red-eyed witch doctor of the Congo, or read with cultivated rapture thin translations from the sonnets of the mystic Lao-tse; now and again crack the hard nutshell of an argument of Aquinas, or catch suddenly the shining meaning of a bizarre Eskimo fairy tale, it will be always the one, shape-shifting yet marvellously constant story that we find.*

J. Campbell

*The most effective way to destroy people is to deny and obliterate their own understanding of their history.*

G. Orwell

At the horizon of our memory, where the contours of history get wiped out, we find the world of myths and mythologems. The longer we move inward into the misty expanse of human memory, phantasmal perceptions and shadows surge back and forth and dissolve more and more into the mists that conceal our primordial experience. Images come into being and disperse along the eternal course of memories from man's very beginning. The myths tell us stories of times when no distinction existed between gods and humans and both wandered side-by-side through a co-inhabited world. The sun of the "timeless" golden age sank into the sea of time, and all we do now is to sense the afterglow[24]. With grief and yearning we may direct our gaze toward the dwindling glimmer

---

[24] Stockland, O. (1969).

21

of a happy time, while we may shiver in the cold winds of our here and now. At the end of the 19th century, Nietzsche stated, "God is dead,"[25] called for the "re-evaluation of all values" and announced the necessity of the godless "Übermensch." The golden age has definitely come to an end. We live our individual lives alone and without the continual presence of gods.

More than a century after Nietzsche, we still try to exist as Über-menschen: autonomous, responsible individuals, independent from god and the rules of a divine world. We live now in linear times while the myths of earlier days enjoy the endless expanse of circular time. We placed ourselves into the center of the universe and are content with our own company, but the bleak memory of humanity's sun-drenched childhood paradise continues to comprise a significant, but partly ignored component to sustain our psychic and mental health. Memorizing the stories and visions that the myths project into our present-day concrete and linear reality requires attention. Every now and then, our mental and psychological health depends upon sips from the well of re-membrance, the collective unconsciousness that is available to all humankind[26], as reflected by our personal and collective childhood.

As a collection of explanatory stories, mythology and mythologems are vital features of every culture. Today the myth has again become a fundamental frame of reference for Western thinking[27]. There are different ways to define the myth. Mythology—from Greek mythos (myth) and logia (study)—refers to the myths of a group of people (such as an ethnic group or a nation) and the collection of stories to explain surrounding nature, history and customs. Many sources for myths have been proposed, ranging from personification of nature and natural phenomena, accounts of possible historical events, and explanations of rituals[28]. Mythologizing is not just an occasional, isolated, ancient, or primitive practice but is perpetually present. The Romanian historian of religion and philosopher M. Eliade observed that for people to have meaningful lives, their life cycle must be placed into a narrative, a story, a

---

[25] Nietzsche, F. (1882).
[26] Metzner, R. (1994).
[27] Frog (2018).
[28] Frazer, J.G. (1922).

myth. Contemporary literature, legends, and the immensely increased popularity of fantasy novels and comics exemplify this. In our times dominated by believes in natural sciences, technology, statistical evidence, and rationality, there unmistakably exists an urgent need for "fantasy," probably reflecting a need to attach to our long-forgotten mythology background. A culture's collective mythology helps to express belonging and shared religious experiences. It encapsulates behavioral models and moral and practical lessons[29]. The myth is thus a fundamentally modern term that we define according to interests and needs[30].

The study of myths dates to ancient history and has accompanied humanity ever since. The 19th century comparative mythology re-interpreted myth as a primitive and failed counterpart of science[31], a "disease of language,"[32] or a misinterpretation of magic rituals[33]. Recent approaches reject conflicts between the value of myth and rational thought, often viewing myths as expressions to understand general psychological, cultural, or societal truths, rather than inaccurate historical units[34]. Eliade argued that a myth narrates a sacred history; that is, a transhuman revelation which took place at the dawn of the Great Time, in the holy time of the beginnings (*in illo tempore*)[35]. Being real and sacred, the myth becomes exemplary, and consequently repeatable, for it serves as a model, and by the same token as a justification, for human actions. In other words, a myth is a true history of what came to happen at the beginning of time. One of the foremost functions of a myth is to establish models for behavior[36]. By telling myths, members of traditional societies detach themselves from the present, returning to the mythical age or the myths that are hidden behind the present, thereby bringing themselves closer to the divine.

---

[29] Eliade, M. (1968).

[30] Frog (2018).

[31] Edward Burnett Tylor (1832 –1917) was an English anthropologist, the founder of cultural anthropology.

[32] Max Müller (1823–1900), was a German-born philologist and orientalist, that lived in England.

[33] James George Frazer (1854–1941) was a Scottish social anthropologist influential in the early stages of the modern studies of mythology and comparative religion.

[34] Kisak, P.F. (2016).

[35] Eliade, M. (1957).

[36] Eliade, M. (1998).

J. Campbell, the American mythologist, writer, and lecturer best-known for his work in comparative mythology and comparative religion, wrote that in the long view of the history of mankind, four essential functions of mythology could be discerned.

"The first and most distinctive—vitalizing all—is that of eliciting and supporting a sense of awe before the mystery of being. The second function of mythology is to render a cosmology, an image of the universe that will support and be supported by this sense of awe before the mystery of the presence and the presence of a mystery.

"A third function of mythology is to support the current social order, to integrate the individual organically with his group. The fourth function of mythology is to initiate the individual into the order of realities of his own psyche, guiding him toward his own spiritual enrichment and realization."[37] All that gives rise to a mythological canon that is an organization of symbols by which energies are gathered toward a focus. For not authority, but aspiration is the motivator, builder, and transformer of civilization, Campbell writes[38]. In addition to protagonists such as Mircea, Campbell and the founder of analytical psychology, the Swiss psychiatrist and psychotherapist C.G. Jung, many central European writers, thinkers, and intellectuals provided studies of mythology. Of particular significance among those are Johann Gottfried Herder (1744-1803), Friedrich Schiller (1759-1805), Friedrich Wilhelm Joseph von Schelling (1775-1854), Jacob Grimm (1785–1863), Sigmund Freud (1856-1939) and Claude Lévi-Strauss (1908-2009). Interest in mythology is thus an essential theme for all cultures, although not always being evaluated highly, e.g. by today's natural sciences.

## 1.1 On the significance of Germanic mythology

In this book, a narrower perspective of the term mythology is selected. It assumes that mythologies are the narratives of cultures and collective psychology that go back to the mythologems of humanity's early times. The focus is further restricted to one of Europe's most important,

---

[37] Campbell, J. (1991).
[38] Campbell, J. (1991).

widespread, and neglected mythologies: the Germanic one. How important can Germanic mythology be when it comes to Europe as a whole? How can the significance of Germanic mythology be evaluated? For a start, we consider the balance of basic European language groups, such as the Latin (e.g., French, Italian, Castilian, etc.), Greek, Germanic (e.g., German, Dutch, Swedish), Slavic (e.g., Russian, Polish, Ukrainian), and Finno-Ugric (e.g., Finnish, Estonian, Hungarian). Among the 730 million Europeans, the proportions among language groups (in decreasing percentage) are as follows: The Slavic speakers comprise about 255 million (35 percent), followed by Romance/Latin speakers[39] comprising about 225 million (30 percent). The Germanic speaking Europeans comprise about 205 million (28 percent), and the Finno-Ugric speakers comprise about 45 million (6 percent). Greek speakers encompass about 13 million of the Europeans (1.8 percent). However, the significance of the myths of various cultural and language groups is not only reflected by language. Frequent invasions of Eastern people into the European heartlands resulted in Germanic, Latin, Finno-Ugric, Slavic and Greek "genes" (including the associated folklore and myths) being incorporated into sedentary populations that used and shared different languages and mythologies[40]. The movement of people and tribes during the barbarian invasions and the Migration Period (376-800; see 2.1) resulted in an extensive blend of genes, folklore, and myths throughout Europe[41]. Germanic tribes spread throughout Europe and northern Africa, as reflected by the large-scale movements of Angles, Jutes, Saxons, Francs, Goths, and Vandals[42], to mention some. It is thus likely that more than 30 percent of the European population are of direct Germanic origin or having earlier on applied a Germanic language. How is this heritage reflected among the mythology understanding of European culture groups?

Any visitor of bookshops or libraries that has selections for mythology and ancient tales will observe that one can find a multitude of literature on Greek and Roman mythology. Also, general books on

---

[39] Including about 23 million Moldavians and Romanians that use a Latin-based language that is strongly influenced by Slavic and Hungarian.
[40] Anthony, D.W. (2007).
[41] Fehr, H. & Rummel, P.v. (2011).
[42] Lopez, R.S. (1962).

myths and mythology are widespread. However, one will find only a few sources of Germanic and maybe scant volumes on Celtic mythology. In vain will one search for literature about Slavonic and Finno-Ugric mythology, although these two groups comprise almost 40 percent of European speakers. And under the headline of Germanic mythology, one will find, at the most, heroic adventures (such as the *Das Lied der Nibelungen* and *Beowulf*)[43] that share limited resemblance to the assumed original Germanic mythological narratives. Consequently, we may ask why more than 70 percent of the mythology of the European population is uninteresting and marginalized for the general public? Why does our knowledge of mythology reflect first of all the Greek, Roman, and Christian cultures? Is it because these cultures are much more important and relevant and richer than others? Do they reflect the mythological essence of Europe as a whole?

In the opinion of the author, many Europeans do not live congruent (in agreement or harmony) with their original inheritance and culture. Ignoring or bypassing them result in that large mythological realms stand vacant and glaring emptiness reigns. Empty spaces have been filled with Greek or Roman myths and culture, the dominion of Christianity and the educated. The lack of congruence between the potential and realized cultural niche may perpetuate maintain dangerous deficiencies. A major psychological incongruence between the potential and realized niche in an individual will, in the long run, give rise to imbalance, distortion, and ultimately to suffering. Not so in populations? Will all Europeans, based upon the dominant Greek and Roman cultures alone, find adequate mythological support for the grand existentialistic questions? It appears that Europeans are forced into a universally accepted cultural scheme dominated by a tradition that only partly reflects the European cultural diversity. The reasons for this in-congruence will be investigated in 7.1 and 7.2. As a consequence, Europeans (and people outside Europe who have their base in European culture) may suffer from alienation and dissociation with their basic and original culture. Alienation and dissociation are the base of many psychological disorders and, thus, cannot be taken lightly. Individuals,

---

[43] *Das Lied der Nibelungen* (1833), *Beowulf: Verse Translation* (2003).

ethnic or religious groups, and nations can become victims of forces that erupt due to a neglected unconscious basement. Should humanity's ultimate goal not be increasing congruence between the ideal (as defined by education and self-definition) and actual self (what we actually realize and are)?

## 1.2 Mythological and archetypical lobotomy?

Throughout this book the term archetype (original pattern from which copies are made) will be applied. It derives from the Latin noun archetypus which is a Latinization of Greek archetupos—first-molded (a compound of arche [beginning, origin] and tupos [meaning pattern, model, or type]). Here, the concept of an archetype relates first of all to the psychological theory of C.G. Jung. An archetype is a collectively inherited unconscious idea, a pattern of thought, an image, etc., that is universally present in the individual psyche[44]. The archetype is a constantly recurring symbol or motif in literature, painting, dreams, or mythology. What effects can we expect when parts of our archetypes are ignored or marginalized, and, as we will see when it comes to Germanic mythology, actively demonized, repulsed, and repressed (see chapter 9)? In the author's opinion, such shortcomings create problems that create major conflicts for individuals inside and between nations, to be illuminated in chapter 7. Processes such as marginalization, demonization, repulsion, and repression obstruct the harmonic development of humans and hinder individuation. They provide a fertile soil for symptoms that at best fill the waiting rooms of psychologists, but usually create wide-ranging sociological and political disturbance, including violence and war.

What appears in our imaginations, daydreams, and dreams originates from and is moulded by our cultural delineation. In order to come unbiased to terms with our inner and outer selves, we have to realize ourselves, on the background of our culture. To become genuinely human implies, in the author's opinion, connection with humanity's collective roots, through one's personal and collective delineation. And

---

[44] Skogemann, P. (1986); Stevens, A. (1994).

as a consequence, our mythological knowledge and pathfinding should reflect and be proportional to our cultural background, our origin, or where we live and come from. Neglecting parts of one's cultural background is like denying the existence of a persona non grata in our heritage, a common challenge for many humans. Many stop investigating their genealogy when they discover undesired or unacceptable ethnic groups, criminals, or "barbarians." Who claims to belong to a barbarian culture when one can enjoy the pleasures of a highly ranked civilization? Neglecting major parts of one's cultural background can be compared to voluntary cultural lobotomy. It may result at best in stillness and tranquillity but will most probably and in the long run result in restlessness, deficiencies, and pathologies. At times it can even result in mind-blowing tragedies (see chapter 7).

## 1.3 Mythology and psychology in a Jungian perspective

In Jungian psychology, archetypes are highly developed elements of the collective unconscious[45]. Being unconscious, the existence of archetypes can only be deduced indirectly by examining behavior, images, art, myths, religions, or dreams. Jung understood archetypes as universal, archaic patterns and images that derive from the collective unconscious[46]. They are autonomous and hidden forms, inherited potentials that are actualized and transformed once they enter the consciousness as images or manifest themselves in behavior on interaction with the outside world[47]. Here, they are given particular expression by individuals and their cultures. Archetypes, their actions, preferences, and imaginary create the very base of mythology and the mythologem, its basic narrative.

Strictly speaking, archetypes refer to the underlying forms or archetypes-as-such from which emerge images and motifs (e.g., the great mother, the old wise man, and the shadow). It is history, culture, and personal context that shape these manifest representations, thereby

---

[45] Here, the part of the unconscious mind which is derived from ancestral memory and experience; it is common to all humankind; as distinct from the individual's unconscious.
[46] Feist, J. & Feist, G.J. (2009).
[47] Stevens, A. (2006).

giving them their specific content. The history, culture, and context of each individual ethnic group or nation are thus essential, conspicuous features that are important to study in order to understand the archetypical expression. These images and motifs are more precisely called archetypal images that find their variable imaginary in the different cultures and ethnic or language groups. However, it is common to use the term archetype interchangeably to refer to both the archetypes-as-such as well as archetypal images.

Jung states that our archetypical legacy is phylogenetically acquired. Phylogenesis—from Greek *phylon* (tribe, clan, race) and *genetikós* (origin, source, birth)—is in the present context the evolutionary development and cultural history of humans. Phylogeny is often represented by models or diagrams delineating an evolutionary history, e.g., through phylogenetic trees. One of these common trees is the relationship and development of our hominine ancestors throughout the last 6 million years, ending with *Homo erectus, Homo neanderthalensis* and us, *Homo sapiens*. In this book it is useful to look at the "phylogeny" of language groups. The Indo-European languages could be represented as a language tree (Fig. 1) where we differentiate among the Anatolian, Celtic (e.g., Scottish, Irish, Breton), Romance (e.g., Romanian, Spanish, Italian, French), Germanic (e.g., Dutch, German, English, Swedish), Slavonic (e.g., Russian, Polish, Ukrainian, Serbian), Baltic, Iranian, Indian and Greek language branches. From the Indo-European roots toward the twigs and foliage of today, we then find former languages such as Anatolian, Britannic and Proto-Celtic, Italic and Latin, western, northern and Proto-Germanic, Balto-Slavic, Indo-Iranian and old Greek, etc. In order to understand where we come from and who we are, we have to move uninterruptedly from where we are today (the foliage and twigs) toward the base of the branch and down to humanity's joint cultural roots (Fig. 1). In anology, we mention our current culture (the foliage and twigs), the mythologies (the branches), the mythologemes (the main trunk) and the archetypes (ther root). Our Indo-European history is stratified, layer by layer. History in German is *Geschichte* (directly translated "a laminated sequence").

Since archetypes are phylogenetically inherited and in analogy to the Indo-European language tree, we have to start our mythology investigation with the current European cultures. From there we can

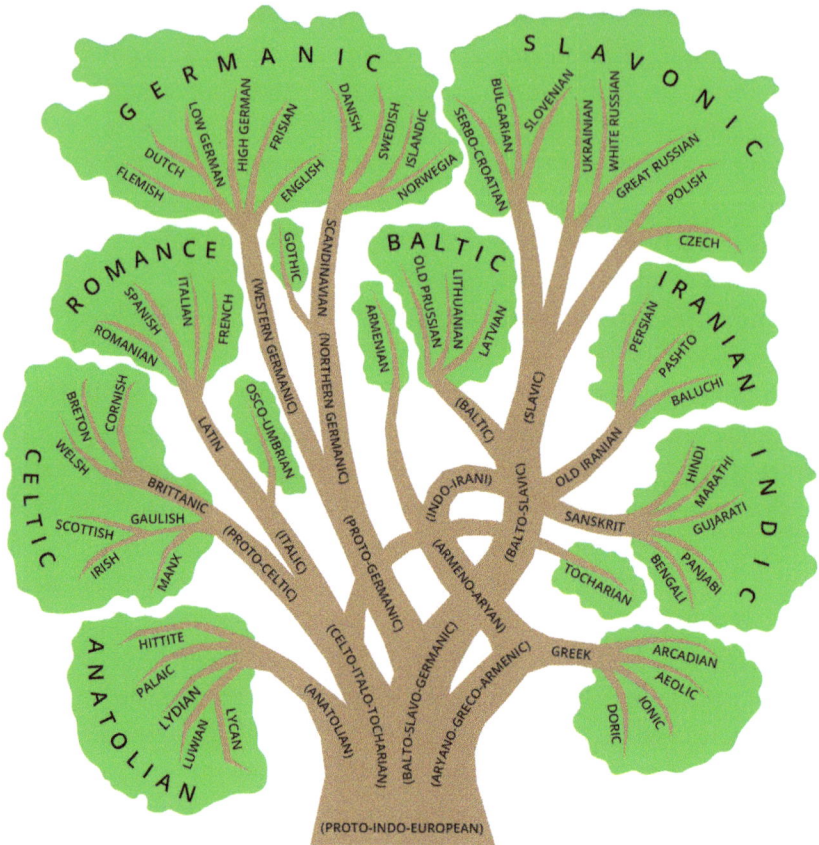

Fig. 1. The Indo-European language branch of the language tree. Nine minor branches are indicated: Anatolian, Celtic, Romance, Germanic, Baltic, Slavonic, Iranian, Indic, and Greek. The branches represent the plethora of today's many Indo-European languages (and mythologies). The 样 base of the stem represents the proto-Indo-European language and the unidentified Indo-European mythologies. The roots of the tree come close to what one may call the archetypes. To investigate one's cultural heritage implies that one searches for the mythologems and archetypes. One progresses more and more from present to past, from the concious to the unconcious. Redrawn from https://www.thedailystar.net/news-detail-126432.

inquire what type of culturally specific images and ideas our ancestors developed. Descending deeper and deeper toward the stem and into the roots of our Indo-European heritage, we can discover more and more the ideas and archetypes that we share with an increasing number of European cultures and ethnic groups. At the very base of the human heritage tree and its roots, we find the common human experiences, our basic archetypes (such as great mother, the old wise man, and the shadow, among others).

The universal nature of Jung's approach to psychology (and any other universal method) demands that education has to honour and reflect, support and amplify the cultural nature of all humans, without any prejudice. The analysis of archetypes and their impact upon our individual and collective lives necessitates knowledge of the entire cultural and genetic inheritance of humanity. This is the ultimate human development ideal of analytical psychology. However, we are all children of our times, continents, countries, religions, and families. We reflect specific cultural imprints, limitations, and prejudices that restrict our ultimate ideal of human education, reflected by the comic playwright Publius Terentius Afer (commonly referred to as Terence, 195/185-159 B.C.E.): "Nothing human is alien to me." Can we enjoy all-embracing lectures and seminars about, for example, widespread European mythologies, e.g., Germanic, Slavic, Celtic, or Finno-Ugrian mythology in any of the educative institutions in Europe? Are European mythology and our cultural roots part of the general education of Europeans? And do we really attempt to educate the entire spectrum of European culture? Not at all. European mythology and culture are, by and large, not taught at graduate schools or at colleges as part of the general training. Some remnants of the classical education in Greek and Latin mythology (and in Scandinavia Norse mythology) are still presented, but the mythological and archetypical literacy does by no means reflect the comprehensive reality of the Europeans. The majority of the Europeans, the people of Slavic, Celtic, Germanic, or Finno-Ugric origin may in vain try to learn about their roots and mythological and archetypal background. And, sadly, this is also the case at Jungian institutions that do not adequately reflect the diversity of ethnic groups, continents, and religions of those that assemble in the auditoria.

## 1.4 Structure and goal

The main goal of this book is to convince the reader that key sectors of our archetypical heritage are suppressed, with negative outcomes for our mental and cultural health and adverse effects on peaceful coexistence (see chapter 10). Some of the suppression is vigorous, resulting in nonacceptable elements of our cultural inheritance not being tolerated (see chapter 7). Other forms are subtler and hardly recognized. This suppression finds support through the unfortunate conduct of the well-educated that favor the Greek, Roman, and Christian inheritance and rationality. This is the quintessence of humanistic education, which has a dark companion: the suppression of "barbarian" cultures and less rational methods of obtaining knowledge. The author wishes to encourage the reader to join forces with those that try to help overcome the detrimental consequences of this restricting, intolerant, and conflict-supporting conduct.

This book deals actually as much with cultural suppression and ostracizing as with inadequate pathways of self-realization and individuation. It is based upon the conviction that humanity's true background is multiethnic and multicultural and that *Homo sapiens* is the one and only human race. Investigating and assimilating the multiethnic and multicultural nature of man is a process that makes humanity truly human. The author points at hidden processes that cast dangerous shadows over human civilization: marginalization, negligence, and suppression of what is regarded as unacceptable and "barbaric" aspects of our heritage. And he points at the consequences that untouched defense mechanisms behind this censorship have for our psyche and the peaceful coexistence of humanity. The book wishes to reduce the archetypical illiteracy that darkens and at times threatens our civilization (see chapter 10).

As the specific object for the generic goal of the book, the author selected Germanic mythology. It also focuses upon Europe, where the author was raised and lives. While dealing with Germanic mythology, the author wishes to ignite some of the readers' dormant mythology "fixed stars" and "star signs" that enable him/her to recognize the Germanic archetypes in European culture and in dreams (Fig. 59). The book can be seen as part of an archetypical literacy project with the ultimate goal of enabling Europeans (and their descendants throughout the world) to recognize the language of the archetypes and the unconscious that persistently attempts to talk to us, whether we comprehend it or not (Fig. 2).

32

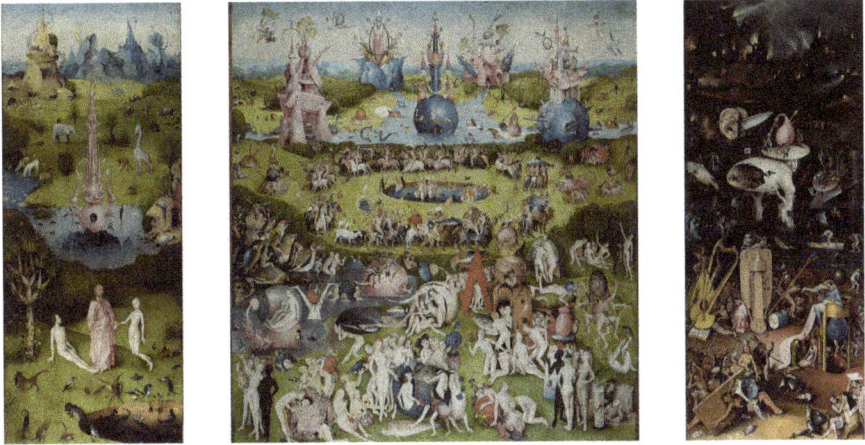

Fig. 2. *El jardín de las delicias/ De tuin der lusten* (*Garden of Earthly Delights*) by Hieronymus Bosch (1450-1516; Museo del Prado, Madrid) displays a symbolic language that is hardly accessible to humans today. We have forgotten the language behind Bosch's symbolism and spiritual perspective. Without specific knowledge, we may not decipher the archetypical language that is exposed to us in new cultures, dreams, or imagination. To communicate in the best possible manner humanity can increase its "linguistic" capacity, in the broadest sense. Without symbolic or archetypic literacy, we may be as much detached from understanding as when confronted with Bosch's imaginary today. Wikimedia Commons.

The book is designed to address four specific goals: First, it introduces the Germanic tribes, the knowledge base of Germanic mythology, Germanic writing and poetry, and asks if all elements of Germanic mythology are lost in central Europe (chapters 1-5). Second, in support of the less knowledgable reader and applying a broad brush, it summarizes main elements of Germanic mythology (chapter 6). Third, it presents the development of Germanic mythology and culture through time, describing ostracizing as the main mechanism for the maintenance of cultural superiority and asks how we can reach an adequate relationship with Germanic archetypes (chapters 7-9). Finally, a treatise on a road map to peace through a balanced archetype geography education forms part four, representing an epilogue. Specific aspects that are not essential, but complementary for understanding the text, are presented in 21 fact boxes throughout the text. The many figures and the at-times lenghty figure legends attempt to add a visual story that parallells the written text.

*Abendspaziergang* (*A Walk at Dusk*) by Caspar David Friedrich (1774-1840; Getty Center, Los Angeles). His head bowed, an introspective man walks alone in the silvery, cold moonlit night while contemplating a megalithic tomb. It is winter, but a grove of lush oaks rises through the mist in the background with the promise of spring. The waxing moon counterbalances the deadly ambience, promising the rebirth of life. The painting embodies a notion of a past that radiates into the present, the melancholy of the contemporary. The male figure could be associated with a priest or shaman, immersed by worship in a red, ceremonial robe. Or it may represent our ego contemplating about the meaning of life. The threat of the archaic megalith grave may reflect our fear of the unknown and suppressed, but the archaic may provide our best support in the coolish darkness of the present. Wikimedia Commons.

# 2. The Indo-European Invasion, the Germanic Tribes and Barbarism

*We all travel, if not in space in time. And since the first strolling teller-of-tales enthralled his audience at the first campfire, we have all loved travellers and travellers' tales. From Gilgamesh through Odysseus to Bilbo Baggins and Frodo, the epic journey and its hero continue to capture our imagination.*

R. Standen

*Sluggish and sedentary peoples, such as the Ancient Egyptians— with their concept of an afterlife journey through the Field of Reeds— project on to the next world the journeys they failed to make in this one.*

B. Chatwin

Who are the Germanic tribes, and from where do they originate? The Germanic tribes are a subgroup of the Indo-European people. We hold actually little direct evidence about both the Germanic tribes and Indo-European people. The main evidence regarding the Indo-European people was provided by comparative language investigations. Despite observing similarities between European languages, the science of linguistics did not develop much until the late 18th century. As there are few historic facts of the origin and movements of the Germanic tribes, we start our account by a short overview on Indo-European languages.

## 2.1 Indo-European languages

The Indo-European languages are a family of several hundred related languages and dialects. There are more than 400 living Indo-European languages, from which the majority belong to the Indo-Iranian branch (Fig. 1). The most widely spoken Indo-European languages by native speakers are Spanish, English, Hindi, Portuguese, Bengali, Russian, and Punjabi, each with over 100 million speakers. Today, 46 percent of the human population speaks an Indo-European language across all inhabited continents. Of the 20 languages with the largest quantities of native speakers, 11 are Indo-European. About two-thirds of the world population speak an Indo-European language, as primary speakers and through their second language (as lingua franca, education language, or official state language).[48] As a result, through language, Indo-European cultural traits (including associated proto-mythology) are a conspicuous and wide-reaching reality for humanity. The Indo-European family includes most of the modern languages of Europe (more than 90 percent; see 1.1). It was also predominant in ancient Anatolia (present-day Turkey), the ancient Tarim Basin (present-day northwest China) and most of Central Asia until the Mongol invasions and medieval Turkic migrations[49].

All Indo-European languages are descended from a single pre-historic language, reconstructed as Proto-Indo-European, spoken sometime in the Neolithic era (about 10200 B.C.E. and ending between 4500 and 2000 B.C.E.). The affinity of European languages and the number of speakers are presented in Fig. 3. Three language groups—the Romance, Germanic and Slavic groups—govern. Celtic, Greek, and Finno-Ugric groups are more distant. The internal language spread in all language groups is significant. Between 3500 and 3000 B.C.E., the Indo-Europeans are meant to be a defined language group (Fig. 4). By 1000 B.C.E., they had split up into nine major divisions: Indian, Armenian, Iranian—such as Sanskrit, Old Persian (from which today's Persian

---

[48] Haarmann (2016).
[49] https://en.wikipedia.org/wiki/Proto-Indo-Europeans; Anthony, D.W. (2007).

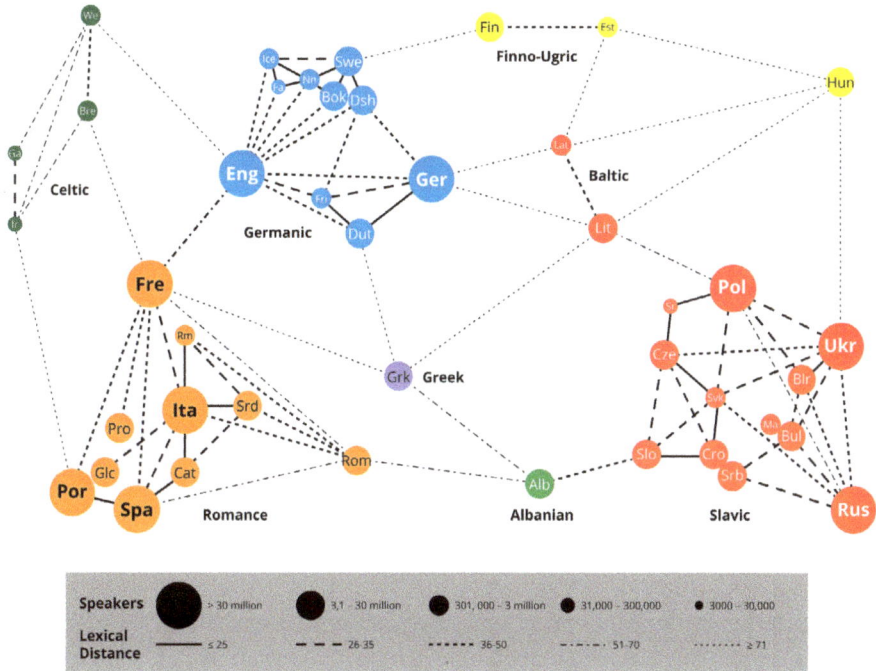

Fig. 3. The number of speakers of and the lexical distance between European languages. Eight separate clusters are identified: Romance, Celtic, Germanic, Finno-Ugric, Baltic, Greek, Albania and Slavic. French, Italian, Spanish, Portuguese, German, English, Polish, Ukrainian and Russian dominate among the 42 identified European languages. Redrawn from https://elms.wordpress.com/2008/03/04/lexical-distance-among-languages-of-europe/

[Farsi] derives)—Germanic, Balto-Slavic—(which split into Baltic (from which developed today's Latvian and Lithuanian—and Old Slavic—from which Russian, etc. is derived)—Celtic (which split into Irish, Gaelic, Breton, and Welsh)—and Albanian, while Hellenic had become Old Greek and Latin. From Latin, the Romance languages, such as the French, Portuguese, Castilian, Catalan, Romanian and Provencal language groups, developed during 800-1200 (not specified in Fig. 4). In line with the Roman tradition, the Romanic languages have a tendency to centralize and focus upon one main language. Many Romanic dialects could have developed into different languages, but while this was the rule among the Germanic languages (see the high diversity in Fig. 4), seemingly no such extensive differentiation took place among the Romanic ones.

ca. 3500-3000 BCE

ca. 1000 BCE

1 A.D. (Anno Domini)

ca. 500

ca. 800-1200

ca. 1300

ca. 1700-1900

Proto-Indo-European

Indian — Armenian — Iranian — Germanic — Balto-Slavic — Albanian — Celtic — Hellenic — Italic

Sanskrit — Old Persian — Avestan — Persian

Middle Indian

Hindustani, Bengali, and other modern Indian languages

N. Germanic — E. Germanic — W. Germanic — French Provençal Italian Spanich Portuguese Catalan Romanian

E. Norse   W. Norse — Gothic — High German  Low German

Swedish, Danish, Gothlandic   Norwegian, Icelandic, Faroese — German  Yiddish

Old Frisian — Anglo-Saxon (Old English) — Old Saxon — Low Franconian

Frisian — Middle English — Middle Low English — Middle Dutch

Modern English — Plattdeutsch — Dutch, Flemich

Greek

Latin

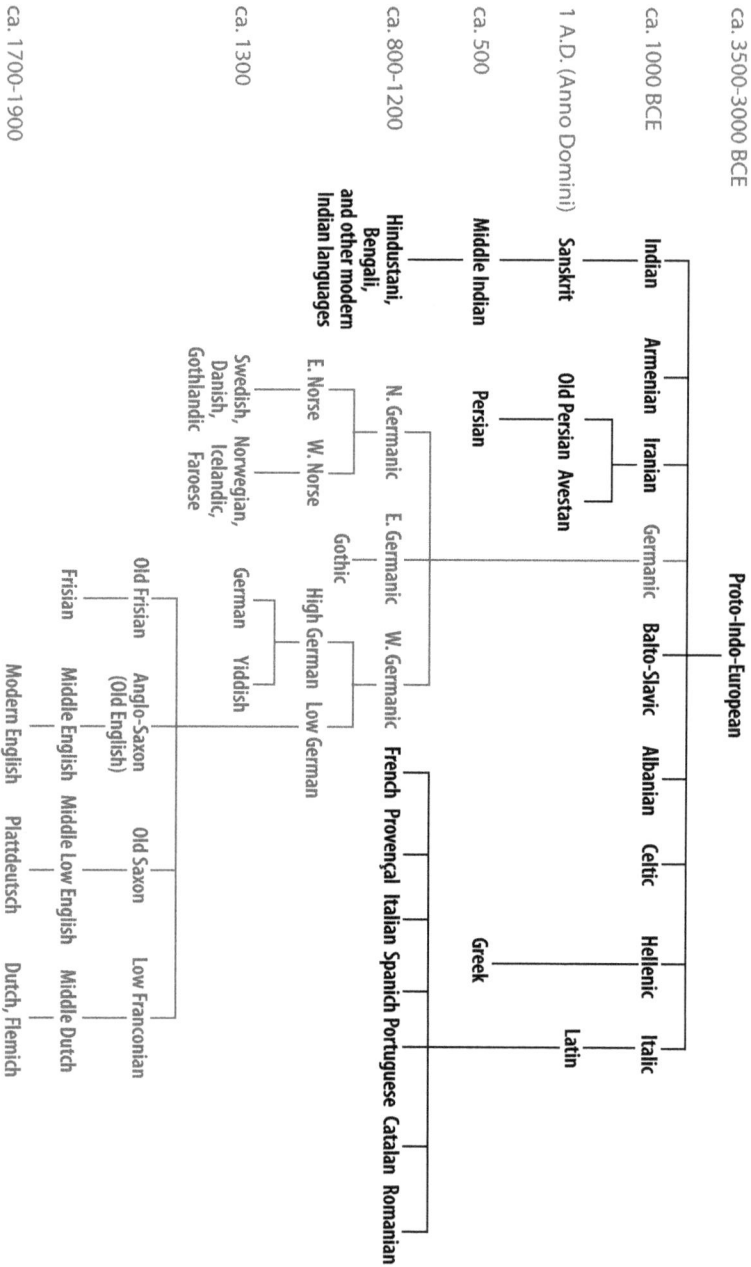

Fig. 4. The Indo-European languages and their development from the proto-Indo-European of 3500 B.C.E. to present. The development of the Germanic languages is indicated in green. They are characterized by an extensive development from 800 and onward. Redrawn from https://norse-mythology.org/indo-europeans-matter/

38

The Germanic branch had a particularly diverse development (Fig. 4). By 800-1200, it had split into three language branches: the Northern, Eastern and Western Germanic languages. The former developed by 1300 into Eastern and Northern Norse, from which today's Swedish, Danish and Gothlandic, and Norwegian, Icelandic, and Faroese developed, respectively. From the Eastern Germanic branch, Gothic arose, but this language became extinct. By 1300, Western Germanic had developed into High German (today's German and Yiddish), while Low German over the years gave rise to a canon of languages. Old Frisian turned into today's Frisian. The Anglo-Saxon (old English) turned into Middle and Modern English. Finally, Low Franconian developed into Middle Dutch and today's Dutch and Flemish. This language diversification is in line with the important political principle among the Germanic tribes: federalism and independence.

## 2.2 The Indo-European invasions and the subjugation of old European cultures

As all other groups, the ancestors of Proto-Indo-Europeans wandered ultimately out of humanity's original home, Africa. Mainstream science assumes that hominids arrived in Central Asia about 40000 B.C.E., i.e. in the middle of the last ice age (Out of Africa theory[50]). One branch spread westward into the central and southern, unwelcoming, ice age that impacted Europe around 30000 to 40000 B.C.E.

The Proto-Indo-European speakers lived during the late Neolithic period, or roughly during the fourth millennium B.C.E.[51] Mainstream scholarship places them to the north and west of the Pontic-Caspian forest-steppe in Eastern Europe, i.e., north of the Caucasus, east of the Black Sea, and west for the Caspian Sea (Fig. 5). By the late third millennium B.C.E., offshoots of the Proto-Indo-Europeans had reached Anatolia, the Aegean, Western Europe, Central Asia, and southern Siberia.

---

[50] https://en.wikipedia.org/wiki/Recent_African_origin_of_modern_humans.
[51] Haarmann, H. (2016).

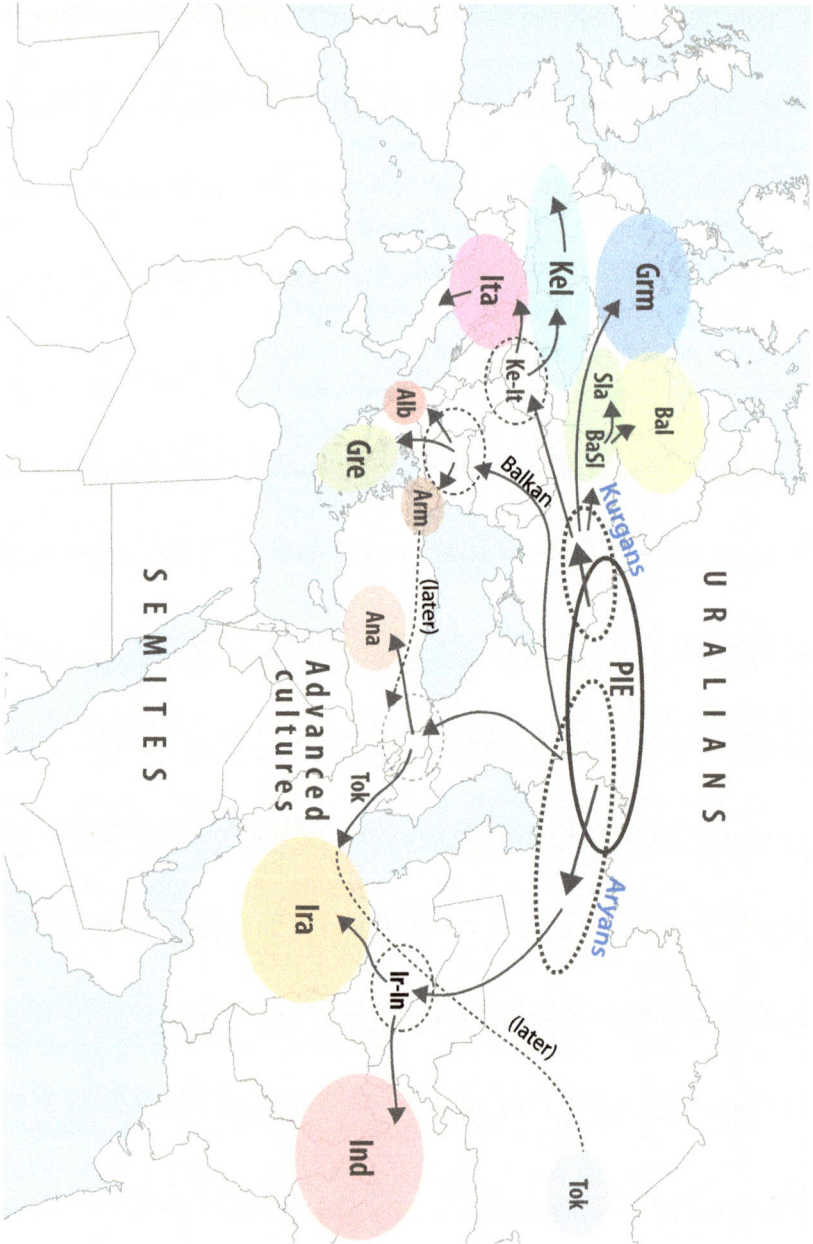

Fig. 5. Projection of possible Indo-European migration routes between the Uralian hunter-gatherers in the north and the Semites and advanced cultures in the south, 3500 to 2500 B.C.E. They leave the assumed proto-Indo-European homeland (PIE) toward the southeast (Iranian, Indian, Tocharian), the northwest (Baltic, Germanic, Celtic, Italic) and the Balkans (Greek, Albanian, Armenian). Redrawn from http://www.hjholm.de/

We assume that their culture was based upon pastoralism, a branch of agriculture concerned with the raising of livestock. Pastoralism generally has a mobile aspect, moving the herds in search of fresh pasture and water. Pastoralism is a successful strategy to support a population on less productive land and adapts well to the environment. For example, in steppes such as the Pontic-Caspian, pastoralists and their animals gathered when rainwater was abundant and the pasture rich, but then they scattered during the drying of the savannah. In the times before agriculture, a "sea of grassland" stretched several thousand kilometers from Mongolia to the woods of Eastern Europe, inviting to navigate the "sea" with "four-legged ships": horses. Changes in climate have often been associated with the movement of Indo-European groups and Germanic tribes. Recent research points out that the year 536 and the following decade was the worst period in historic times, caused by a volcanic eruption on Iceland[52], with implications for the Migration Period (2.3).

We assume that the Indo-European invaders were patriarchal. Patriarchy is a social system in which males hold primary power and predominate in roles of political leadership, moral authority, social privilege, and control of property. In the domain of the family, fathers or father figures hold authority over women and children. Some patriarchal societies are also patrilineal (inheriting or determining descent through the male line, such as the Greeks and Romans). This implies that property and title are inherited mainly by the male lineage, and descent is reckoned exclusively through the male line. In central Europe, these expanding patriarchal pastoralists met upon a flourishing matricentric (gravitating toward or centered upon the mother) cultures that were based upon agriculture and subdued them. Old Europe is a term coined by the Lithuanian archaeologist Marija Gimbutas (1921-1994) to describe what she perceived as a relatively homogeneous pre-Indo-European Neolithic culture in southeastern Europe, located in the Danube River valley. In Gimbutas' model of European prehistory, the Danubian culture forms a core that she envisions as a relatively advanced matrilineal (inheriting or determining descent through the female line)

---

[52] http://www.sciencemag.org/news/2018/11/why-536-was-worst-year-be-alive.

civilization, dominated by females and fertility goddesses. Gimbutas terms the patriarchal invaders from the Pontic-Caspian steppe as the Kurgan culture[53], which she identifies with the Proto-Indo-European language. A suppression of the culture of Old Europe was the consequence. Here is not the place to argue for or against Gimbutas' controversial model (see 6.5), but it is mentioned because it can explain why the gods' home and fortress Asgard in Norse mythology (see 6.5) is characterized by a remarkable balance between the patriarchal Aesir (true-born children of the Indo-European pasturist invasion) and the matricentric Vanir (fertility gods attached to localities). Thus, the sedentary gods of Old Europe became tightly entangled with some of the patriarchal pasturist invaders and their flying sky gods, providing a balanced and unique heavenly matrix for the Germanic people. As a consequence, balanced male and female values were represented within Asgard (6.5; Fig. 26).

The anticipated movement of the various Proto-Indo-European groups between 3500 and 2500 B.C.E. into western and eastern directions is illustrated in Fig. 5. The Proto-Indo-European heartland is situated between the Uralian hunters and gatherers (with a significant influx of Neanderthal genes) in the north and the advanced cultures of Mesopotamia and the Semites in the south. The Proto-Indo-European tribes divided themselves into the westbound Kurgan and the eastbound Aryan branch (see Box I). The Aryans are the original core for the Iranians, the Indians, and Tocharians, who inhabited the oasis city-states on the northern edge of the Tarim Basin (modern Xinjiang, China) in ancient times[54]. The Kurgans supported four branches. The northern-most branch gave rise to the Balto-Slavic, Slavic, Baltic and Germanic tribes. The central branch supported the Italo-Celtic, Celtic, and Italic tribes. The Balkan branch included the Albanian, Greek, and Armenian (migrating eastward later) tribes. The southbound movement gave rise to the Anatolian tribes (such as the Hittites).

---

[53] The noun Kurgan is first attested in Old East Slavic, which borrowed the word from an unidentified Turkic language or languages. Following its use in Soviet archaeology, the word is now widely used for tumuli (burial mound) in the context of archaeology.

[54] Barber, E. W. (1999).

## Box I: Who were the Aryans?

In present-day academia, Indo-Iranian and Indo-European have, for the most part, replaced the term Aryan. Drawing on misinterpreted references in the Rigveda by Western scholars in the 19th century, the term Aryan was adopted as a racial category through the work of Arthur de Gobineau (1816-1882). His ideology of race was based on an idea of blonde northern European "Aryans" who had migrated across the world and founded all major civilizations, before being degraded through racial mixture with local populations. During the time of the Third Reich, the term Aryan obtained a specific German and Nordic connotation. Alfred Rosenberg (1893-1946), one of the principal architects of Nazi ideology, argued for a new "religion of the blood." It was based upon the supposed innate qualities of the "Nordic" people to defend their "noble" character against racial and cultural degeneration. These "nobles" were collectively and inaccurately called Aryans and are the basis of Nazi Aryanization race policy.

The Aryanization race theory was combined with the fatal and steadily applied aphorism *mens sana in corpore sano* (a healthy mind in a sound body; by the Roman poet Juvenal). The annihilation of the "racially inferior" Untermenschen (subhuman [a term that became infamous when the Nazis used it to describe "inferior people" such as Sinti/Roma, Jews, Slavic people and mental retarded/handicapped]) was sanctified like the removal of a sick organ in an otherwise healthy body. This led to the direct extermination of 11 million people. The Aryan master race attempted to keep its purity by making soap out of the bodies of the Untermenschen, as Arthur Koestler sarcastically remarked[55].

According to the Indo-Aryan migration model of Marija Gimbutas (1921-1994), the Aryans were those Indo-Europeans who turned eastward for their region of origin (Pontic–Caspian or Kazakh steppe) and gave rise to three major Indo-European cultures: the Iranian, Indian and Tocharian (extinct people of the Tarim Basin, China) cultures. Gimbutas defined the Indo-Europeans who moved westward as the Kurgans (see 2.2). The term Aryan, a term meaning "noble," which was used as a self-designation by Indo-Iranian people, was wrongly applied in Europe.

---

[55] Koestler, A (1977).

## 2.3 The movement of the Germanic tribes

Around 100 B.C.E., the authors of classical antiquity first mention Germanic tribes. At times there are doubts if some of these tribes were of Germanic or Celtic (e.g., the Teutons) origin. The Latin term *germani* was designed by the Romans to characterize what they considered wild and uncivilized groups of people that tried to or invaded the Roman Empire from the north. Germani is thus a xenonym, i.e., the name has been created by another group of people. The region they came from became Germania in Latin. In Germania, a suite of tribes, such as the Suebi, Cheruski, Goths, Kimbri, Vandali, Langobardi, Teutoni, etc., resided (Fig. 6, top). The tribes never used the encapsulating term *germani* themselves. They had probably no generic name for them as a group or potential "nation." They were just different tribes that potentially were able to communicate with each other. The *germani* thus never existed: it is a Roman, synthetic, and xenonym term[56]. *Germani* is an ostracizing Roman projection to characterize wild people outside the realm of the civilized world. Throughout this book, we will frequently take note of how ruling and dominating groups ostracize to self-importantly segregate themselves from nondesirable or interest groups (see chapter 8).

The first time historic sources mention the Germanic tribes is when the Kimbri invaded the Roman Empire 113 to 101 B.C.E. The Kimbri were an ancient people, either Germanic or Celtic, who together with the Teutons and Ambrons fought the Roman Empire. They were initially successful, particularly at the battle of Arausio, in which a large Roman army was killed, after which they raided large areas in Gallia and Hispania. In 101 B.C.E., during an attempted invasion of Italy, the Kimbri were defeated. Roman sources identify these Kimbri with a group that lived in Jutland, but strong evidence for this connection is lacking.

---

[56] In recent times various languages attempt to exchange xenonyms by applying endonyms (e.g., Persian › Farsi; Peking › Beijing; Eskimo › Inuit; Lapp › Sami). Take note that some nations vigorously object to endonyms to prevent independence.

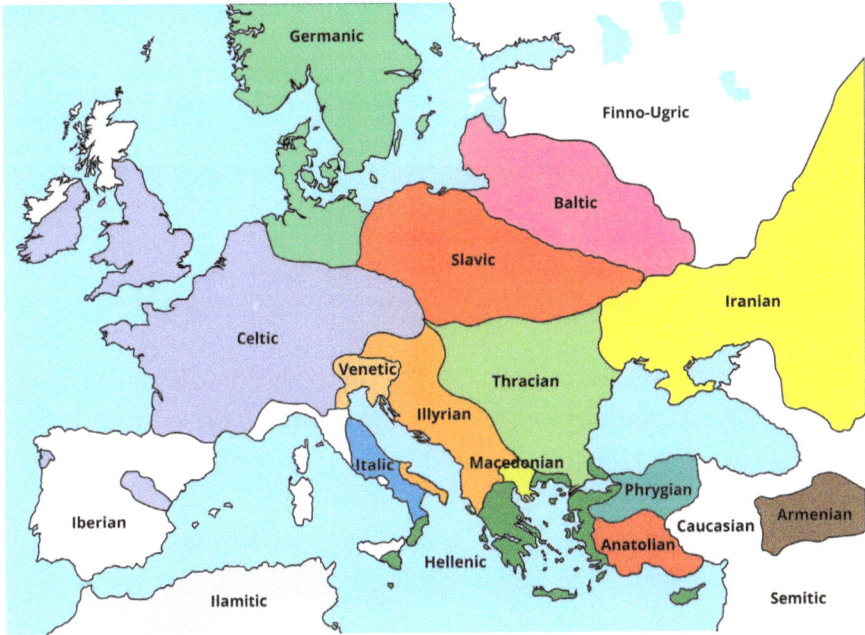

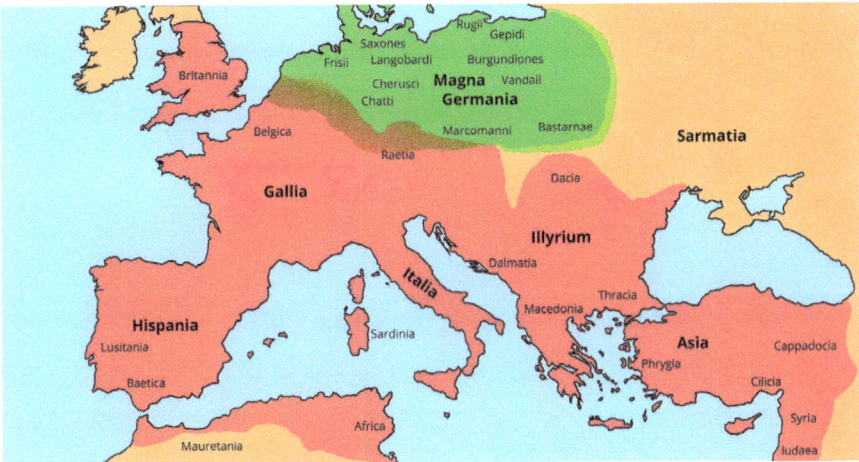

Fig. 6. Distribution of people in Europe by 500 B.C.E. (above), Germanic heartlands of Magna Germania 300 (below). Magna Germania dominates in the north and northwest of the Roman Empire. Redrawn from https://en.wikipedia.org/wiki/Germanic_peoples

We think that the Germanic heartlands around the birth of Jesus were southern Scandinavia and northern Germany, and the tribes were spreading into eastern regions of Europe toward the Danube (Fig. 6, below). The Roman term *Magna Germania* was established by 200 for what today is mostly Germany and western Poland. Tribes such as the Chatti, Frisii, Cherusci, Langobardi, Marcomanni, Vandali, Burgundians, and Gepidi were identified. Some of these tribes will we meet again later, when they moved throughout Europe.

The Migration Period, also known as the Migration of People or Barbarian Invasions, was a period of large-scale migrations, invasions, or war in Europe. This period was marked by profound changes both within the Roman Empire and beyond. The Migration Period started with the invasion of the Huns in 370, followed by Germanic tribes (such as the Goths, Vandals, Angles, Saxons, Lombards, Suebians, Frisians, Jutes and Franks), Avars, Magyars and Slaves. It lasted approximately until 800, and in the middle of it the word experienced its worst-ever period (536 and beyond[57]) that took more lives than the plague. Climate change, mass death, and utmost distress are significant aspects of the Migration Period. These invasions shaped the map of today's Europe and influenced populations and cultural life profoundly. The Western Roman Empire with its center Rome dissipated. Britons, Angles, and Saxons dominate today's Great Britain. The Frisians, Saxons, Burgundians, Francs, Alamannians and Thuringians dominate what today (for the most part) is called Germany.

## 2.4 Rome, the Barbarian Invasions and nation states

The Romans called themselves lords of the world. All the trade and skills, all the art and learning of the known world were theirs. Beyond the borders of the Roman Empire, the world was given over to wild barbarians, who were neither skilled in the arts of war nor of peace nor anything else. That the civilization of Rome could collapse seemed

---

[57] http://www.sciencemag.org/news/2018/11/why-536-was-worst-year-be-alive.

impossible. Yet, the invaders triumphed, Rome fell, and the mighty empire crumbled into dust. Eastern Rome, the Byzantine Empire, continued the Greek-Roman-Christian culture tradition for another 1,000 years until it fell to the Ottoman Turks in 1453. Eastern Rome kept the self-conception of representing the civilization par excellence. Thus, they selected the Greek term ortho (straight, upright, right, or correct) for their interpretation of Christianity—orthodoxy (right opinion). After the fall of Rome, orthodoxy termed Constantinople the second Rome, the true center of Christianity. After 1453, Russian orthodoxy claimed that Moscow was from now on the third Rome, i.e., the very center of civilization. Russian orthodoxy continued the self-proclaimed cultural uniqueness and cultural arrogance of Rome's classic times, as reflected in the fundamental Soviet communistic assumption that Moscow and Russia were the main center of civilization in the last century.

Did Rome and civilization fall due to the barbarian invasions, as frequently stated? No, the decline of Rome was rather the natural and inevitable effect of being a high culture over several centuries. Rome suffered from cultural exhaustion, immoderate greatness, and was undermined culturally by its prominent foreign legionnaires, coming from varied and extensive lands beyond the border. The Barbarian Invasions were a part of the decline that started with internal dissolution, profound religious and ethnic diversity and cultural fatigue. The Migration Period, accompanied by climate challenges, brought up a set of questions regarding ethnic identity, language, countries, and relationships among neighbouring states that complicates European politics up to now. It concerns in particular how we apply the term nation-state. This is a type of state that conjoins a.) the political entity of a state to b.) the cultural entity of a nation. The term nation-state implies that a.) and b.) coincide, in that a state has chosen to adopt and endorse a specific or dominating cultural group associated with it. The Migration Period brought new cultural and ethnic structures to Europe. However, how culture and ethnicity are interpreted can give rise to complications, e.g., the assumption of genetic or cultural superiority (see Box II). This brings us to an issue, strongly associated with the Germanic tribes, that

## Box II: Tribes, ethnic groups, Pan-Germanism and Pan-Slavism

A tribe is viewed, developmentally or historically, as a social group existing before the development of, or outside, states. A tribe is a group of distinct people, dependent on their land for their livelihood, who are largely self-sufficient, and not integrated into or as a national society. The Germanic tribal societies were organized largely on the basis of social, especially familial or descent, groups (clans, kinship). Over time some of these developed into nations and states.

In the 18th century, J.G. Herder was one of the first scholars to set off to study various ethnic groups. He viewed tribes as coherent biological (racial) entities, using the term to refer to discrete ethnic groups. He believed that the Volk (people) was an organic whole, with a core identity and spirit evident in art, literature, and language. These were seen as intrinsic characteristics unaffected by external influences. Language, in particular, was seen as the most important expression of ethnicity. He argued that groups sharing the same (or similar) language possessed a common identity and ancestry. The Romantic ideal that there had once been one single German or Slavic people who originated from a common homeland and spoke a common tongue helped provide a conceptual framework for political movements of the 18th and 19th centuries. Those groups that lacked a homeland, such as Jews and Gypsies, were considered less developed people. To concepts of these days belongs Pan-Germanism and Pan-Slavism. Pan-Germanists originally sought to unify all the German and possibly also Germanic-speaking peoples in a single nation-state, known as Großdeutschland. Anti-Eastern and Western sentiments were strong. Pan-Slavism is a movement that crystallized in the mid-19th century and whose ideology concerned the advancement of integrity and unity for the Slavic people. It sought to unite those people for the achievement of common cultural and political goals. Pan-Slavism had strong anti-Western sentiments. By destabilizing multiethnic political structures, endorsing national states or political mergers, and promoting opinions regarding ethnic superiority, these "pan" ideas have brought distress and aggression to Europe. Few ideas have been (and are) more strongly supported than that of the national state and ethnic supremacy. Few ideas have resulted in more loss of lives, wars, and human misery. The political stability and prosperity after World War II was based upon the weight given to supranational bodies such as the UN, NATO, and EU. Today's tendency to emphasize the national state, separate currencies, border controls, and ostracizing of ethnic minorities, religions, migrants, and refugees opens the door for decreased political stability. It is a regression, not a pathway to sustainable and peaceful future.

Attention should be paid to "pan-terms" and political "pan-ambitions" that are connected to ethnicity and culture. Despite good original intentions, Pan-Germanism turned into Nazism, and Pan-Slavism supported the Soviet interpretation of communism, two movements that despise independent citizens. Both ideologies deplored those who did not directly belong to a particular ethnicity and culture for individual freedom, personal integrity, or even lives. It may be time to renew our memory of the tolerance and freedom of the Germanic federal system.

is essential throughout this book and which needs careful attention: barbarian culture, the primitive, and our interpretation of what we consider civilized.

## 2.5 Barbarism, the primitive and civilization

The term barbarian is a common stereotype that refers to a person who is perceived as uncivilized. Barbarians can be any member of a nation judged by some to be less civilized, but may also be part of a certain "primitive" cultural group (such as nomads), social class both within (such as criminals) and outside one's own nation (such as immigrants). In times of confrontations and wars, entire nations may be called barbarians. The term originates from the Greek word *barbarous,* which over time, got the meaning "whoever is not Greek is a barbarian" (in a clearly pejorative manner). It is suggested that *barbarous* (literally "babbler") is an onomatopoeia (a word that sounds like what it represents), based upon children's first attempts to speak in old Greece. It is in the confrontation between the expanding Greek settlements (trading) along the shores of the Black Sea and the Scythian and other tribes of the Pontic Steppes (agriculture) that the Greek developed the term *barbarous.* The term has become our civilization's dark shadow[58]. The Romans and Christians had similar attitudes, adopted and remodeled the term. Italians in the Renaissance often called anyone who lived outside their country a barbarian. This tradition of derogatory characterization continued to our times. For example, the communist leader Rosa Luxemburg (1871-1919) wrote about "socialism or regression into barbarism."[59] Today the word is used either as a general reference or to a member of a nation or group viewed as inferior. Alternatively, but to a far lesser degree, barbarians may instead be admired and romanticized as noble savages. A most important principle at all times is to keep the barbarians out of civilized societies. Comparable notions are, of course, also found in non-European civilizations, notably in the Middle East, China, and Japan.

Christianity further developed the Roman assumption that their cultivated empire was destroyed by barbarian invasions, but in an additional, downgrading manner. Not only culture and language played a role, but also religion. Christianity thus introduces the terms pagans or heathens, all being primitive people, savages, or barbarians. In Latin, the term *paganus* characterizes originally a person who lives in a rural area. The term heathen signifies originally a person who lives in a heath or moorland. Over time, both heathen and pagan took on the meaning of "a person having no (civilized) religion." In essence, the term deals with educated and Christians versus those that have less education and/or are unbelievers. Also, the terms reflect the arrogance of culture-defining

---

[58] Ascherson, N. (2007).
[59] Rosa Luxemburg's "Junius Pamphlet" of 1916.

towns toward an assumed less civilized countryside, a tradition that continuously enjoys support throughout Europe. Modern English reflects this attitude well: Farmers rear pigs, calves, cows, and sheep (belonging to the subjugated, barbarian Saxonians); and the meals of the dominating classes contain pork, veal, beef, and mutton (food of the "civilized" Norman/French-inspired overclass).

## 2.6 Conclusion

The invasion of the proto-Indo-Europeans into Europe shaped the culture and language landscape of Europe, as we know it today. In turn, some of these European languages and cultures spread throughout the world. The curse of the term barbarian, transferred from the Greeks over the Romans, the Roman Catholic Church, and the Renaissance (see 7.2) continues unobstructed into our times, suggesting that Germanic culture is suspect to be primitive and barbarous. This deeply rooted term penetrates our culture and gives raise to social suppression, political unrest, and ostracizing the undesirable. This will be elaborated in chapters 7 and 8. We, the self-proclaimed, educated cultural chosen, pursuing the Greek, Roman, Christian, and Renaissance culture line, suppress a vital source of psychological health: the life-giving primitive and archaic, be it Germanic, Slavic, Turkish, or Finno-Ugric. In order to stay seemingly cultivated, rather than psychologically healthy, we ostracize: We keep our personal and cultural realms clean by keeping the barbarians at a stance. Today's customary assumption that Germanic tribes were barbarians, i.e., uncivilized and primitive people, prevents us from investigating the shadow of our own civilization. Thus, we need to learn more about the widely ignored knowledge base for the original Germanic culture and mythology.

Indeed, we deal with dark gods (see page 34) that probably were just gods before, but in our times their image is darkened: They talk to us from the depth of their graves. The threat of the dark gods can be mirrored in our fear of the unknown, but they may also reflect repressed contents of the unconscious. The gods may just wish to tell their stories, reflecting their epic journey through the times. They may be our best friends (see chapter 9).

*Without title* (last Stilleben) by Paul Klee (1879-1940; Zentrum Paul Klee, Bern). No other painter was able to decipher the ultimate idea or archetypical structure, *das Ding an sich* (behind what we observe when confronted with what we call reality) than Klee. Shortly before Klee died, he depicted some of the forms and symbols from humanity's cosmos. A statue and a coffepot stand on a small, yellow table that is covered with symbols and runic structures, associated with an angel (of life or death?). The background is an abyss of darkness. We all have a knowledge base of archtypic structures that talk to us in preferences, inclinations, and dream visions. Wikimedia Commons.

# 3. The Knowledge Base
# of Germanic Mythology

*What you have inherited from your fathers, earn over again for yourselves or it will not be yours.*

J. W. v. Goethe

*Wholeness is not achieved by cutting off a portion of one's being, but by integration of the contraries.*

C.G. Jung

Before providing some basic information about the written sources dealing with Germanic mythology, we briefly mention the important, unavoidable terms "source criticism" and "information evaluation." Evaluating an information source is essential in relation to the validity of the subject[60]. Any source may be forged or corrupted. Strong indications of the originality of the source increase its reliability. The closer a source is to the event that it intends to describe and the more the author has personal experience of what is written, the more one can trust it to give an accurate description. A primary is more reliable than a secondary source. If a number of independent sources contain the same message, the credibility of the message is increased. The tendency of a source is its motivation for providing some kind of bias. Tendencies should be minimized or supplemented with opposite motivations. Not only do we have to ask what sources of information exist regarding Germanic mythology, but also how independent and reliable they are. What measures do we take to evaluate the reliability of sources? Do we detect an intention, purpose, and motive with the source? These basic questions accompany us throughout this chapter.

---

[60] Thurén, T. (1997); Olden-Jørgensen, S. (2001).

## 3.1 Latin texts

Romans always wrote with the intention to show up for and to influence other Romans. The truth (as compared to today's ideal: that a statement is known to be correct, i.e., in accord with reality, as confirmed by evidence) was never a Roman virtue. In Rome, one should impress, strengthen public reputation, and get support for one's (political) plans. Thus, one has to watch out when applying evidence by Roman writers.

One of the main and early Latin sources regarding the Germanic tribes is *Commentarii de Bello Gallico* (*An Account of the Gallic Wars*) by Gaius Julius Caesar (100-44 B.C.E.), written as a stylish, third-person narrative. Caesar describes the battles and intrigues that took place in the nine years he spent fighting the Germanic and Celtic peoples in Gaul who opposed progress, i.e., Roman conquest. The "Gaul" that Caesar refers to is for the most modern France, Belgium and Switzerland. On other occasions, he refers only to that territory inhabited by the Celtic peoples known to the Romans as Gauls. The book is valuable for the many geographical and historical claims that can be retrieved from the work. Notable chapters describe Gaulish custom, their religion, and a comparison between Gauls and Germanic peoples. In the spring of 55 B.C.E., Caesar's soldiers attacked a large group of Germanic refugees during an armistice. During early summer, he crossed the Rhine and invaded Germania; later, he even invaded Britain. These operations had little military purpose, but the Senate was impressed, and that was what mattered. Caesar's Gallic Wars was not a document intended to make life miserable for trainees of Latin through 2,000 years, but to pave the road for Caesar's political career. Thus, Caesar selected the seemingly more objective third-person, an unemotional and exalted language. He worked hard to create alliterative catch phrases (such as *veni, vidi, vici* [I came; I saw; I conquered]). We learn a good deal about the Germanic tribes, but more about Caesar.

The main Latin source of information about the Germanic tribes is the famous *De origine et situ germanorum* (*On the Origin and Situation of the Germanic Peoples*, in short: *Germania*) by Gaius Cornelius Tacitus (55-107). It is a historical and ethnographic account on the Germanic tribes outside the Roman Empire. Tacitus' writings are known for their dense prose that seldom glosses the facts. *Germania* begins with a description of the lands, laws, and customs of the Germanic peoples. It describes some individual tribes. They are divided into three large branches, deriving their ancestry from the sons of the god Mannus, their common forefather. Tacitus mentions that the Germanic tribes all had common physical characteristics, such as blue eyes, reddish hair, and large bodies. They were vigorous at the first onset, but not tolerant of exhausting labor. They were tolerant of hunger and cold, but not of heat.

Tacitus describes the Germanic leadership as merit-based and egalitarian. He mentions that the opinions of women are given respect and he describes a form of folk assembly, rather similar to the public *things* recorded in later Germanic sources[61] (see 5.1 and Box VII). In these public deliberations, the final decision rests with the men of the tribe as a whole. Tacitus mentions that women often accompany their men to battle and offer encouragement. He says that the men are often highly motivated to fight for the women because of their fear of losing them to captivity. Tacitus says that the Germanic people are mainly content with one wife. He explicitly compares this practice favorably, perhaps since monogamy was a shared value between Roman and Germanic cultures. He also records that adultery is rare and that an adulterous woman is shunned afterward by the community.

Volumes have been written about to which extent Tacitus is reliable or not, in particular because we have so few written accounts about the Germanic tribes from these days. Tacitus might have wanted to stress the dangers that the Germanic tribes posed to the Roman Empire. They were potentially different from the Germanic tribes of Scandinavia, as based upon later Norse sources. Alternatively, all Germanic tribes may have developed and changed over the 1,000 years between the authoring of *Germania* and the Norse texts (see 3.3). Tacitus himself had never traveled in the Germanic lands, and all his information is second hand, at best. His book may also be part of his political career. He wanted to make an impression on the Romans rather than delivering a precise account. That the Romans were cultivated compared with the wild barbarians was crystal-clear, but the Roman citizens could learn from

---

[61] A *thing* was the governing assembly of a northern Germanic society, made up of free people of the community and presided over by law speakers.

virtues of these primitive folks. *O tempora, o mores* (Oh, the times! Oh, the customs!) is a typical, Roman phrase: from the very start of the Roman Empire, the virtues were seen in decline, and increasing decadence seemingly spread over 500 consecutive years of Roman dominance. The term *Germani*, as used by Tacitus, does not necessarily coincide with the modern linguistic definition of Germanic peoples, as some of the described tribes were probably Celts. *Germani* was a cumulative concept for those wild, uncivilized tribes lingering outside the northern borders of the Roman Empire.

## 3.2 Early Christian texts

Various sources that deal with the Germanic people exist from about 900 to 1,300, under strong influence of Christianity. Again, one has to ask: What is the intention, purpose, and motive behind these accounts? Despite interests to describe the conditions in the Germanic territories, in particular those of the "wild" Saxon tribes, the Roman Catholic Church had, first and foremost, to show that pagans and heathens were primitive people and that Christianity presented progress and culture. Information about Germanic believers and their mythology provided by Christian sources is thus highly tendentious, opinionated, and unreliable. To obtain reliable knowledge about the Germanic tribes, one is forced to read conscientiously between the lines.

*Gesta Hammaburgensis ecclesiae pontificum* (*Deeds of the Bishops of Hamburg*) is a historical treatise by Adam of Bremen (born before 1050; died between 1081 and1085). The book is one of the most important sources of early medieval history of Northern Europe. It covers the entire period known as the Viking Age. The text focuses on the history of the Hamburg-Bremen diocese and its bishops that had jurisdiction over the missions to Scandinavia.

The writings of Adam von Bremen are an important knowledge source of Norse paganism, including the alleged practice of human sacrifice. The description of the temple in Uppsala is one of the most famous excerpts of the *Gesta*: "In this temple, entirely decked out in gold, the people worship the statues of three gods in such a manner that the mightiest of them, Thor, occupies a throne in the middle of the chamber; Wotan and Frikko have places on either side ... Thor, they say, presides over the air, which governs the thunder and lightning, the winds and rains, fair weather and crops. The other, Wotan—that is, fury[62]—carries out war and imparts to man strength against his enemies. The third is Frikko, who bestows peace and pleasure on mortals." What is described are the three most strongly venerated Norse gods in Uppsla: Thor, Odin and Freyja.

The Temple at Uppsala was a religious center of the ancient Norse religion once located at what is now Gamla Uppsala (Old Uppsala, Sweden). Theories have been proposed about the implications of the descriptions of the temple and the findings (or lack thereof) of the archaeological excavations in the area. Recent findings suggest extensive wooden structures and log lines that may have played a supporting role to activities at the site, including ritual sacrifice (probably necromancy; see Box VIII). Adam von Bremen wishes to underline that there is a need for more culture and civilization in his diocese. If human sacrifice were generically carried out in the holy grove at Uppsala, or anywhere else, can still be discussed. Tacitus mentions it, and the Arabian traveler Ahmad ibn Fadlan (877-960) famously describes the sacrifice of a female slave as part of a Volga Viking ship burial in today's Ukraine that he witnessed in 922 (see 3.6). It may be that Adam von Bremen's writing first of all wished to underline the impression that Germanic tribes in Scandinavia needed to be liberated from their barbaric habits, i.e., to be converted to Christianity.

In *Abrenuntiato Saxonica* (Old Saxon baptismal pledge) from 789 and *Deutsches Bußbuch* (penitential book) by Burchard von Worms (965-1025), we can learn about magic beliefs diffusing from pagan times into the Christian era of medieval Germany. A penitential is a book or set of church rules concerning the Christian sacrament of penance, a manner of reconciliation with God[63] that was first developed by Celtic monks in Ireland in the sixth century. It consists of a list of sins and the appropriate penances prescribed to find them. It served as a type of manual for confessors. Deutsches Bußbuch indicates that pagan Germanic beliefs were common in Germany, also on the west side of the Rhine. This

---

[62] Wodan, id est furor.
[63] https://en.wikipedia.org/wiki/Penitential.

despite a thousand years of Roman and Latin influence and domination in the region, including several hundred years under the Roman Catholic Church[64].

*Gesta Danorum* (*Deeds of the Danes*) is a patriotic work of Danish history, by the 12th century author Saxo Grammaticus (1150-1220). It is the most ambitious literary undertaking of medieval, Christian Denmark and is an essential source for the nation's early history. Consisting of 16 books written in Latin, *Gesta Danorum* describes Danish and to some degree Scandinavian history in general, from prehistory to the late 12th century. In addition, *Gesta Danorum* offers singular reflections on European affairs from a uniquely Scandinavian perspective. *Gesta Danorum* was, first of all, written to increase the fame of Danish kings and is thus only partly reliable.

All in all, the early Christian texts shed a scarce light upon the culture and mythology of the Germanic tribes. The common opinion in these records is as follows: The old pagan times were over—Thank God—and a civilized future had just begun. There was no reason to describe the old barbaric rites and culture now that the new day has dawned. A progressive, promising future had to be a Christian one.

## 3.3 Norse and Anglo-Saxon texts

Compared with Germany, the transition from Germanic (or Celtic) paganism to Christianity was rather smooth on the British Isles and in Scandinavia. This is partly due to the Hiberno-Scottish mission that started with Saint Columba in the sixth century, introducing "Celtic Christianity"[65]. By 678, it had arrived in Friesland and it reached central and southern Germany during the first half of the eighth century. Celtic Christianity, which was distinguished by its organizations around monasteries rather than dioceses, selected an almost opposite strategy for its mission compared to the Roman Catholic Church. The latter followed in the Roman footprints and applied military force, political synchronization, destruction, and conversion of holy sites, forced baptism, and centraliza-

---

[64] Hasenfratz, H.-P. (1992); Hasenfratz, H.-P. (2011).
[65] Murphy, G.R. (2013).

tion through kings and the Holy See. Peaceful coexistence, conversion by setting an example and help of any kind through the monasteries were the main strategy of the Hiberno-Scottish mission. In Scandinavia, resistance against Christianity and centralized kingdoms was vehement and resulted in emigration to Iceland and Greenland. According to the Icelandic "Landnámabók" (Book of Settlements), the settlement of Iceland began in the year 874 when the Norwegian chieftain Ingólfr Arnarson became the first permanent settler. In the following centuries, mainly Norwegians and to a smaller extent other Scandinavians settled in Iceland, bringing with them thralls of Gaelic origin. Landnám (Old Norwegian, to take land, i.e., settlement) was a strategy to continue pagan beliefs, based upon the strictly federal structure of the Norse people. Germanic paganism and Christianity lived side by side in Scandinavia and Iceland for hundreds of years. This is the main reason why the sources of Germanic mythology flow much richer in Scandinavia. Central Europe is much closer to Rome and thus exposed to force and the centralistic, Roman, and Catholic tradition. Consequently, the richest sources for Germanic mythology are Old Norse and Anglo-Saxon texts. And indeed, these are rich sources! Here, only a short overview that regards the *Codex Regius, Edda* (the Younger, Snorri or Prose-Edda), *Beowulf* and *The Dream of the Rood* is provided.

The *Codex Regius* (*Royal Book*; Icelandic: *Konungsbók*) contains a suite of Norse poetic work in an Icelandic Middle Age manuscript. The codex was written around 1200 and contains the "Older" or "Poetic Edda." It is the sole source for most of the poems it contains. Nothing was known of its whereabouts until 1643, when it came into the possession of Brynjólfur Sveinsson (1605-1675), then Bishop of Skáholt, Iceland. In 1662, he sent it as a present to King Frederick III of Denmark (1609-1670), hence the name. It was kept in the Royal Library in Copenhagen until 1971, when it was brought back to Iceland. It is now kept in the Árni Magnússon Institute for Icelandic Studies in Reykjavik (Fig. 7). Since air travel was not to be entirely trusted with such precious cargo, it was transported by ship and came back to its place of origin, accompanied by military escort! J.R.R. Tolkien frequently lectured on the subject of the *Codex Regius* during his decade long career as an Oxford professor. The text became a quarry for themes and figures for his oeuvre (see Box III).

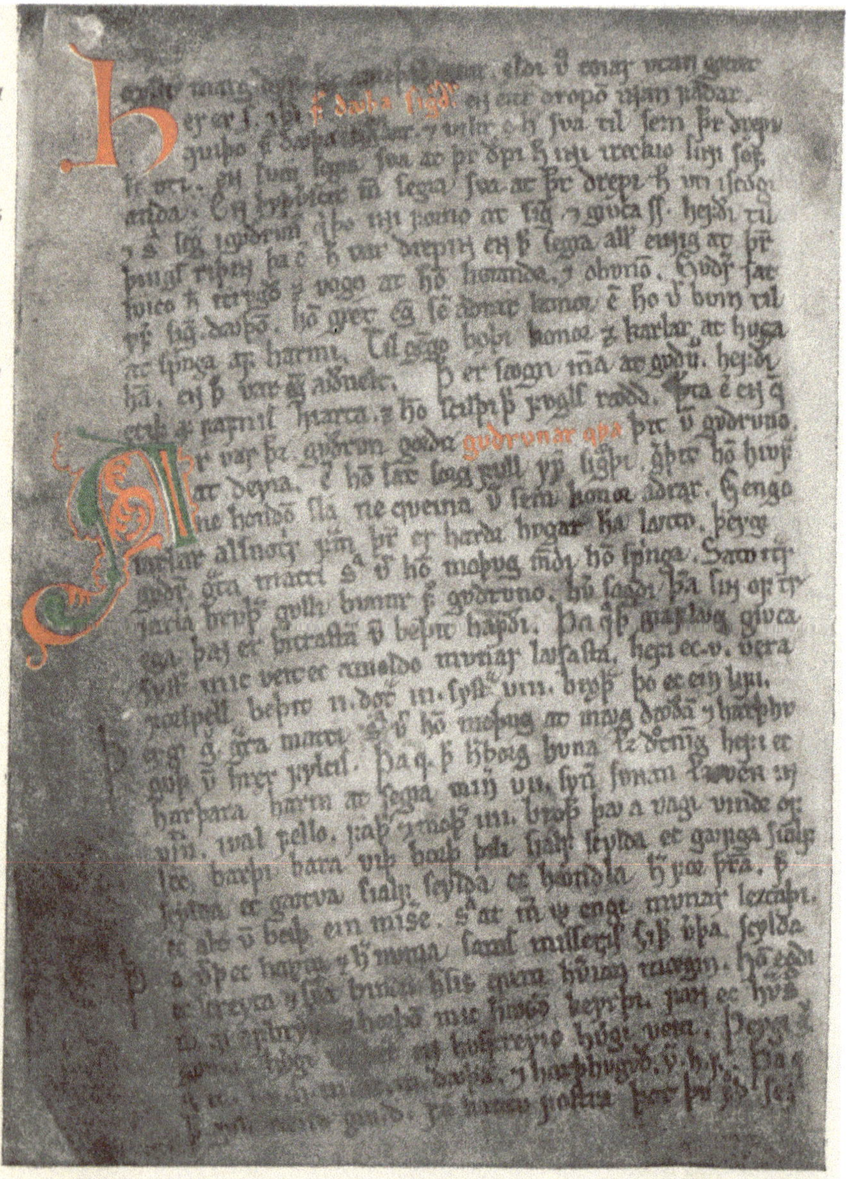

Ein Blatt aus der ältesten Handschrift der älteren Edda,
dem Codex Regius
der königl. Bibliothek zu Kopenhagen, Nr. 2365.
(XIII., vielleicht schon XII. Jahrhundert.)

Fig. 7. Page of the *Völuspa, Codex Regius*. Wikimedia Commons.

## Box III: Snorri or Shakespeare?[66]

In the late 1920s, the legendary writer J.R.R. Tolkien (1892-1973) provoked an argument. Opposing him, among others, was another legendary writer, C.S. Lewis (1898-1963). Tolkien had not yet written *The Hobbit* or *The Lord of the Rings*. Lewis had not yet written *The Chronicles of Narnia*. They were both debating the appropriate curriculum for English majors at Oxford University, where they both taught.

Tolkien believed too much time was spent on dull and unimportant writers like Shakespeare, whom Lewis revered. Tolkien thought students should read Snorri Sturluson.

Who?

And not only Snorri, but also the other fine authors of the Icelandic saga and Eddic poems. And the students should read them in Old Norse. ... It's even better in the original, Tolkien said. He had been reading Old Norse since his teens. He loved the cold, crisp, unsentimental language of the sagas and their bare, straightforward tone like wind keening over ice. Reading Snorri and his peers was more important than reading Shakespeare, Tolkien argued, because their books were more central to (the English) language and ... the modern world. Egg, ugly, ill, smile, knife, fluke, fellow, husband, birth, death, take, mistake, lost, skulk, ransack, brag, law, bylaw, axle, crook, raft, plough, leather, thorp, skerry, ombudsman, heathen, and hell are common English words that all derive from Old Norse. As for Snorri's effect on modernity, it was soon to mushroom.

The *Prose Edda*, also known as the *Younger Edda* or *Snorri's Edda*, is an Old Norse work of literature written in Iceland in the early 13th century. It is assumed that the work was written, or at least compiled, by the Icelandic scholar and historian Snorri Sturluson (1178-1241) around the year 1220[67]. It begins with a section on

---

[66] Extract from "Song of the Vikings" by Brown, N. M. (2012).
[67] Gudmundsson, O. (2011).

the Norse cosmogony, pantheon, and myth. This is followed by three distinct books: *Gylfaginning*, *Skáldskaparmál*, and *Háttatal*. Sturluson, undoubtedly the greatest European author of the 13th century, planned the collection as a textbook. It was to enable Icelandic poets and readers to understand the subtleties of Norse alliterative verse (see 4.2), to grasp the meaning behind the many kennings (see 4.2 and Box VI) that were applied in skaldic poetry and which in the new Christian time were on the verge to be forgotten.

The *Prose Edda* was originally referred to as simply *Edda*. The title changed to *Prose Edda* in modern collections to distinguish it from the collections titled *Poetic Edda* that is largely based on *Codex Regius*. In the 13th-century versions of the *Edda* were still known in Iceland, but scholars speculated that there once was an *Elder Edda* that contained the pagan poems that Snorri quotes in his *Prose Edda*. When *Codex Regius* was discovered, it seemed that this speculation was correct—and so the name *Younger Edda* came into common usage, despite later studies showed that the *Prose Edda* was composed first and connected to an unknown original. By far the greatest knowledge on Norse mythology derives from the two *Eddas* (see chapter 6).

Another rich source of information is one of the most important works in Anglo-Saxon literature, *Beowulf*, an epic, heroic poem in Old English (Fig. 8), consisting of more than 3,000 alliterative lines. It is the oldest surviving long poem in Old English and is commonly cited as one of the most important works of Old English literature. It was written in England sometime between the eighth and the early 11th centuries. The author was an anonymous Anglo-Saxon poet. The poem is set in Scandinavia. Beowulf, a hero of the Geats (Goths), comes to the aid of Hrothgar, the king of the Danes, whose mead hall (feasting hall) in Heorot has been under attack by a monster known as Grendel (a giant or dragon?). After Beowulf slays him, Grendel's mother attacks the hall and is then also defeated. Victorious, Beowulf goes home to Geatland (Götaland in modern Sweden) and later becomes king of the Geats. After a period of 50 years has passed, Beowulf defeats a dragon but is fatally wounded in the battle. After his death, his attendants cremate his body and erect a tower on a headland in his memory. Like in *The Song of the Nibelungs*, written down around 1200 in the Bohemian-Austrian region, the epic tradition of a "good story" is placed into a Germanic context,

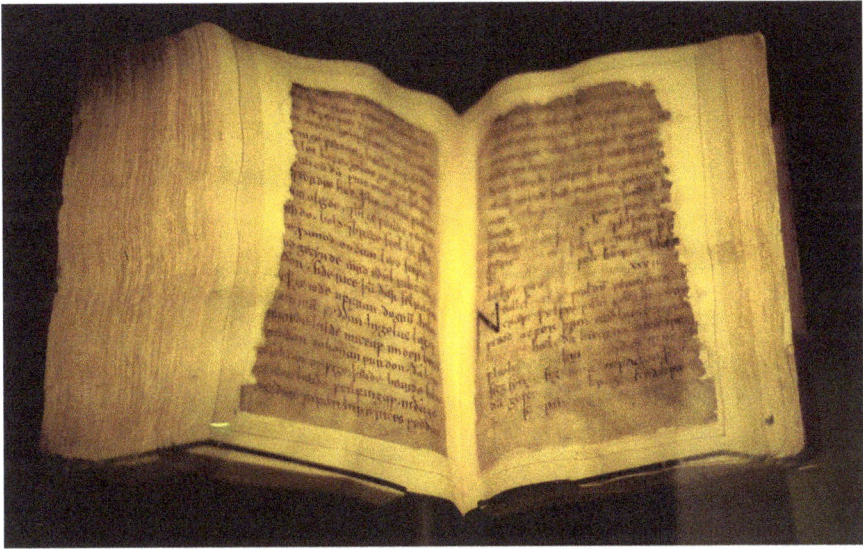

Fig. 8. Page of *Beowulf*. Wikimedia Commons.

with clear reference to Germanic mythology (e.g., Midgard Serpent [dragon, see also Box XX], Ragnarök, Balder's burial, see chapter 6).

On the British Isles, texts and monuments exist from the long transition period between Norse and Christian believes, reflecting the knowledge base of Germanic mythology[68]. The eighth-century Ruthwell Cross (showing Latin, futarc, and futhorc writing [see 4.1]) and the Christian poem *The Dream of the Rood* (unknown author) are of significance here. The poem belongs to the corpus of Old English literature. Like most Old English poetry, it is written in alliterative verse. The term rood derives from the Old English word rod (pole, staff, etc.). More specifically it means crucifix in this context but may also point at the pole/stave of the Volva, Odin, and the alliterative meter of Germanic poetry (see 4.2). Preserved in the 10th century Vercelli Book, the poem is considered one of the oldest works of Old English literature. The name of the poem (rod/pole) and the cross indicate clearly that the ultimate pole, the world tree Yggdrasil, and the cross share similarities[69]. Both are

[68] Murphy, G.R. (2013).
[69] Murphy, R.G. (2013).

essential for a god's sacrifice (see Box XI). The Rothwell cross shaft carries both the Norse and Latin writing of the two worlds that it combines. The shaft appears to combine the image of the crucified Christ with that of Odin/Wotan bound upon the Tree of Life. In the poem, the heroic lord or warrior fixes himself to the rod/pole/cross, which again unequivocally hints at Odin. Thus, the *The Dream of the Rood* and the *Ruthwell Cross*, in words and design, reflect attempts to understand Christianity through a base in the Germanic tradition. A similar combination of Germanic pagan symbols and the new Christian religion is also found in Norwegian stave churches (Fig. 9) and early medieval round churches in southern Scandinavia.

Fig. 9. Carvings around the north wall portal of Urnes Stave Church, Norway. Entangled snake- or dragon-like animals and foliage on the wall of this early medieval church appear to reflect the worm Nidhögg at the root of Yggdrasil (see 6.2; Box XX). Entering the church can be interpreted as entering the world tree, in which Hoddmimis Holt is hidden (Liv and Livtrase, the not-yet-born humans who will become the onset of a future lineage of man of the New Earth; see 6.2 and 6.5.7). Christianity is thus interpreted as the New Earth. Wikimedia Commons.

## 3.4 East Germanic texts

The only existing evidence for the East Germanic language is the "Gothic Bible" or "Wulfila Bible". In the fourth century bishop Ulfilas (or Wulfila; 310-383) translated it from Latin into Gothic language, spoken by the Eastern Germanic (Gothic) tribes. During the third century, the emigrated Goths lived on the northeast border of the Roman Empire, in what is now Bulgaria, Romania, and Ukraine. During the fourth century, the Goths were converted to Christianity (Arianism[70]), largely through Ulfilas efforts, who invented an alphabet, created for the purpose of translating the Bible. It is completely different from the "Gothic script" of the Middle Ages, a script used to write the Latin alphabet (see 8.2). Ulfilas translated in Nicopolis ad Istrum (today's Veliko Tarnovo in northern Bulgaria). In the fifth century and onward, the Bible was translated into Armenian, and thereafter followed Syriac, Coptic, Old Nubian, Ethiopic, and Georgian translations. The very onset of translating the Bible was thus initiated by a barbarian Germanic tribe. For the next major translation into a Germanic language (Martin Luther), we had to wait until the 16th century. The Wulfila Bible, although fragmentary, is the only extensive document in an ancient East Germanic language and one of the earliest documents in any Germanic language (Fig. 10). On behalf of Swedish scientists, the text was stolen by Swedish troops during the Thirty Years War from the Abbey of Werden in Germany and transported to Uppsala, where it is today. The Gothic version of the Lord's Prayer from about 450 is even today understandable.

Text box 1. The start of the Lord's Prayer in Gothic (left) and English right).

| | |
|---|---|
| Atta unsar | Our Father |
| thu in himinam, | in heaven, |
| weihnai namo thein. | hallowed be your name |
| Qimai thiudinassus theins, | Your kingdom come, |
| wairthai wilja theins, | your will be done, |
| swe in himina jah ana airthai | on earth, as it is in heaven |

---

[70] Arianism is a nontrinitarian Christological doctrine which asserts the belief that Jesus Christ is the Son of God who was begotten by God the Father at a point in time, a creature distinct from the Father and is therefore subordinate to him, but the Son is also God.

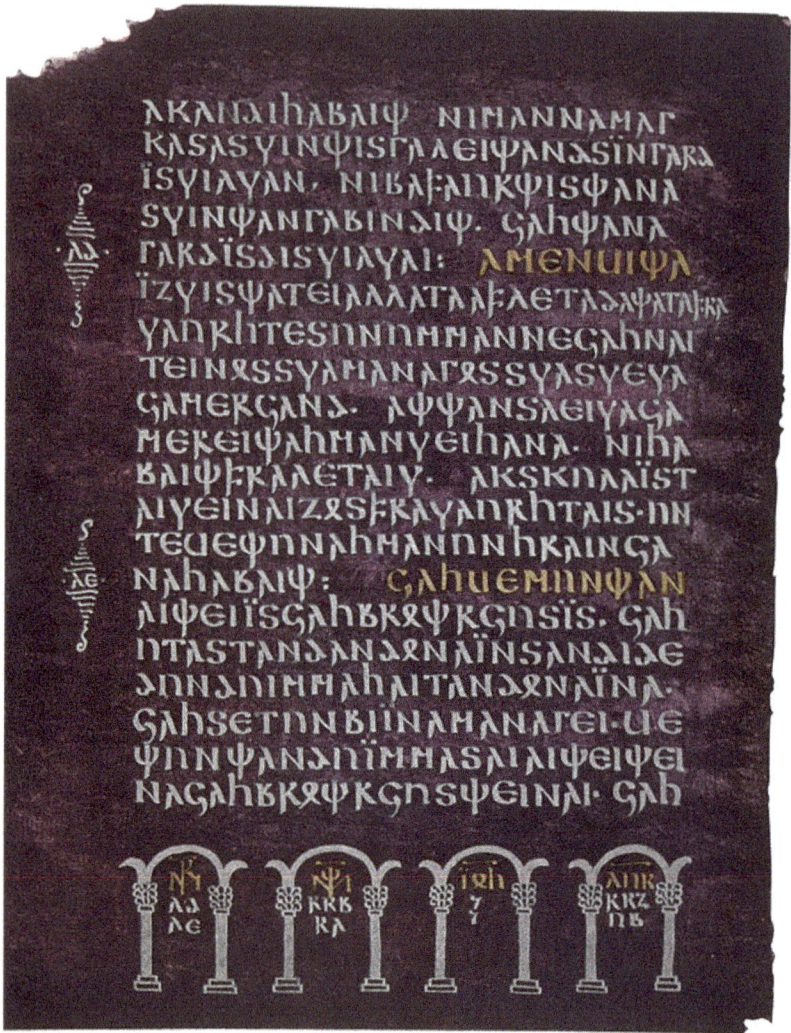

Fig. 10. Page of the Wulfila Bible. Wikimedia Commons.

Unfortunately, we do not have any written sources regarding the culture and beliefs of the Goths from their pagan times. East Germanic culture, language, and genes dissolved for good into the expanse of Europe.

## 3.5 Central-European texts

West of the Rhine and south of the Danube, the influence of Latin, Rome, and the Catholic Church "romanized" the Germanic tribes, and that influenced their writing so much that almost no Germanic texts are preserved from this region. The lack of texts could be interpreted as a sign of the low cultural standards of the Germanic tribes but reflects rather ideological suppression[71]. The Germanic mythology became suppressed, the veneration groves became church sites, and the holy trees were cut. The *thing* (Old Norse, English, and Icelandic), the governing assembly of Germanic societies, made up of the free people of the community (see Box VII) and the Germanic matrimonial partnership (see Box XIV) were abolished. The Germanic culture went into dissolution and became encased into the subconscious and unconscious.

The oldest but utterly isolated discovery of Germanic gods in central Europe is an inscription on the Nordendorfer Runenspange (a silver brooch with rune inscriptions) from the sixth century, found in Bavaria. The inscription is in Elder Futhark (see 4.1). Three gods are mentioned on the brooch. The words *wodan* and *wigithonar* were interpreted as the names of Wotan and Thor ("Weihe-Donar", *wigi* = Germanic *$\bar{w}$igian [consecrate] or "Kampf-Donar" [*wigi* = Germanic *$\bar{w}$igan fight]). Interpretations of the short text vary widely, but it is obvious that central Germanic gods were known, if not consecrated, by the Germanic Aleman tribe in the sixth century.

After the failed Roman attempts to include the eastern Rhine region (cf. the greatest military defeat of Rome under Publius Quinctilius Varus, 9 B.C.E.), it took more than 700 years before the Germanic tribes east of the Rhine became part of European, Christian mainstream history. Charlemagne (742-814) subjected the obstinate Continental Saxons living in what was known as Old Saxony (east of the Rhine) in a long series of campaigns, the Saxon Wars (772–804). The Saxon Wars resulted in the incorporation of Saxony into the Frankish realm, forcible

---

[71] Andalusia could serve as an analogy. Due to eradication of Muslim texts by the massive suppression by Christianity, one cannot find much written after 780 years of highly developed Arabic culture. Which in many respects became a base for Christian European culture because the translated classical Greek texts were steadily used in the highly advanced institutions in Andalusia.

conversion to Christianity and expulsion of some of the population to northwestern France. All holy trees and columns, such as the Irminsul (Old Saxon [great/mighty or arising pillar], a pillar which is attested as playing an important role in the Germanic paganism of the Saxon people) were destroyed (see Fig. 48). Charlemagne and the German National Saint Bonifatius (675-754) were the ultimate, uncompromising messengers for the centralistic Roman Catholic Church, the most famous, fanatical, and disrespectful holy tree loggers and eradicators of the Germanic faith. Not a single holy tree has ever been reported to have been cut by the tolerant and peaceful Hiberno-Scottish mission that did not have a demand for supremacy and absolute power. The presence of Irish-Scottish Christianity and the fact that some Germanic people had already had converted to Christianity was ignored in history. Christianization is interpreted by complete surrender to the Roman Catholic Church and the central power of kings. The epic poetry of the Saxons that seemed to have existed did not survive Christianization.

Some elements of Germanic mythology were preserved in the Middle High German epic poem *The Song of the Nibelungs*. The story tells of the dragon-slayer Siegfried at the court of the Burgundies, how he was murdered and of his wife Kriemhild's revenge. *The Song of the Nibelungs* is based on pre-Christian Germanic heroic motifs that include oral traditions and reports based on historical events and individuals of the fifth and sixth centuries (e.g., the defeat of the Burgundies by the Huns in 437). Germanic mythology sneaked into the epos. For example, Hagen von Tronje is one-eyed, good in warfare, and has prophetic powers. Obviously, he has been provided with the attributes of Wotan/Odin. Old Norse parallels of *The Song of the Nibelungs* legend survived in the *Prose* and *Poetic Edda*, the *Völsungen Saga*, and other sagas. *The Song of the Nibelungs* suggests that there has been a Germanic mythology similar to the Norse one, also in Central Europe. Alternatively, these elements could have been imported from Scandinavia.

However, in the Merseburger Zauberprüche (Merseburg Incantations or Merseburg Charms), two medieval magic spells (charms or incantations), written in Old High German provide us with evidence of an existing Germanic mythology in Central Europe, similar to the one found in Scandinavia. The Merseburger Incantations are the only known examples of Germanic pagan belief preserved in this language. They were discovered in 1841, but they were written in the ninth or 10th century. The manuscript is stored in the library of the cathedral chapter of Merseburg, hence the name. Each charm is divided into two parts. A preamble tells the story of a mythological event. The actual spell follows in the form of a magic analogy. In their verse form, the spells are of a transitional type. The lines show not only traditional alliteration (see 4.2), but also the end-rhymes introduced in the Christian verse after the ninth century. Dealing with Germanic mythology the second Merseburg charm is of particular significance.

Text box 2. One of the Merseburg Incantations in Old High German (left) and English (right).

| | |
|---|---|
| Phôl ende Wuodan fuorun zi holza, | *Phol and Wodan were riding to the woods,* |
| dû wart demo balderes folon sîn fuoz birenkit. | *and the foot of Balder's foal was sprained.* |
| Thû biguol en Sinthgunt, Sunna era swister. | *So Sinthgunt, Sunna's sister, conjured it.* |
| Thû biguol en Frîja, Folla era swister. | *and Frija, Volla's sister, conjured it.* |
| Thû biguol en Wuodan, sô hê wola conda: | *and Wodan conjured it, as well he could:* |
| Sôse bênrenki, sôse bluotrenki, | *Like bone-sprain, so blood-sprain,* |
| sôse lidirenki: | *so joint-sprain:* |
| Bên zi bêna, bluot zi bluoda, | *Bone to bone, blood to blood,* |
| lid zi geliden, sôse gelîmida sîn. | *joints to joints, so may they be mended.* |

Paraphrased, these verses tell that Phol is with Wodan when Balder's horse dislocates its foot while riding through the forest. Wodan offers an invocation: "Bone to bone, blood to blood, joints to joints, so may they be mended." Figures that can be clearly identified within Continental Germanic mythology are Uuôdan (Wodan) and Frîia (Frija). Comparing to Norse mythology, Wodan is well-attested as the cognate of Odin. Frija is the cognate of Frigg, also identified with Freyja. In the present context Phol is another name of Balder[72]. The Merseburger

---

[72] The *Prose Edda* tells that Balder became king of Westphalia during Odin's march for Sweden.

Incantations suggest close linkages between Norse and Continental Germanic mythology. And they reflect some of the alliterative word magic (e.g. "bên zi bêna, bluot zi bluoda", text box 2) that is part of the atavistic, shamanistic tradition that has and, in some regions, still is part of the Germanic people's heritage.

## 3.6 Non-European texts

Arabs who encountered Scandinavians who had journeyed eastward depicted them as handsome people but filthy and barbaric. More than 1,000 years ago, the diplomat Ahmad ibn Fadlan recorded a meeting with a strange race that he called the *Rusiyyah* (eastern Germanic tribes, now commonly known as Volga Vikings)[73]. Ahmad ibn Fadlan first met the Norse warriors as they traveled across the Russian and Ukrainian steppes, sailing their long ships down the Volga River and investigating trade with the Arab world. How were the Norsemen perceived through the eyes of a non-European? The records of Ahmad ibn Fadlan are said to be the most complete written accounts (outside of Icelandic books), but they concern only the eastbound Norsemen who used the Baltic Sea and adjacent rivers to visit what is modern-day Russia and Ukraine for trade. Ahmad ibn Fadlan was fascinated by what he perceived to be their barbaric lifestyles. He wrote that they did not purify themselves after excreting or urinating. Neither did they wash themselves when in a state of "ritual impurity" (after coitus) and did not even wash their hands after food. He attested that they were the filthiest of all Allah's creatures.

The reaction of Ahmad ibn Fadlan is a mixture of horror and fascination. In addition to the lack of hygiene, the men were tattooed and performed ship burial rituals that included killing a female slave. Ahmad ibn Fadlan may have failed to report important qualities of the Norse culture of these times: Too strong was his challenge with these "savages." However, other Arab scholars also shared some observations of these

---

and Norway. The kenning Phol is hidden in the name Westphalia. See Nemenyi, G.v. (2004).
[73] https://en.wikipedia.org/wiki/Ahmad_ibn_Fadlan. The Rusiyyah or Rus' people originated in what is currently coastal Middle Sweden around the eighth century and that their name has the same origin as Roslagen in Sweden.

saqalibah (a term translated as "fair-haired, ruddy-complexioned population of Central, Eastern and North-Eastern Europe"). Some wrote they were handsome, clean, and well-dressed. They were generous to each other, honored their guests and treated well those who sought refuge with and came to visit them. They do not allow anyone to annoy or harm guests.

For an Arab such as Ahmad ibn Fadlan, accustomed to the secluded privacy of a walled home, strict separation between genders in public, and strict cleanliness, the Norse culture was a significant challenge that influenced his impressions. If not, particular aspects of the Norse culture would have presented Arabic authors with a plethora of positive and impressive characteristics that may have dominated their accounts.

## 3.7 Scientific investigations of Germanic Mythology

After the discovery of *Codex Regius* in 1643, the interest in Germanic mythology increased. In particular in Germany, many were searching for written remains of the Germanic past. The Merseburger Incantations, the Nordendorfer Runenspange, and elements from the heroic songs and epics *Nibelungenlied*, *Hildebrandslied*, and *Heliand* belong to the few proofs of the existence of a Germanic mythology in Central Europe. Were there more? A most important, by all means eminent, figure to find out was Jacob Grimm, the founder of basic German(ic) antiquity and German philology. In 1835, he published one of the most significant textbooks on the topic and the first exhaustive treatment of the subject[74]. It traced the mythology and beliefs of the ancient Germanic peoples from their earliest attestations to their survivals in modern traditions, folktales, and popular expressions. The structure of this breakthrough of literature science is encyclopedic. The articles and chapters are discourses of philological, historical, folkloristic, and poetic aspects of pre-Christian Germanic religions. In many instances, Grimm mixes the North and Central Germanic variants to one religious entity, which is most likely incorrect (see 7.4). An important figure for spreading the knowledge

---

[74] Grimm, J. (1835).

about the Germanic times is Karl Joseph Simrock (1802–1876), a German poet and writer who is primarily known for his translation of texts such as the *Nibelungenlied* and the *Edda* into modern German. Simrock established his reputation by his excellent modern rendering of the old German texts. He was expelled from Prussian civil service for writing a poem in praise of the revolution in France. Both Grimm and Simrock made essential contributions to the understanding of the Germanic past.

An important follower of the Grimm tradition was Viktor Rydberg (1828-1895), the Swedish author of *Investigations into Germanic Mythology*, a two-volume work published in Swedish in 1886 and 1889[75]. Rydberg is considered the last and poetically most gifted of the mythological school founded by Jacob Grimm.

Summarizing, we can state that strong evidence of a Central European Germanic mythology cannot be provided. Some books try to summarize one German mythology[76], but these works are rather speculative and mix Norse mythology with Central European elements. It is thus unclear what the mythological differences between the Western, Eastern and Central Germanic tribes were. But there are indications that they shared similarities.

## 3.8 Conclusion

Reliable information about a plethora of Germanic tribes and their mythology is sparse and spread over 1,500 years and the expanse of the entire European continent. Changes continuously take place over time and space. One coherent Germanic mythology did probably not exist. Germanic mythology is a comprehensive term for myths associated with historical Germanic paganism, including Norse, Anglo-Saxon, and Continental Germanic mythology. These mythologies were potentially different, if we knew them in sufficient detail. They ultimately derive from the mythology of the proto-Indo-Europeans and have probably much in common. From the anticipated three, basic Germanic mythologies, we know only one well: Norse mythology. The lack of

---

[75] Rydberg, V. (1889).
[76] e.g. Herrmann, P. (1898).

indisputable evidence for a Central European Germanic mythology has resulted in that mythological material being "borrowed" from Icelandic sources in order to create a more comprehensive mythology for Central Europe. This is in particular the case for Germany. The original German mythology was annihilated and eradicated by the Roman Empire, Charlemagne, and the Roman Catholic Church. During times when the German Nationalist movement was strong, Germanic mythology in Central Europe has been regrettably misused to serve narrow German nationalistic goals (see 7.4 and Box XV).

*Dans i storstuen* (*Girls Dancing*) by Halfdan Egedius (1877-1899; National Gallery of Norway, Oslo). Norwegian folk dances encompass a strong passion for rhythm and beat, pointing at the alliteration of the Norse literature tradition. The pounding of staves of the old times is mimicked through inciting tramping on wooden floors, resulting in vibrant echo. Two girls with their flying skirts, engirdled by their compatriots and in the darkness of the barn, are seized by the rhythm and the round dance of life. The contrast between the bright summer evening outside and the internal, personal experience points at seizure and profound emotion. Do we hear the thundering stave of the Völva, the vision and prophecies of the seeress from the poetic *Edda*? Is this whirling dance of excitement, accompanied by the hammering pulse of life, a radiating memory from the Norse times? Copyright: National Gallery of Norway, Oslo.

# 4. Old Germanic Literature and Poetry

*Weite Welt und breites Leben,*
*Langer Jahre, redlich Streben,*
*Stets geforscht und stets gegründet,*
*Nie geschlossen, oft gerundet,*
*Ältestes bewahrt mit Treue,*
*Freundlich aufgefasstes Neue,*
*Heitern Sinn und reine Zwecke:*
*Nun, man kommt wohl eine Strecke*[77]

J. W. v Goethe

The Germanic tribes developed a characteristic, unprecedented form of writing and poetry. The Norse literature was rich and diverse. Nowhere in Europe could so many people read and write than in Scandinavia and Iceland during early medieval times. With the introduction of Christianity and Latin writing, a wealth of literature was produced, in particular in Iceland. The splendor of this period radiates into our times. Even today

---

[77] Spacious world, capacious life,
Years with honest effort rife,
Tireless searching, firmly founded,
Never ended, often rounded,
Old traditions, well respected,
innovations not rejected,
noble aim, with cheer professed:
Well, we're sure that we've progressed.

Iceland is an extremely literate society, as demonstrated by the about 300 books published annually (about 880 books per million inhabitants). These are remnants of the previously so rich Norse tradition. It may have been different in other parts of the Germanic regions, but it may be wise to accept the notion that the Germanic barbarians were not necessarily illiterate. Here we focus briefly upon a few aspects of Germanic writing and poetry and figure out if archetypal patterns can be detected[78]. We investigate what runes and alliteration are before we end in a brief excursion into the spectacular modernity of Norse poetry[79].

## 4.1 Runes

Runes (Proto-Norse runo, Old Norse: rún) are the letters developed by Germanic tribes in a set of related alphabets known as runic alphabets. They were used to write various Germanic languages before the adoption of the Latin alphabet and for specialized purposes thereafter. In the name rune we find the German verb raunen (whispering, sharing a secret). Thus, the runes had not only a communicative but also a spiritual and secret role. The term rune suggests an element of air, breath, and a hardly recognizable message. That fits well with the Aesir gods that follow and hover the Germanic tribes through the skies (see 6.5).

The Scandinavian rune variants (see Fig. 11) are also known as *futhark* (derived from their first six letters of the alphabet: F, U, Þ, A, R and K). The Anglo-Saxon variant is *futhorc*. The earliest runic inscriptions date from around 150. The Latin alphabet generally replaced runes during Christianization, by approximately 700 in Central Europe and 1100 in Northern Europe. However, the use of runes persisted for specialized purposes in Northern Europe, for example during the late medieval times in the city of Bergen. Until the early 20th century, runes were used in rural Norway and Sweden for decorative purposes and on runic calendars (Norwegian: *primstav*). Even today, Icelandic magical staves, symbols called Galdrastafur (*galdr*, Old Norse, spell, incantation) are credited with magical effects preserved in various *grimoires* (book

---

[78] Bodkin, M. (1934).
[79] Hallberg, P. (1962).

ᚠᚢᚢᚦᚠᚱᚻᚷ

f   u   th   a   r   k   g

ᚹᚺᚾᛁᛜᛢᛈ

w   h   n   i   J   ch   p

ᛉᛋᛏᛒᛖᛗᛚ

x       b   e   m   l

ᛜᛟᛞᛟᚨᛦᛠ

ng   oe   d   o   ae   y   ea

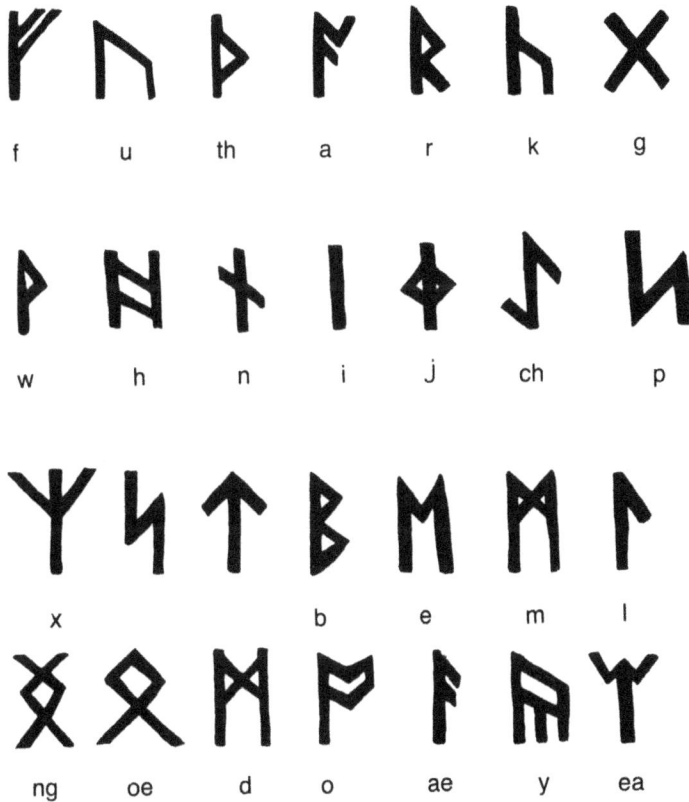

Fig. 11. Overview of one of several runic alphabets. Also described are the pronounciation of each rune, the meaning that can be attributed to the rune, and the Latin letter that is associated with the rune. Wikimedia Commons.

of spells)[80]. For more information about interest in runes in modern times, see Box V.

Historically, the runic alphabet is a derivation of Old Italic scripts of antiquity, with the addition of some innovations. Migrating Germanic tribes picked up the art of writing during their movements through central and southern Europe (see 2.3). Which variant of the Old Italic family in particular gave rise to the runes is uncertain. Suggestions

---

[80] https://en.wikipedia.org/wiki/Icelandic_magical_staves.

Fig. 12. Rune stone "Ölstastenen" at Skansen, Stockholm. The rune stone comes from Uppland in Sweden and is from about 1000. It is repainted in order to provide an impression of what the stone might have looked like. Snakes or dragons dominate the design (see Box XX). Take note of the cross on top, combined with the dragons. The text says: "Björn, Ödulv, Gunnar and Holmdis raised this stone after Ulv, Ginnlögs husband. And Åsmund stroke." Wikimedia Commons.

include Raetic, Venetic, Etruscan, or Old Latin as candidates. Runes can be written as we use Latin letters to mark specific events (Fig. 12), often on large rune stones[81] or to indicate specific ownership, see for example the Golden Horns of Gallehus[82]. Runes can also be signs for some specific sounds or they can be used as a sign for the specific concept which names they carry (similar to Japanese *katakana* and *hanji* or Egyptian hieroglyphs; see Fig. 11). They can also mean numbers and be magic signs. Thus, the rune *feoh* could mean f, but also the god Freyr, gold, wealth, and abundance. The rune rad could denote r, a ride, vehicle, and journey. And as a last example we mention the rune mann, denoting m, man, human being, or the moon. Except for a short period in the Middle Ages, runes were not used for everyday communication and literature. Based upon the German term *Buchstaben* (letters), which is related to runes, one can speculate that runes may have had a ritual, oracle-type function (see Box IV).

---

[81] Jansson, S. B. (1980). Runstenar. STF, Stockholm.
[82] https://en.wikipedia.org/wiki/Golden_Horns_of_Gallehus.

## Box IV: Runes, oracle sticks and I Ching?

Longish, vertical carved lines (similar to rods or staves) can be seen as the basic structural element of runes. In German, letters are Buchstaben (from Proto-Germanic *bōks; see English book), which means rods or staves[83]. Another theory focuses upon the strong central stroke of runes (Old Norse stafr). This implies that the term "letter" is connected to runes in German. It is possible that throwing staves was used to obtain an oracle. The arrangement of the staves created patterns that potentially were interpreted as runes with a fixed, sacred, and particular symbolic meaning (see 4.1). In German, to read is *lesen*, but the verb has two meanings. It is either "to read" or "to pick something up" (e.g., Beerenlese). Buchstaben *lesen* could thus mean both to read letters or to pick staves (oracle sticks, in case they were thrown during oracle-type ceremonies). Thus, "to read" and "letters" in German may refer to oracle application of runes in former times.

The religious context of runes resulted in their symbolic application and prevented their use to write literature. Staves could have had an application that is similar to the application in the book *I Ching*. This is an ancient divination manual and the oldest of the Chinese classics, possessing a history of more than two and a half millennia of commentary and interpretation. The *I Ching* is an influential text read throughout the world, providing inspiration to the worlds of religion, psychoanalysis, business, literature, and art[84]. Runes and oracle sticks may share parallels with the application of *I Ching*.

Runes were and are popular, though for different reasons than during Germanic times. Increasing interest in runes at the end of the 19th century was strongly reflected by a range of esoteric movements (see Box V). For a detailed account of Germanic neopagansim (Asatro[85]) and German ultranationalist movements, see Schnurbein (2018). The Nazi

---

[83] https://de.wikipedia.org/wiki/Buchstabe.
[84] Smith, R. J. (2008).
[85] modern Asatru are expressions of old Norse religion and folklore from 1960 and onwards.

and *völkisch* movements actively exploited elements developed by bizarre and eccentric groups (see Box V). In Fig. 11, we recognize the oe or othala (oethel) rune (Proto-Germanic *ōthalan [heritage; inheritance, inherited estate]) that has been used by the neopagan Deutsche Glaubensbewegung (German Faith Movement) and similar organizations in Germany and abroad[86] (see Box XVI). This rune is still used by related movements in Europe today, on the shoulder straps of the Ukrainian merchant marine and, astonishingly, as an insignia of the rank of sergeant major in the German *Bundeswehr*. Several contemporary fascist and white racism movements apply the victory rune of the god Tyr[87]. Odinists and followers of Asatru (see 7.8) use runes, usually without any relation to National Socialism or white racism. Icelandic magical staves (Galdrastafur) are anew applied in Iceland.

## Box V: Völkisch movement, rune mysticism and Nazi symbolism

Völkisch movement (*Völkische Bewegung*) is the German inte-pretation of a populist interest group with a romantic focus on folklore and the naturally grown community in unity (as opposed to a refined and sophisticated society characterized by diverging interests). *Gleichschaltung* (the process of successively establishing a system of totalitarian control and coordination over all aspects of society = Nazification of state and society) is the instrument to create unity. In line with J.G. Herder, the *völkisch* movement is characterized by the one-body-metaphor (*Volkskörper*) for the entire population. The ideological core of the *völkisch* movement was an aggressive National Socialism, anti-Semitism, and social Darwinism. In the struggle of existence only the superior, valuable races win. This is in opposition to the tolerant and friendly coexistence of people that inspired Herder.

---

[86] Emberland, T. (2003).
[87] For example Nordic Resistance Movement; https://en.wikipedia.org/wiki/Nordic_Resistance_Movement.

In 1908, the Austrian occultist, mystic, and *völkisch* author Guido von List (1848-1919) published *Das Geheimniss der Runen* (*The Secret of the Runes*)[88]. In his book, List published a set of 18 so-called Armanen runes, based on the Younger Futhark (see 4.1) and runes of List's own introduction. In the esoteric tradition of the times, these were allegedly revealed to him in a state of temporary blindness after cataract operations on both eyes. The use of runes in Germanic mysticism played a certain role in Nazi symbolism. The fascination with runic symbolism was mostly limited to Heinrich Himmler (1900-1945) and shared less by the other members of the Nazi top leadership. Consequently, runes appear mostly in insignia associated with the Schutzstaffel (SS), the paramilitary organization led by Himmler (two Sig Runs, see Fig. 10).

Runes are popular in Germanic neopaganism (see 7.8) and to a lesser extent in other forms of New Age esotericism[89]. Various systems of runic divination have been published since the 1980s[90]. For example, today's neo-Nazi Nordic Resistance Movement applies the victory rune of the god Tyr. For more information, see Schnurbein (2018).

## 4. 2 Alliterative verse, *heiti* and *kennings*

Old Norse poetry is characterized by alliteration, which is a stylistic literary device. It is identified by the repeated sound of the first consonant in a series of multiple words and the repetition of the same sounds in stressed syllables of a phrase. Alliteration comes from the Latin word *litera* (letters of the alphabet). The German/Scandinavian term for alliteration is *Stabreim/stavrim*, which is a form of rhyme that directly accounts for a main element of Germanic poetry and literature. The term derives from the German/Scandinavian word *Stab/stav* (stick, pole, stave) and illustrates a.) the manner in which runes are carved/cut/scratched and

---

[88] List, G.v. (1914).
[89] Nemenyi, G.v. (2003).
[90] https://en.wikipedia.org/wiki/Runes.

b.) the meter of poetry (which could have been accompanied by beating a wooden stick onto the floor or ground). Germanic seers (such as the Völva [see chapter 6]) and the god Odin (see 6.5.1) are applying sticks/poles. The Latin-based term alliteration unfortunately removes the immanent meaning of the term and camouflages its nature. The term *Stabreim/stavrim* was introduced by Snorri Sturluson, the author of the *Prose Edda*: *stafr* (stave, syllable [Scandinavian *stavelse*]). The entire Germanic poetry used alliteration until the Christian tail rhyme took over. The Old English *Beowulf*, the Old Saxonian *Heliand*, the Old High German *Hildebrandslied* and the Old Norse poetic *Edda* are all based upon alliterative long lines. Germanic poetry was orally communicated (often in a stunt manner) and thus needed an audience of listeners, not readers. Alliteration (with a unique rhythmic meter) was important in times when memorizing rather than writing was a core element of the literary tradition.

Through the use of phraseological twin-forms, alliteration is an important part of our everyday rhetoric. **D**onald **D**uck, **M**ickey **M**ouse, **g**ood as **g**old, **b**usy as a **b**ee and **f**riend and **f**oe are examples. Alliteration was and is an important element to memorize and make significant points. We refer here to two recent examples from important speeches.

"... they will not be judged by the **c**olor of their **s**kin but by the **c**ontent of their **c**haracter," said Martin Luther King, Jr..

"... because **b**rave men and women have been ready to **f**ace the **f**ire at **f**reedom's **f**ront," articulated Ronald Reagan.

If we listen carefully to rap texts, we can clearly discover that alliteration is an important element for the rhythm and the content of what is communicated (twin-forms, beat of syllables, deep-felt terms, strong and accentuated personal take of the communicator). The old skaldic poem forms have thus not completely disappeared: We use their techniques daily.

The Old Norse poetic vocabulary was expanded by *heiti* and *kennings* (Box VI). A *heiti* (Old Norse [name, appellation, designation, term]) is a synonym used in Old Norse poetry in place of the normal word. For instance, Old Norse poets might use *jór* (steed) instead of the

## Box VI: *Kennings* and *heiti*: some examples.
## A selection of kennings of the gods Odin and Freyja
## and *heiti* circling the term *hlíf* (shield)

Odin
Alføðr = Allfather, Father of All
Bøðgæðir = Battle Enhancer
Faðr galdr = Father of Magical Songs
Fimbultýr = Mighty God
Foldardróttinn = Lord of the Earth
Galdraføðr = Father of Magical Songs
Gangleri = Wanderer
Geirtýr = Spear God
Hangadróttinn = Lord of the Hanged
Hangagud = God of the Hanged

Freyja
Daughter of Njørðr
Sister of Freyr
Wife of Óðr,
Mother of Hnoss
Possessor of the fallen slain
Possessor of Brísingamen
Van-deity
Vanadís
Fair-tear deity
Syr (meaning sow)

Hlíf
eldr hlífar = fire of shield (sword)
flagð hlífar = giantess of shield (ax)
flagða hlífar = shaker of axes (warrir)
flagðs hlífar = noise of ax (battle)
galkn hlífa = monster of shields (ax)
grand hlífar = destruction of shield (ax)
gnýr hlífa = roar of shields (battle)
gim hlífar = fire of shield (sword)
hlíf-él = shield-shower (battle)
valdr hlífar = holder of shield (warrior)

prosaic *hestr* (horse). *Kennings* are highly condensed metaphorical ways of referring to a deity, a place, or an object. In the Merseburg Incantations (see 3.5) Phol is a *heiti* of Balder. Some of the 170 *kennings* of Odin are provided in Box VI. In the modern sense, *heiti* are distinguished from *kennings* in that a *heiti* is a simple word, whereas a *kenning* is a circumlocution in the form of a phrase or compound word. Thus, *mækir* is a *heiti* for sword (the usual word in prose is *sverð*), whereas *grand hlífar* (destruction of shield) and *ben-fúrr* (wound-fire) are *kennings* for sword (see Box VI). Indeed, Old Norse applies a flowery language that has, as compared to today's language use, a theatric elegance.

## 4.3 Germanic poetry

Old Norse poetry encompasses a range of verse forms written during the period from the eighth to the 13th centuries. Most of the Old Norse poetry survived in Iceland, but there are also 122 preserved poem lines in Swedish, Norwegian, and Danish rune inscriptions (e.g. Fig. 12). Poetry played an important role in the social and religious world of the Norse peoples. In Norse mythology, the book *Skáldskaparmál* (language of poetry, the second part of Snorri Sturluson's *Prose Edda*) tells the story of how Odin brought the mead of poetry to Asgard, which is an indicator of the significance of poetry within the contemporary Scandinavian culture. The role of writing with runes had a different goal from writing stories. They were condensations of content, "words of power," magical formulas, or word sorcery.

Old Norse poetry is conventionally, and somewhat arbitrarily, split into two types—Eddic and skaldic poetry. Eddic poetry includes the poems of the *Codex Regius* and a few other similar ones. Skaldic poetry is usually defined as everything else. There exist glorious examples of modern poetry harbingers by Norsemen and in a style which was first continued in Europe by the end of the 19th century. Brutal and rough men who owned outspoken poetic hearts created these marvelous poems. Here we mention Egill Skallagrimsson (904–995), a poet, warrior, and farmer. He is also the protagonist of the famous *Egill's Saga*, written by an unknown author (but probably by Snorri Sturluson).

Apart from being presented as a warrior of immense might, violence, and recklessness in literary sources, Egill is also celebrated for his poetry, considered by many historians to be the finest of the ancient Scandinavian poets. *Sonatorrek* (the irreparable loss of sons) has been called the birth of Nordic personal lyric poetry. Egill is old and loses his last son at sea. Life lost its meaning, and in his immense grief, he withdraws into a room, locks the door, and wishes to die. His daughter convinces him to leave the room and to compose a poem in honor for his beloved son. He does so, and on short notice he selects the very complicated format of a *dråpa*, the most splendid type of skaldic poetry.

Egill Skallagrimsson survives, and *Sonatorrek* became one of his best-known poems. Egill is not like Jeremiah in the Old Testament, who—full of agony and lament about the fate his Almighty has burdened him with—gets crushed by his unempathetic, brutal and one, and only god, Jehovah. On the contrary, Egill blames his chosen main god, Odin, for the loss of his sons. He breaks his oath to Odin, liberating himself from the power of the god. The Germanic gods wander with humans in concert through the world, and thus they are somehow partners, equals (although with different roles and power). Mentally Egill is thus a free, secularized, and modern man who can choose his gods or abandon them. Being free and self-determined is the highest of the Germanic virtues. In contrast, penance and remorse are highly valued by Christianity. "Better be a wolf of Odin than a lamb of God" is a slogan that can be found on T-shirts in support of Odinism and white supremacy. Here it reflects the autonomy of a person as related to God, selecting rather the independence of the wolf character than becoming the sacrificial embodiment of God.

*Sonatorrek* is in general assumed to be Europe's first purely subjective lyric. Subjectivism is the philosophical belief that our own mental activity is the only unquestionable fact of our experience. A thousand years before subjectivism would enter European philosophy, lyrics, and provide the base for secularization, the barbarian Egill

Skallagrimsson took the position and example of modern man. *Sonatorrek* represents a form of stunt poetry, it has immediacy, and it is sketchy. "Modernity is the transient, the vanishing, the accidental," writes Charles Baudelaire (1821-1867) a thousand years later[91]. *Sonatorrek* is "a poem of unparalleled psychological depth, poetic self-awareness and verbal complexity."[92] It is composed by the wildest barbarian one can imagine: Egill had lots of blood on his hands. But he was self-determined, relying just on himself and absolutely determined to stand on his own feet, even without a god. Old Germanic literature and poetry encompassed characteristics that precede modern literature and clearly deserves far greater attention of Europe's culture elite.

## 4.4 Conclusion

In this short and cursory account on Germanic runes, literature and poetry we illustrate that Norse manuscripts and poetry between 900 and 1300 belong to the highlights of European literature. Elaborately ornamented stones with runic inscriptions are found all over Scandinavia (e.g. Fig. 12), but those in central Europe, if they existed, have disappeared. It is made clear that this rich literature reflects archetypical patterns and carries the insignia of modernity. This remarkable realm of mainly Norse, but actually world literature, regrettably appears to be mostly of academic interest outside Scandinavia. If we loosen the ropes of our cultural straitjackets we can select literature more objectively according to their significance (see Box III). We have a European treasury that plays, maybe unconsciously, a significant role in modern European culture. Our barbarian Germanic ancestors may have pioneered much of what is summarized by the term "modernity." Academic tradition demands that all originators are considered adequately for their contributions to culture in its entirety. This principle should also be mandatory in the wide-ranging fields of culture. Credit where credit is

---

[91] http://www.bc.edu/bc_org/avp/cas/fnart/fa257/baudelaire1.html.
[92] Larrington, C. (1992).

due implies that Europeans should improve their cultural literacy, which appears heavily compromised by the ideals of our humanism-influenced education. A serious attempt to obtain a balanced view on culture demands a more eclectic orientation. Along these lines, Norse and Old Anglo-Saxon literature has to become a matter of necessity in our literature curricula. C.S. Lewis represented a traditional, narrow-minded yesterday, the outsider I.R.R. Tolkien the future and modernity (see Box III).

*Slindebirken* (*Birch Tree at Slinde*) by Thomas Fearnley (1802-1842; National Gallery of Norway, Oslo). The majestic tree stood on the burial mound Hydneshaugen, in the majestic Sognefjord in western Norway. It contains a grave from the fifth century. Each Christmas evening, the farmers poured beer over the roots of the assumed holly tree and never used an ax or knife on it. A holly tree, reflecting the memory of Yggdrasil, with roots deep down in the memory of the past? By noticing and respecting the remnants of our cultural past we pave the ground to increase our cultural and archetypal literacy. Copyright: National Gallery of Norway, Oslo

# 5. Are all Elements of Germanic Mythology Lost in Central Europe?

*Unexpressed emotions will never die. They are buried alive and will come forth later in uglier ways.*

S. Freud

*If you can prove receptive to this "call of the wild," the longing for fulfilment will quicken the sterile wilderness of your soul as rain quickens dry earth.*

C.G. Jung

We have already indicated that a main segment of the European civilization, the representations of original Germanic culture, has been and is neglected, demonized, repulsed, and repressed. What did not comply with the "rules" and accepted standard by the ruling classes and cultures was (and is) suppressed. During this process, major ethnic-based segments of the European population became "homeless" as their original archetypical representations were not a selected part of the accepted European cultural canon. After more than about 2,000 years of variable, at times downright, suppression we could thus expect that most elements of Germanic mythology are lost from Central Europe while some of them still may be detectable in Scandinavia. Is this really the case? No, elements of Germanic mythology are evidently alive, also in Central Europe.

## 5.1 Federal state structures and independent citizens

One of the main characteristics of the Germanic tribes was their strict organization in federal systems. In the pre-Christian clan culture of Scandinavia the members of a clan were obliged to avenge injuries against their dead and mutilated relatives. A balancing structure was necessary to reduce tribal feuds and avoid social disorder. In the North Germanic cultures the balancing institution became the *thing*. Similar assemblies are reported also from other Germanic people. The exceptionality of the Germanic *thing* was already noted and described by the Romans (e.g., Tacitus) and depicted on a relief on the Marc-Aurel column in Rome, raised in 193 (Fig. 13).

The *thing* was the governing assembly of a Germanic society, made up of the free men of the community of a region, province, or land, presided over by law speakers (judges). Close relatives, often the oldest brother, represented free women. There were hierarchies of *things*, so that the local *things* were represented at the higher-level *thing* of a

Fig. 13. A Germanic council—considered early evidence of what would become known as the *thing* (assembly) —depicted on the victory column of Marc Aurel on Piazza Colonna, Rome. As villages are burned down, women and children are captured, displaced, and men are killed, the emotion, despair and suffering of the "barbarians" in the war are represented intensely in single scenes. The pictorial language of the column is unambiguous: Imperial dominance and authority are emphasized. Wikimedia Commons.

province or land. At the *thing*, disputes were resolved and political decisions made. The place for the *thing* was often also the place for public religious rites and commerce. The *thing* met at regular intervals, legislated, elected chieftains and kings, and judged according to the law, which was memorized and recited by the law speaker. In reality, the most influential members of the community, the heads of clans and wealthy families dominated the *thing*, but "one-man-one-vote" was the general rule.

There are today two important democracies that directly continue the Germanic *thing* system into the present. The most important one of these is Switzerland, the other the Isle of Man. The Confoederatio Helvetica has kept much of the Germanic *thing* system alive since the 14th century. Free men (and of course now also women) vote frequently and regularly. Until recently, they did so at specified locations under open skies. The people and their approximately 2,300 municipalities are the very core, the highest political authority of the Swiss state. This decentralized, federal principle permeates the entire Swiss political system. Swiss citizens can bring their opinions to bear at federal, cantonal, and communal levels: They can vote on a wide variety of issues and elect their representatives to the Federal Assembly. No other country gives its citizens more opportunities to express their views in popular votes on the entire range of issues than Switzerland. The Swiss system, based upon the Rütli oath of 1291 (Fig. 14) that brought the original cantons into a federal system in the 13th century, is very close to or most probably a continuation of the Germanic *thing* system[93]

---

[93] Citation form Friedrich Schillers drama "Wilhelm Tell"
  Wir wollen sein ein einzig Volk von Brüdern,
  in keiner Not uns trennen und Gefahr.
  Wir wollen frei sein, wie die Väter waren,
  eher den Tod, als in der Knechtschaft leben.
  Wir wollen trauen auf den höchsten Gott
  und uns nicht fürchten vor der Macht der Menschen.
  We want to be a single People of brethren,
  Never to part in danger nor distress.
  We want to be free, as our fathers were,
  And rather die than live in slavery.
  We want to trust in the one highest God
  And never be afraid of human power.

Fig. 14. *Rütlischwur* (Oath of Rütli), the legendary turning point in the pursuit of independence, when the Confoederatio Helvetica (Switzerland) was founded by the original kantons Uri, Schwyz, and Unterwalden. After the establishment of the federal state, the Rütli oath became associated with the Swiss Federal Charter, a document dated to 1291. Every August 1, the Swiss National Day, the oath is reenacted to commemorate the forming of the Old Swiss Confederacy. The oath of Rütli is deeply entrenched in the Swiss people and the very basis of the world's strictest democracy. Fresco from the Tellskapelle (1879/80), Lake Lucerne, by Ernst Stückelberg (1831-1903). Photo: Paul Wassmann.

Another example of a ruling form that directly stems from Norse times is The High Court of Tynwald (Manx Tinvaal) on the Isle of Man. It is the oldest continuous legislature and parliament in the world. On the National Day the mostly independent representatives meet on the traditional embankment under open skies to vote. Behind the name Tinvaal, we find the term *thing*.

In the case of the Isles of Man, the connection to the Germanic *thing* system is obvious, but who among the Swiss would address in public that the world's most highly developed, modern democratic state is a direct successor of a barbarian past? For cultivated people who officially selected the stylish Latin for Confoederatio Helvetica as the name for their state, this statement could be far too bold. One rather continues to think that the great democratic tradition is a prolongation of the classic times of Greece and Rome, and that our present political systems are reflections of the classic tradition, not a prolongation of what is assumed as our primitive and barbaric past.

A similar trend is also reflected in the concept of the independent Germanic farmer and clan leader. Free Germanic men were basically farmers, longing for decentralized independence, supporting or heading their clan. No symbolic type represents this better than the fabled figure of Swiss freedom fighter Wilhelm Tell. Independent, freedom-loving, strong, stubborn, skilful, and resolute, he fights for his people's rights, his progeny, and against feudalistic suppression of foreign powers. The fundamental core of Europe's modern political reality (for which people had to fight for lengthy periods of time) reflects most likely more the ideals of Europe's Germanic past than the so called cradle of civilization, the antique Greece (see Box VII). Several of today's highly appreciated qualities of modern European societies were preceded by Germanic civilization. Honor whom honor is due. It may involve a revision of our historical perspectives and an evaluation of our reeducation and cultural backdrop. Our modern societies reflect more closely the Germanic desire of independence from central powers. It turned out to become a long, vicious fight to withdraw from centralism, kings, and popes. The internal independence of prosperous cities, Magna Carta, the Hanseatic League, and Protestantism reflect the Germanic ideal of independence.

## Box VII: Do today's democracies and parliaments derive from Greece?

Democracy is a system of government in which all nationals are involved in making decisions about the state's affairs, typically by voting to elect representatives to a parliament or similar assembly[94]. Democracy is further characterized by a government in which the supreme power is vested in the people and exercised by them directly or indirectly through a system of representation, usually involving periodically held free elections. The term originates from Greek

---

[94] Oxford English Dictionary.

*dēmokratía* (rule of the people) and was founded in the fifth century B.C.E. by the Athenians in classical Greece. Also other cities, such as Corinth, Megara, and Syracuse, had democratic regimes during part of their history. The various short-lived democratic episodes happened inside a period of less than 150 years until Alexander the Great brought this system of government to an end. Modern democracy was launched through the French Revolution, and full legal right to vote for adult citizens was achieved in most modern democracies in the late 19$^{th}$ and early 20$^{th}$ centuries (e.g., through suffrage movements).

Do today's democracies in essence reflect the *dêmos krátos* (people power), based upon a little flash in Greek history? Or do they potentially reflect the long-lasting Germanic *thing* system (see 5.1, Fig. 13), masked by a fashionable Greek term? Is it possible that modern democracy is based upon the law and federal system of the Germanic tribes that were subdued by the arising central power execution of kings and Christianity from the end of the Migration Period to early medieval times? In Europe these centralistic structures waned due to the achievements of various medieval, Renaissance, and modern organizations that seem to favor (and are based upon?) the Germanic federal system (e.g., the Hanseatic League, free imperial cities, Magna Charta, Swiss federal cantonal system [Fig. 14], the French Declaration of the Rights of Man and of the Citizen, etc.). They prepared the ground for today's representation of people by free and equal election, i.e., our democracies and parliaments. It seems thus likely that today's democracies and parliaments have more in common with the Germanic *thing* system, which after all functioned over lengthy periods of time. The *thing* system gradually weakened until the end of the Icelandic *thing* at Thingvellir (874-1271), but it continued uninterrupted on the Isle of Man. Today's democracies and parliaments reflect rather the memory of the suppressed Germanic assemblies (*Althing*) than the short *dêmos krátos* of Athens, generally held as the first democracy in 508 B.C.E. Does the *thing* represent the original democratic "archetype"? Then our modern democracies should pay justice to this and be called *thingocracies*. Honor to whom honor is due.

## 5.2 Six days in a week

Almost all of our weekdays are directly linked to our Germanic ancestry. We have Sunday and Monday, meaning days that get their names from the sun (*sunna* in old High German) and the moon (*mani* in old Norwegian). The name Tuesday (Dienstag [German], Zischdig [Alemannian], tirsdag [Scandinavian]) is the day of the god Tyr/Ziu/Tiw (see 6.6.1). Wednesday (onsdag [Scandinavian]) is the day of the god Wuodan (Wotan) and/or Odin (see 6.5.1). Thursday (Donnerstag [German], dunnschdig [Alemannian], torsdag [Scandinavian]) is the day of the god Thor, Donar, and Tor (see 6.5.3). Friday (Freitag [German], Friidig [Allemanian], fredag [Scandinavian]) is the day of the goddess Freyja (see 6.5.2) or Frigg (the distinction between Freyja and Frigg is problematic, and the names may have their origin in a Germanic, common goddess). If we are aware of it or not, we have lots of Germanic gods with us in our daily life that, despite resistance, have survived in our daily language. But most probably we hardly think about the celebration of four Germanic gods and goddesses when we live through our weeks.

## 5.3 Place names throughout Europe reflect Germanic gods

We find an astonishing number of place names in Europe that reflect Germanic gods. In everyday life we do not take note of these names, in particular when the names are based on *kennings*. The god Odin or Wotan can be found in place names such as Odense, Osmussaar, Odensö, Odensberg, Bad Godesberg, Gudensberg, Odisheim, Woensdrecht, Wambrook, Wanborough, Wednesfield, and Woodnesborough. British names starting on "grim" (such as Grimsby) are based upon a *kenning* for Odin (see Box VI). For Thor, we find Thursley, Thurstable, Thorsager, Thorsvåg, Thorshavn, Torsö, and the many Donnersberg. For Freyja, we find Frøihov, Frövi, and an entire range of place names that are based upon *kennings* for Freyja (see Box VI): Gefn, Hörn, Mardöll, Skjálf, Sýr, Thröng, Thrungva, Valfreyja, and Vanadís. The god Balder is found in Balleshol, Balestrand, Balsfjorden, Baldrsberg, Baldersby, Balderton, and Pule Hill (from the *kenning* Phol). The god Tyr is present in Tisvilde, Thisted, Tyrsjön, and may be Duisburg, Tylö, and Tyrol (through a combination Tyr-Odal or Tyr-Ull). For *thing* meeting places, we find Thingstede,

Thingstow, and Thingvold. Place names derived from Germanic gods are distributed all over the Germanic regions of Europe.

## 5.4 Symbols, tradition, and words

The main Germanic god Wotan/Odin (see 6.5.1) shows up in our cultures seemingly quite often, but in a more subtle, indirect, and symbolic manner. We find clear signs of an idolization of Odin not only in English, but also in northern Germany and Scandinavia. Odin is associated with the horse. The Indo-European invaders arrived with horses (which were unknown in Old Europe, where cows and bulls dominated)[95]. Horses were traditionally sacrificed for the veneration of Odin. Old farmhouses in northern Germany have often crossed-horse profiles at the end of the roof ridge (Fig. 15). In the region of Central Europe where Germanic paganism continued until the end of the eighth century and where resistance against Christianity was strongest, Lower Saxony and Westphalia, we find a white horse in the flags (Fig. 16). The Dala horse from Dalarna in Sweden is a traditional carved, painted wooden horse statuette. In the old days, the Dala horse was mostly used as a toy for children, but it may reflect, along with the use of runes, a hidden tradition of the veneration of Odin.

Fig. 15. Decoration on a farmhouse in Mecklenburg-Vorpommern, northern Germany. Stand the crossed horse heads for a former veneration of Wotan/Odin? Wikimedia Commons.

Almost everywhere we see horseshoes. They protect doors or roof trusses. When kept as a talisman, a horseshoe is

---

[95] Anthony, D.W. (2007); Haarmann, H. (2016).

Fig. 16. The coat of arms of Lower Saxony, Germany. According to German folklore, the banner of Widukind, the last pagan king of the Old Saxons, was a jumping black horse on a yellow field. After the defeat of Saxony and conversion to Christianity, the banner was changed to a jumping white horse on a red field. Whatever the colors, the connection to Wotan/Odin is obvious. Wikimedia Commons.kimedia Commons.

said to bring good luck. Some believe that to hang it with the ends pointing upward is good luck as it acts as a storage container of sorts for any good luck that happens to be floating by. Others believe that the horseshoe should be hung with the ends pointing down, as it will then protect and release its luck to the people below it. Do horseshoes reflect the suppressed and hidden god Odin?

Gandalf is a fictional character and one of the main protagonists in J.R.R. Tolkien's novels *The Hobbit* and *The Lord of the Rings*[96] trilogy. Tolkien thought of Gandalf as an "Odinic wanderer" (Fig. 17). Commentators have compared Gandalf to Odin in his "Wanderer" guise—an old

Fig. 17. Depiction of Gandalf, a fictional character in novels by J.R.R. Tolkien. He thought of Gandalf as an "Odinic wanderer." Take note of the stave/stick and the magnificent shadow of the god, pointing at Odin's/Wotan's ambivalence. Wikimedia Commons.

man with one eye, a long white beard, a wide brimmed hat, and a staff. Thus, we may conclude that the wandering Gandalf with his staff/pole

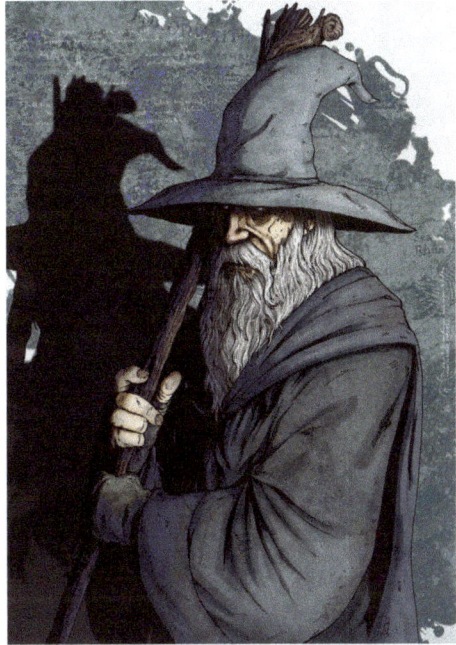

---

[96] Tolkien, J.R.R. (1937). The Hobbitt; Tolkien, J.R.R. (1955). The Lord of the Rings.

Fig. 18. Common jewelery throughout Europe and popular since Norse times: Thor's hammer. Photo: Wikimedia Commons.

is Odin on his way through our times.

Women and men use relatively modest pieces of jewelry that look like a hanging cross or minianvil. Such jewelry was also very popular in Norse times and is called Thor's hammer, a symbol for Mjölnir (see 6.5.3, Fig. 18). The jewelry can be bought throughout Europe, and thus symbols of Thor are with us everywhere.

The Yule goat (Jul = Christmas in Scandinavian) is a Scandinavian and Northern European Christmas symbol and tradition, and Thor may be behind it. In Norse mythology, goats pull the chariot of Thor. Its origin may be Germanic paganism and has existed in many variants during Scandinavian history. Between Christmas and New Year's Day, people wearing masks and costumes (called Julebukker = Yule goats) would go from door to door, where neighbors receiving them attempt to identify who is under the disguise. Modern representations of the Yule goat are typically made of straw[97]. Also, the goddess Freyja is represented in Scandinavia through the traditional Christmas boar. It represents probably her boar Hildisvini (see 6.5.2). Do the Yule goat and the Christmas boar reflect a subdued veneration of Thor and Freyja?

The lesser-known goddess Ostara has her time around Easter (see 6.6.3). Theories connect Ostara with records of Germanic Easter customs, including hares and eggs. Our entire range of Easter celebration and decoration, beside what takes place in or outside of churches, can reflect Germanic (or Slavic?) pagan symbolism.

---

[97] Similar to the Christmas sheaf, probably a fertility symbol and a gesture to feed even the birds during the holy midwinter period.

Fig. 19. Depiction of the fabled Alruna for a medieval manuscript. This popular medical plant throughout times appears here as either mandrake man or woman. There exists a range of names, such as "Master of the life breath" (Old Arabic), Satan's apple, Manroot, Devil's testicle, or Circe's plant. The alruna has obvious connections to graveyards, execution sites, and Odin's focus to obtain knowledge from the afterworld. Folio 90 from the *Naples Dioscurides*, a seventh-century manuscript of Dioscurides De Materia Medica. Wikimedia Commons.

The term rune is part of the German and Scandinavian name for the plant *Mandragora officinarum* or Alruna, the rune for all (English mandrake, probably an alteration of mandragora, Fig. 19). The term rune signifies that the plant has secret qualities and points at Odin, the provider of the runes and ultimate secrets (see 6.5.1). Some alrunes are exhibited and resemble a person who hangs on a tree (Odin?). Because mandrakes contain deliriant and hallucinogenic alkaloids and the shape of their roots often resembles human figures, they have been associated with a variety of superstitious practices throughout history. They have long been used in magic rituals, today also in contemporary pagan traditions such as Wicca (modern witchcraft) and Odinism (Germanic

Neopagan Asatru). It was used as an anesthetic for surgery and to treat melancholy, convulsions, and mania in ancient times. When taken in sufficient quantities, it is said to excite delirium and madness. The mandrake should be preferentially picked at graveyards, close to gallows and a full moon (see 6.5.1). A black dog was bound to the plant, and, at fair distance, a horn signaled the dog to come. The reason for this was the mandrake's deadly scream when it was pulled out of the soil. The mandrake is widely known from the literature, ranging from *Macbeth* to *Harry Potter*. The qualities of the mandrake, the term rune in alruna, the hallucinogenic or deathly characteristics, the connection to graveyards and gallows point at Odin and his divination rituals connected to necromancy (see Box VIII).

## Box VIII: Initiation and necromancy

To foretell events or discover hidden knowledge, necromancy is the practice of magic, involving communication with the deceased for the purpose of divination (soothsaying, fortune saying, prophecy). The term necromancy is adapted from Greek *nekromanteia*, a compound of *nekros* (dead body) and *manteia* (prophecy or divination).

In Norse times, necromancy in the form of pretended hanging was an initiation procedure, a matter of worshipping the connection to the afterworld. Odin is connected to death and is said to be present when people die. He wishes to obtain knowledge from the spirits of those transgressing to the other world. The god needs media for news from the afterworld. Therefore, Odin stays close to the gallows and is present during pretended hangings. Just as the impressionists turned from being painters to huntsmen of fugitive notions and moods[98] on the hunt to catch the essential, Odin lurks like a hunter of the fugitive around the gallows and places where people die. Some of the bodies found in Scandinavian bogs have ropes around their necks. Frequently, these are interpreted as the bodies of executed persons, but they may also be the result of failed pretended hangings. The meaning of the world tree *Yggdrasil* can be interpreted/translated as the "gallows of the terrible"

---

[98] Guy de Montpassant, La vie dún paysagiste, 1886.

(see 6.2). This points at that pretended hanging and self-divination on the world tree, executed by Odin, represented such an overshadowing event in Germanic mythology that *Yggdrasil* is named after this incident (see Box XXI).

A second aspect of necromancy is that Odin applies human skulls for divination. He takes care of the head of decapitated wise giant Mimir (see 6.5.7). He drinks daily from Mimir's well, which encompasses all secrets of the world (representing humanities collective remembrance; Fig. 39).

## 5.5 Subterranean creatures

In almost all European countries, there are reports or imaginations about dwarfs. The word comes from Old English *dweorg*, the Old High German *twerc* (German Zwerg) and Old Norse *dvergr* (Norwegian *dverg*). The Germanic word derives perhaps from the Proto-Indo-European *\*dhwer* (harm, deceive). In Germanic mythology, a dwarf is a small, human-shaped being that dwells in mountains and in the earth, and is variously associated with wisdom, mining, and crafting. Dwarfs are often also described as short and ugly, although some scholars have questioned whether this is a later development stemming from comical portrayals of the beings (Fig. 20). The concept of the dwarf strongly influenced modern popular culture.

Dwarfs have an important role in folklore and imaginations of children, but not only with them. In Iceland, the Faroese, and Scandinavia, we find several categories of subterranean creatures. The Icelandic Elf School (Álfaskólinn) teaches students and visitors about

Fig. 20. Two dwarfs as depicted in a 19th century edition of the *Poetic Edda* poem *Völuspá* by Lorenz Frølich (1820-1908). In Gjellerup, K. (1895). Den ældre Eddas Gudesange (Thanning og Appel 1973). Wikimedia Commons.

Icelandic folklore. The school teaches about the hidden people and the 13 different kinds of elves that the school believes inhabit Iceland. Roads are constructed by taking care of stones and rocks where elves and dwarfs live. If a road is completely necessary, the elves will generally move out of the way, but if it is deemed superfluous, "very bad things" might happen.

In the form of garden gnomes, a figurine of a small humanoid creature, usually wearing a pointy hat, dwarfs are displayed for the purpose of ornamentation on front lawns or in gardens. These figurines originated in 19th-century Germany, where they became known as *Gartenzwerge* (garden dwarfs). However, garden gnomes have been common in Europe at least since the Renaissance. Garden gnomes are typically males, often bearded, usually wear red hats and often have pipes. They are particularly popular in Germany, where we can find approximately 25 million *Gartenzwerge*. Garden gnomes became, partly with a critical and ironical undertone, the epitome of philistinism, a sign of bad taste and kitsch. Still, the Germanic, subterraneous creatures are all around us.

## 5.6 The Wild Hunt and other wild pursuit manifestations

The *Wild Hunt* is a European folk myth involving a ghostly or supernatural group of huntsmen passing in wild pursuit. The hunters may be either elves or fairies or the dead, and the leader of the hunt is often a figure associated with Wotan (e.g., *Wuotis Heer* [Wuodan's Army] of central Switzerland and Swabia). It is a phantasmal group of huntsmen with horses and dogs that cross the skies or chase along the ground (Fig. 21). In Scandinavia, there exist a similar phenomenon, *Åsgårdsreia*, frequently experienced around Christmas. Seeing the *Wild Hunt* or *Åsgårdsreia* was thought to signify catastrophes such as war, plagues, or death of the person who witnessed the manifestation. People encountering the *Wild Hunt* might also be abducted to the underworld or the fairy kingdom. The phenomenon basically represents Odin marching with his elite soldiers, *einherjer*, preparing for Ragnarök (see 6.7).

The Wild Hunt is an impressive segment of Carl Maria von Weber's (1786-1826) epochal opera *Der Freischütz* (1821). A Freischütz (freeshooter) in German folklore is a gunman who is contracted by the devil to obtain a certain number of bullets destined to hit without fail

Fig. 21. *Aasgaardreien* (*The wild hunt*) by Peter Nicolai Arbo (1831-1892; National Gallery, Oslo). This dramatic motive is based on a phenomenon and sturdy undercurrent deriving from our Germanic ancestors that continues all the way into the present. Odin, *valkyries* and the *einherjer* storm through the skies, preparing for the final battle at Ragnarök. Copyright: National Gallery, Oslo.

whatever object he wishes. Six of the magic "free bullets" are thus subservient to the gunman's will, but the seventh is at the absolute disposal of Beelzebub himself. When the two main male protagonists of Weber´s opera, Caspar and Max, prepare for moulding the seventh bullet in the Wolfs Glen, deep in primordial woods, the scary and life-threatening Wild Hunt appears. In contemporay performances corpses dangle from the trees in the Wolf Glen, suggesting that it is a place for necromancy (see Box VIII). We are in the realm of Wotan/Odin.

Also the term nightmare (German *Alptraum*; Norwegian *mareritt*) should be mentioned as an example of a Germanic mythology manifestation. A nightmare has nothing to do with a female horse. The word derives from the Old English *mare*, a mythological demon or goblin that torments others with frightening dreams. It is riding on the victim's chest (Fig. 22). The word nightmare is a cognate with the older German term *Nachtmahr*. "Alp" derives from German *Alben* (or Elfen; English elves). The prefix "night-" and "ritt" stresses the dream aspect of the

Fig. 22. *Nachtmahr* (*The nightmare*) by Johann Heinrich Füssli (1741-1825; Detroit Institute of Art). The Old English *mare*, a mythological demon or goblin, torments the chest of the victim, providing frightening dreams: nightmares. Wikimedia Commons.

expression. Thus, a simple term can be based upon an entire set of mythological views deriving from a Germanic past that we do not directly access anymore.

## 5.7 Symbols and Festivals

Symbols that directly reflect Germanic paganism are common throughout Europe. The fires around St. John's Day at the height of summer probably reflect Germanic paganism. Elements of Christmas celebrations show evident signs of Germanic times. The traditions of the Yule log, Yule goat, Yule boar, *Jule-øl* (beer) and Yule singing still provide indications for the significance of the midwinter celebrations of pre-Christian times (defined by the lunisolar calendar). This holy Germanic midwinter period was transferred to Christianity. The holy 13 nights start with Christmas Day or winter solstice. In English, the final celebrations in this period is reflected in Shakespeare's comedy *Twelfth Night*, or *What You Will*. The late medieval age and visionary Norwegian poem *Draumkvedet* (*The Dream Poem*) is one of the best-known medieval ballads from Scandinavia, with first written versions from the 1840s[99]. The protagonist, Olav Åsteson, falls asleep on Christmas Eve and sleeps until the 12th day of Christmas. After he wakes up, he rides to church to recount his dreams and his journey to the afterlife over the bridge *Gjallarbrui* (*Bifröst*, see 6.2) to the congregation. The events share similarities to elements of other medieval ballads: a moor of thorns, a tall bridge, and a black fire. After these visions, the protagonist is also allowed to see hell and some of heaven. The poem concludes with the specific advice of charity and compassion, to avoid the various purgatory trials of the afterlife. Obviously, midsummer and winter festivals in Northern Europe to a large extent reflect pagan Germanic elements.

## 5.8 Fantasy literature and movies

Historically, most works of the fantasy genre were written pieces of literature. Since the 1960s, a growing segment of the fantasy genre has taken the form of films, television programs, graphic novels, video games, music, and painting. Symbolism frequently plays a significant role in fantasy literature, often through the use of archetypal figures inspired by earlier texts, mythology or folklore. One can argue that fantasy literature and its archetypes fulfill a function for both individuals and society, and the messages are continually updated for current societies. In times when religion loses its impact on people, rationality has become mandatory, technology solves many challenges, and citizens experience existential challenges due to climate change, there seems to be an increasing need for mythology which is frequently channeled through the fanatsy genre.

J.R.R. Tolkien played a significant role in the popularization and accessibility of the fantasy genre with his highly successful books. Rarely does one consider modern fantasy without conjuring the memory and

---

[99] Stockland, O. (1969).

image of Tolkien's creations. An ancient body of Anglo-Saxon myths, particularly *Beowulf,* influenced Tolkien, who was a keen reader of Norse literature and mythology (see Box III). In the fantasy genre there also exists a suite of popular movies and TV series that draw profoundly from Germanic mythology. Examples of these medieval fantasy epics are *Game of Thrones, Excalibur, Dragonslayer, The Barbarians,* and *Valhalla Rising,* etc.

## 5.9 Freemasonry and Germanic Mythology

In 2016, indications were launched that elements of Germanic mythology could have survived into the present in the most unlikely and unexpected disguise: Freemasonry. The Norwegian amateur historian Arvid Ystad published the book *Frimurene i Vikingtiden (Freemansons in Viking Times)*[100], suggesting that the origin of the first three degrees in Freemasonry contain elements of the initiation rituals of Freyja, Odin, and Thor. Several of the strange ceremonies in Freemasonry, such as the rope around the neck and the leather slipper on the right foot of the novice, are argued to derive from Germanic initiation rituals. The rope could, for example, reflect necromantic initiating rites (see Box VIII). The ceremonies to release individuals out of slavery (Norwegian *frelsesølet* [salvation beer]) or to recognize sons (Norwegian *ættleidinger* [adoption]) contained rules for the use of one leather slipper (Gula- and Frostating laws of the Norwegian Viking Age).

These observations and a wealth of additional ones shed new light on the origin of Freemasonry that (at least in central Europe) most often has been placed in the realm of the Crusades or Egypt. But it could also be a remnant of the Danish Viking period in Scotland and England, where modern Freemasonry came into being, through "mason lodges" centered on the building of medieval cathedrals. Ystad's work sheds light upon secret religious tradition connected to guilds that are not publicly known. For example, the religious direction of metallurgy craftsmen became today's alchemy[101] and that of the stonemasons Freemasonry. Secret religions of other guilds have probably existed but are not publicly known. The original Germanic mythology appears to have created a veritable core.

---

[100] Ystad, A. (2016).
[101] Eliade, M. (1978).

## 5.10 Conclusion

Impressions of a hidden, subconscious Germanic tradition and mythology suggest that many elements of Germanic mythology have made it into the present. A sturdy undercurrent, deriving from our Germanic ancestors, continues into the present in a suite of forms: parliaments, place names, summer and winter celebrations, rituals, weekdays, symbols, and folklore, etc. At the surface, we are seemingly dominated by a continuation of the Roman Empire, Christianity, and the Renaissance, but below prevail influence-rich rudiments and structures of the neglected, demonized, repulsed, and repressed Germanic culture that influence our cultural present-day reality.

The archetypes of cultures are like old watercourses along which the water of life has flowed for centuries, digging deep channels, says Jung[102] (see also 10.2). The cultural landscape of Europe is thus characterized by a multitude of cultural riverbeds that may have dried up under the influence of today's dominating culture. The cultural landscape and vegetation of central Europe comprises hardly visible archaic river valleys that, ephemerally hardly detectable, shape the cultural topography of Europe.

Myths can be subtle and static such as the imperceptible archaic valleys. They may play a modifying role by softly, and at the surface unnoticed, influencing the vegetation and features that cover the central cultural landscapes of Europe. Scholars in the field of cultural studies are now investigating the idea of how formerly rejected and suppressed mythological elements are working themselves into modern discourses. Modern formats of communication allow for widespread exchange across the globe, thus enabling mythological discourse and exchange among greater audiences than ever before. Various elements of myth can now be found in television, cinema, and video games. Exploring the web for Norse mythology key terms such as Odin, Thor, Valhalla, *einherjer*, Volva, etc., exposes an astonishing plethora of imagery. Germanic mythology is thus not lost, but it is transformed and covered under an ephemeral cover vegetation of our present-day culture.

---

[102] Jung, C.G. (1936).

*Jonsokbål* (*Bonfire Celebrating Midsummer Night*) by Nikolai Astrup (1880-1928; National Gallery of Norway, Oslo). The custom of lighting bonfires and gathering for games and dancing on Midsummer Night was and is a living tradition with symbolic connotations from the Germanic past. The picture points at humanity's interdependence with nature and the magic forces of nature. Experiencing bonfire celebrations during Midsummer Nights seemingly provides us with a faint note of the time when nature religion was at the center of our life experience. A time when we lived closer and with nature, not trying so hard to subject nature like today. Copyright: National Gallery of Norway, Oslo

# 6. Elements of Germanic Mythology

*In imitating the exemplary acts of a god or of a mythical hero, or simply by recounting their adventures, the man of an archaic society detaches himself from profane time and magically re-enters the Great Time, the sacred time.*

M. Eliade

*Myths are public dreams, dreams are private myths.*

J. Campbell

Because of the lack of reliable information from Central Europe, the main focus in this chapter will be placed upon western Germanic or Norse mythology, with the two *Eddas* as the main source of information (see 3.3). The reader should be aware that Central Europe probably had some different traditions, gods, and goddesses[103]. We present a short summary of a considerable amount of literature that addresses less informed readers. Information has been obtained from books[104] and the web. The chapter serves as a help to those who lack basic knowledge and who wish to learn more about the main elements of Germanic mythology. Throughout the chapter, parallels between the gods and today's reality

---

[103] For an attempt of a German mythology, see Hermann (1898).
[104] Davidson, H.R.E. (1964); Egerkrans, J. (2016); Engelmann, E. (1889); Golther, W. (1895); Engelmann, E. (1895); Enoksen, L.M. (2008); Gimbutas, M. (1982); Hasenfratz, H.-P. (1992); Hedeager, L. (2011); Herrmann, P. (1898); Herrmann, P. (1903); Jacoby, E. (2011); Nemenyi, G.v. (2003); New Larousse Encyclopedia of Mythology (1959); Simek, R. (1998); Simek, R. (2004); Simek, R. (2006); Steinsland, G. (2005); Wagner, W. (1901).

are made, including placing Germanic mythology into psychological context.

The poetic *Edda* starts with the poem *Völuspa* (Old Norse *volva* [seeress]; *spá* [prophecy, vision]), meaning the vision and prophecies of the seeress. The speaking person is the *Völva*, sometimes Anglicized as *Vala* or Germanized *Wala*, the main shaman and seeress in Norse mythology (*volva* means "wand carrier" or "carrier of a magic staff" [Old Norse *volr*]). She represents the portal to the collective unconsciousness that is frequently associated with females and "the mothers" (see 6.6.4). The poetic *Edda* starts vehemently and cataclysmic with this archaic woman: the *Völva* ascends from the abyss of the collective unconscious and materializes out of the dawn of time. And one can almost hear the magical, enervating beat of her staff, emphasizing the heavy alliterative nature of the verses.

> *Hearing I ask from the holy races,*
> *From Heimdall's sons, both high and low;*
> *Thou wilt, Valfather, that well I relate*
> *Old tales I remember of men long ago.*

> *I remember yet the giants of yore,*
> *Who gave me bread in the days gone by;*
> *Nine worlds I knew, the nine in the tree*
> *With mighty roots beneath the mold[105].*

In only 65 unprecedented alliterated stanzas, the *Völva* hammers the entire cosmography and time development of the world into our souls: from the creation over the Twilight of Gods (Ragnarök) to the creation of the New Earth. Her verbalizations are from the abyss of human memory, the archaic realms, the dawn of time. Her words are indisputable and as if carved in granite. The *Völva* is from before the times the gods reigned. In *Völuspa*, she teaches both Odin and humans the history and fate of the world. In Germanic mythology, gods do not

---

[105] All original text citations in this chapter are from The Poetic Edda (1936), translated by H. C. Bellows), http://www.sacred-texts.com/neu/poe/poe03.htm.

decide fate. It is the collective unconscious, ruled by females and the mothers, that determines fate. Gods and humans are subjected to a common destiny, despite their different powers and roles.

In the following, we follow the pathways the *Völva* describes and foresees in *Völuspa*. Her dramaturgy is the Norse metaphorical variety of the Theatrum Mundi[106]. In sections 6.1 to 6.4, we introduce the creation of the world and the structure of the Germanic cosmos. In sections 6.5 and 6.6, we describe the Germanic goods and their domain. Sections 6.7 and 6.8 provide insights into the Twilight of Gods and the emergence of New Earth.

## 6.1 The creation of the world

In the beginning there was no earth, no heaven, no grass, and no holding ground. There were neither sea nor cool waves. There was only the primordial void, the yawning abyss: *Ginnungagap* (gaping abyss, yawning void). Twelve frosty rivers ran from the north out of *Nifelheim* (Mist Home, Mist World), which is one of the Nine Worlds, the home of fog and ice (see Box IX). The source of the rivers was the well *Hwergelmir* (bubbling spring), one of the three major springs at the primary roots of the cosmic tree Yggdrasil (see 6.2).

From the south flew glowing sparks from *Muspelheim*, the devastating fire, another of the Nine Worlds (see Box IX). The ice melted a little. Through the power of fire seeds started to sprout in the white frost. A giant grew up, the enormous Ymir, the ancestor of all *jötnar* (plural of *jötunn*, frost and rock giants, see 6.4). Also Audhumbla, the primeval cow that was created in Ginnungagap, came into being. From her udder, four streams of milk flowed, and Ymir was drinking from them.

Audhumbla licked the salty white frost, her only food. After licking an entire day, in the evening the hair of a male appeared. At the second evening, his head appeared, and at the third, the entire figure emerged. This was Buri, the first god in Norse mythology, handsome and tall. Buri

---

[106] Theatrum Mundi is a metaphorical concept developed throughout Western literature and thought, apparent in theories of the world such as Plato's Allegory of the Cave, and a popular idea in the Baroque Period among certain writers.

got a son, Borr, and with the *jötunn* woman Bestla, he had three sons: the gods Odin, Vili and Ve, forming a triad (Proto-Norse *\*wodaz, wiljô* and *wīhą*[107]).

Ymir was sweating in his sleep, and the giants arose from his body. In order to create the world, Odin, Vili, and Ve killed Ymir. The majority of the first giants drowned in the streams of his blood, but Bergelmir (mountain troublemaker or bear troublemaker, a frost giant) and his wife survived in a trough. From them derive the frost giants in Jotunheim, the giants' home.

The sons of Borr threw the body of Ymir into the middle of Ginnungagap. His blood let, they flow as streams and rivers all the way into the ocean. From his flesh they made the firm earth. They piled his bones into the mountains. His teeth became the stones, while his broken bones became the screes. Then they took his skull and arched it over the world so that the sky limited the world upward. At each corner of the world, a dwarf carried the vault of the earth. They designated part of the world as Jotunheim for the race known as the *jötnar*. Because of the giant's malevolence toward humans, the brothers took Ymir's eyebrows to form a protective wall around the center of the earth. This sheltered area was called Midgard, and house of the human race (Figs. 23, 24; Box X).

The brain of Ymir they threw into the air, and the clouds appeared. They fixed sparks from Muspelheim to the sky, and they became stars. Out of Ymir's hair grass, plants, bushes, and the woods were made. Odin, Vili, and Ve snatched glowing embers from the realm of Muspelheim and created the sun and moon. These were placed above the world to illuminate the earth and gave them stable living homes.

One day the sons of Borr came across two fallen trees. One was an ash and the other an elm. From these trees Odin created the first man and woman and gave them the essence of life. Vili gave the thought and feeling, and Ve gave them the ability to hear, speak, and see. Their names were Ask and Embla. Also later on, Odin, Vili, and Ve created the means to measure and record time. The light and dark phases of the earth were ruled by night and day. Odin set them in the sky on chariots that circled

---

[107] Approximately inspiration, cognition and divine will; https://en.wikipedia.org/wiki/Vili_and_Vé.

Fig. 23. The World Tree Yggdrasil. Crafted by the copper engraver Oluf Olufsen Bagge (1780-1836). Take note of the bridge Bifröst between Asgard, Midgard, and Helheim, the Midgard Serpent and the mountains of Jotunheim. Wikimedia Commons.

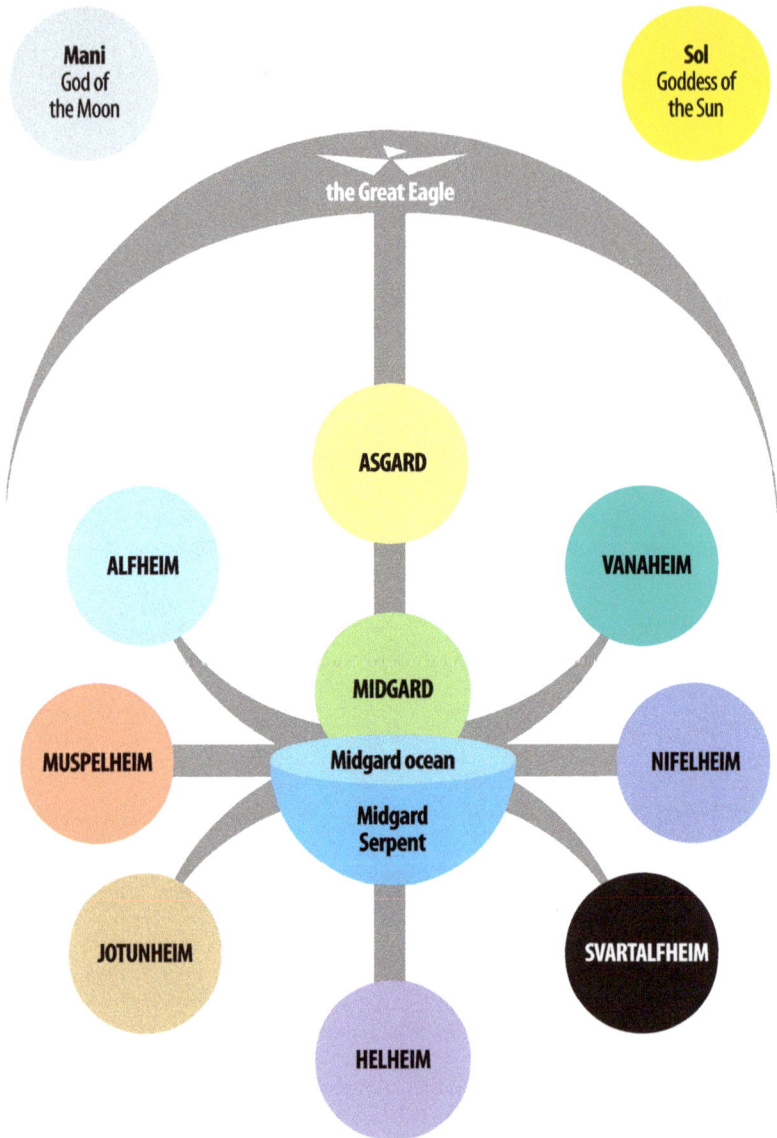

Schematic depiction of the Germanic world tree, the ash Yggdrasil and the nine word homes (see also Box X). See "the nine in the tree", page 110).

the world every two half days. The chariot of the night is pulled by the horse Hrimfaxi (frost mane); that of the day is drawn by the mare Skinfaxi (shining mane).

## 6.2 Cosmography and the World Tree Yggdrasil

In Germanic mythology, gods and humans do not live in diametric worlds. They live in concert in a world separated into Niu Heimar (Old Norse [nine homeworlds; see Box IX]), unified by the world tree Yggdrasil (Fig. 23). The term *heimr* (home or homestead) means here the world (including parts where no humans live). All nine homeworlds are not listed completely in surviving texts but are mentioned in various myths. The most important part of the world consists on three parts: Asgard (garden of the gods), where the patrilineal Aesir and the matricentric Vanir reside; Midgard (middle garden), where the humans live; and Utgard (out garden), where the *jötnar*, giants, and trolls live (Figs. 23, 24).

Midgard is engirdled by a primordial ocean, in which the gods have thrown the Midgard Serpent (Old Norse: *Jormungandr*, huge monster), obviously representing the uroboros[108]. The center of the three "gardens" and "homesteads" is the cosmic tree Yggdrasil. There is a connection between Midgard and Asgard. This is the burning rainbow bridge Bifröst (also called shivering path or Asbru [bridge to the Aesir]) that is watched by the god Heimdall, who is mentioned at the very start of *Völuspa* (Fig. 23). Heimdall is the guardian of the gods and possesses the resounding horn Gjallarhorn (Old Norse [yelling horn or the loud sounding horn]), owns the golden-maned horse Gulltoppr, has gold teeth, and is the son of Nine Mothers. Heimdall is attested as possessing foreknowledge, keen eyesight and hearing. He keeps watch for the onset of the end of time, Ragnarök, while drinking fine mead in his dwelling Himinbjörg (Old Norse heaven's castle), located where Bifröst meets Asgard. The gods ride over Bifröst to the humans and the dead soldiers to Valhalla and Folkvang (see 6.5.1). The soul journey of the initiated or shamans takes place along the same pathway (e.g., the poem *Draumkvedet*, see 5.7). The Völva continues

*An ash I know, Yggdrasil its name,*
*With water white is the great tree wet;*
*Thence come the dews that fall in the dales,*
*Green by Urth's well does it ever grow.*

---

[108] Symbolizing the recycling and renewing of the universe.

## Box IX: The sacred number nine and the "homeworlds" of Germanic mythology

Like the *ennead* (a group of nine deities) in Egyptian mythology, the numbers three and in particular nine are significant in Norse mythology. Both numbers (and multiplications thereof) appear throughout surviving attestations of Norse paganism, in both mythology and cultic practice. Odin hangs for nine nights on Yggdrasil. Thor takes nine steps backward before the Midgard Serpent kills him. Along with the number 27, both numbers figure in the lunar Germanic calendar (3 x 9). Before the adaption of the Julian calendar, the Germanic calendar was lunisolar, as reflected in the Germanic term *mēnoth-* (month; Old English monath, Old Saxon manuth, Old Norse manathr), being a derivation of the term *menth* (moon). The Runic calendar that developed in medieval Sweden was lunisolar, fixing the beginning of the year at the first full moon after winter solstice (similar to the timing of Easter).

The nine "homeworlds," unified by the world tree Yggdrasil (see Fig. 24) are:

**Asgard**, the home of the Aesir.

**Alfheim** (home of the fairies) or **Ljósálheim** (home of the light-elves).

**Vanaheim**, (home of the Vanir, gods associated with fertility, wisdom, and the ability to see the future).

**Midgard**, the world inhabited by and known to human.

**Muspelheim** (home of fire), a world of fire and lava and home of the *jötunn* Surt. The sun and the stars originate from Muspelheim.

**Nifelheim** (mist home/world), a world of darkness, ice, and snow, and home of the dishonorable dead, overlaps with the term *Helheim* (see below).

**Jötunheim** (home of the *jötunn*) or **Útgard** (out yard), stronghold of the giants.

**Hel(heim)**, the home of the death goddess Hel, the resting place for those souls who do not go to Valhalla or Niflheim (see above).

**Nidavellir** or **Svartálfheim** (world of darkness, home of the dwarfs).

Yggdrasil is an immense ash tree, the axis mundi, and considered very holy (Fig. 23, Box X). The gods go daily to Yggdrasil to assemble their meetings, the *thing*. The branches of Yggdrasil extend far into the heavens. The name Yggdrasil derives from Old Norwegian *ygr* (fierce, terrible) and *drasill* (steed, gallows). *Ygr* is one of Odin's many *kennings*, (see Box VI). Yggdrasil could thus mean the "terrible Odin's gallows or horse," a rather peculiar name for a World Tree. It points at Odin's self-sacrifice on the World Tree (see 6.5.1. and Box XXI). Yggdrasil is seen as a place for initiation. Pretended hanging was a typical initiation procedure in Norse times (Box VIII), and the nine-day, intentional hanging of Odin on the Yggdrasil signifies an essential aspect of Norse mythology (see 6.5.1 and Box XXI). Odin is described as both riding the tree or hanging himself on it. Both are intentional, well-controlled procedures.

The dew that falls from Yggdrasil provides life to every living creature on earth. Thus, all generations have to thank the tree. Nobody can imagine what the ash is suffering. Stags graze in the foliage and remove it continuously. From their antlers rains falls down to Hwergelmir, and that is the reason that the well never dries up. The bark of the tree is old, and the wood is rotten. An eagle has his nest up in the tree. He looks into the world and knows much. The squirrel Ratatosk (Old Norse drill-tooth) runs up and down the trunk and invents gossip that creates animosities between the eagle and the worm Nidhögg (Old Norse malice striker).

Deep inside the trunk of Yggdrasil rest the seeds of the future. Once the Völva was asked who would survive Ragnarök, the twilight of gods (see 6.7). "Liv and Livtrase are the names of the pair of humans that wait inside the Holt of Hoddmimis," was the answer. Liv (life, the female) and Livtrase (the one that fights for life, the male) are not yet born, but they will become the onset of a future lineage of man. Hoddmimis Holt is Old Norse/Proto Germanic and is difficult to interpret, but it may be a *kenning* of the well of Mimir (Mimisbrunnr) at one of Yggdrasil roots and wood or a grove (holt). Hoddmimis Holt points at the role Yggdrasil will play for the creation of the New Earth after Ragnarök (see 6.8).

Yggdrasil has three mighty roots that stretch deep into the collective unconscious. The three representations of the collective unconscious are

## Box X: The world tree: a main pillar of many cultures

The world tree is a motif present in several religions and mythologies, particularly in Indo-European and Siberian religions. The world tree is represented as a colossal tree, connecting the heavens, the terrestrial world, and, through its roots, the underworld (Fig. 24). It is also connected to the motif of the tree of life. Specific world trees include, for example the oak in Slavic, Finnish, and Baltic mythology, the sacred fig Ashvattha in Hindu mythology and the Irminsul (see 3.5) in central Germanic mythology. There were sacred trees close to houses in Norse times and even today a *tuntre* (prominent tree close to the main residence) is an important aspect of Scandinavian countryside courtyards. A prominent tree was the essential center of Germanic sanctuaries and *things*.

The conception of the tree rising through a number of worlds is found in northern Eurasia and forms part of the shamanistic lore[109]. It seems to be a very ancient conception, perhaps based on the Pole Star, the center of the heavens, and its connection to the world (*axis mundi*). Among Siberian shamans, a sacred tree may be used as a ladder to ascendto the heavens. In the mythology of the Samoyeds, the world tree is also the symbol of Mother Earth, who is said to give the Samoyed shaman his drum and help him travel from one world to another. The cosmic tree was one of the most important elements in Latvian mythology and Lithuanian folk painting.

Trees and treelike symbols are central in most religions, ceremonial traditions, or paintings. We have the holy Irminsul of the Saxons in the Teuteburger Woods that was cut down by Charlemagne (see 7.2; Fig. 48). We have the tree of knowledge in the center of Paradise. Dionysus, the god of wine, ritual madness, fertility, theater, and religious ecstasy sailed from the east with a ship into the Greek culture, with a grapevine as the mast. We have the Christmas tree and the maypole. There is the Jewish tree of life (*Etz ha Chayim*) in the Kabbalah. The world tree, such an Yggdrasil, is indeed a main pillar in many cultures.

The majority of the sacred and ritual trees in the history of religions are only replicas, imperfect copies of this exemplary archetype, the Cosmic Tree. Thus, all these sacred trees are thought of as situated at and projected into the Center of the World[110].

---

[109] Eliade, M. (1964).
[110] Eliade, M. (1961).

represented by wells: Hvergelmir, Mimirsbrunnr and Urdabrunnr. The root of Hvergelmir reaches down into the middle of Nifelheim. The teeth of Nidhögg gnaw on the root of the tree of life every day. The second root reaches down to the well of Mimir (see 6.5.6), the wisest of all who remembers everything what has happened in the world (the well of remembrance). The third root reaches down to the well of the *nornes*, Urdabrunnr, where the three women decide about destiny (see 6.3).

There is lasting significance of the evergreen Yggdrasil in northern Europe[111]. The trees image did not only survive through absorption into the cross, but northerners identified the new truth of their adopted religion in the symbols, narratives, and churches (Norwegian stave churches [Fig. 9] and Danish/Swedish Round Churches). Visiting these churches can be linked to entering Yggdrasil, and maybe one gets reborn in the New Earth, like Liv and Livtrasi. There appears to be a connection between Yggdrasil and the evergreen Christmas tree with its heavenly lights and red fertility apples from the tree of life/knowledge in Paradise.

## 6.3 Female beings associated with fate

Mystic and supernatural female characters inhabit major stretches of the Norse and probably Germanic universe. They are associated with the collective unconscious, fertility, and fate. They are well-known in German literature. In J.W.v. Goethe's drama *Faust II*, three females (mothers) appear when the protagonist descends into the underworld, ending with the famous epitome of human existence: "*das ewig Weibliche zieht uns hinan*"[112]. It is thus the eternal female that is the agent leading to development. Against the exisiting state of things in a patriarchal world, Goethe worked up the significance of the female, reflecting his genius. In today's world, the female, not the male, provides development and progress.

In Norse mythology, a *dis* (lady, goddess, plural *disir*) is a ghost, spirit, or deity associated with fate who can be both benevolent and

---

[111] Murphy, G.R. (2013).
[112] The eternal feminine, draws us upward.

antagonistic toward mortals. *Disir* comprise an entire range of female characters. Their original function was possibly that of fertility goddesses who were the object of both private and official worship (*disablot*; a blot [Indo-European *bhle/*bhlo* = to swell] is a sacrifice to the gods or a sacrificial holiday). Their veneration may derive from the worship of the spirits of the dead. The *disir*, like the *nornes*, the *fylgjur* (see below) and *vættir*[113] are almost always referred to collectively, i.e. in plural.

The *nornes* are female figures in Germanic mythology that rule the destiny of gods and men. The best-known are the three *nornes* Urd, Werdandi, and Skuld (fate, happening [see German: *werden*] and necessity [see English: shall], or past, present, and future, respectively).

*Thence come the maidens, mighty in wisdom,*
*Three from the dwelling, down 'neath the tree;*
*Urd is one named, Werdandi the next,—*
*On the wood they scored,— and Skuld the third.*
*Laws they made there, and life allotted*
*To the sons of men, and set their fates.*

They are often represented in the following manner: Urd spins the threat of life, Werdandi takes it over the lap and hands it over to Skuld, who ultimately cuts it when lifetime is over. They draw water from the well Urdabrunnr and pour it over the roots of Yggdrasil so that its branches will live forever. These *nornes* are powerful maiden giantesses (*jötnar* from Utgard). Beside these three *nornes*, there are other malevolent and benevolent *nornes* who visit newborn children's cradels in order to determine their future (in the days before name-giving).

Among these mighty female creatures associated with Jotunheim, Utgard and the collective unconscious are also the *fylgja* (plural *fylgjur* [to accompany]). This is a spirit that accompanies a person in connection with fate and fortune. A *fylgja* can be considered as a *dis*, i.e., a ghost goddess that is attached to fate. It is similar to the Fetch, a supernatural double or an apparition of a living person in Irish folklore. A *fylgja* has

---

[113] Nature spirits that are divided up into "families," including elves, dwarfs, *jötnar*, and *valkyries.*

Fig. 25. Graphic depictions from helmet plates depicting various Germanic warriors. Upper left: a dancing warrior and a bear warrior (*berserk*?); upper right: an ax warrior and a constrained wolf (*ulfhethnars*?); lower left: two warriors with a swine on the helmets; lower right: a warrior fighting with two bears (*berserk*?). From the Vendel Period (550-790; between the Migration Period and the Viking Age). From Mörbylånga municipality, Öland, Sweden. Picture 39 on page 90 in Kongl. Vitterhets Historie och Antiqvitets Akademiens Månadsblad (1872). Wikimedia Commons.

similarities with the *doppelgänger* (literally "double-goer", a look-alike or double of a living person, an evil twin), and sightings are regarded as omens, usually for impending death. In northern Norwegian narratives, approaching death can be heralded through the appearance of manifestation of the *fylgja/doppelgänger*.

In some instances, the *fylgja* can take on the form of the animal that shows itself when a child is born. Men who were viewed as leaders would often have a *fylgja* to show their true character. This means that if they had a "tame nature," their *fylgja* would typically be an ox, goat, or boar. If they had an "untamed nature," they would have *fylgjur* such as a fox, wolf, deer, bear, eagle, falcon, leopard, lion, or a serpent. *Fylgjur* could also mark transformations between human and animals, i.e., shape shifting. These transformations are often hinted at when sagas mention berserkers or *ulfhethnars* transforming into animals or imitate animalistic characteristics (Fig. 25).

## 6.4 Giants and dwarfs

Utgard is the realm of giants, dwarfs, and elves that engirdles both Asgard and Midgard. Utgard and its mighty population of powers are a permanent threat to humans and gods: The unconscious can invade Midgard and the conscious homeland (Fig. 23). The giants, dwarfs, and elves all come from hostile realms, dominated by mountains, rocks, caves, and ice. The giants have many names. They can be called *jötunn* (eaters [from Indo-European *etunar*], *thurs* [strong, from old Indian *tura*], or troll [from Middle High German *trüllen*, to roll]).

The *jötnar* are mythological races that live in Jötunheim. They were banished there by the Aesir, who refused them entry to their world, Asgard. However, the *jötnar* frequently interact with the Aesir, as well as the Vanir. They are usually in opposition to, or in competition with them, but also interact with them in a nonhostile manner. Some *jötnar* even intermarry with the Aesir and Vanir, and many are named as parents or grandparents of Aesir such as Thor and Odin (Fig. 26). This creates complex relationships, not only between the Aesir and Vanir, but also between these gods and the giants and the conscious and unconscious. The Germanic "heaven" shares similarities with life and the world. It is a multicultural and mixed pursuit, not a straightforward, top-down regulated pantheon of gods that exists detached and elevated over the human world. The Germanic world is not strict and unilateral; it resembles life with all its meandering and contrasting realities.

The *jötnar*, *thurs* and trolls are forceful and naïve and wish in particular to get hold of Freyja, the goddess of fertility and love (see 6.5.2). In contrast, taking secrets, knowledge, gold, and riches from the giants is one of the main activities of the gods. The greatest threat for the

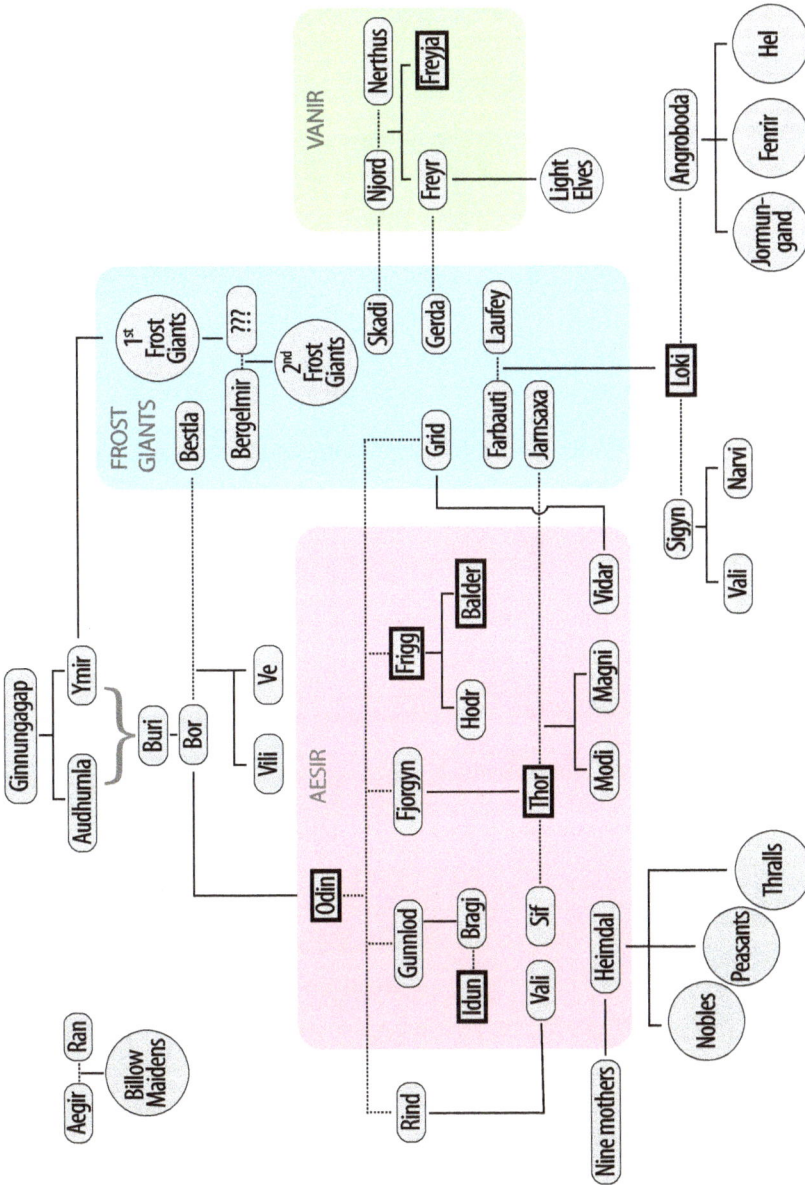

Fig. 26. The creation and genealogy of Germanic gods, giants, and humans, from Ginnungagap to nobles, peasants, thralls, and Lokis offspring with the *jötunn* woman Angerboda. Take note of the coexistence of Aesir, Vanir, and giants in the Germanic universe. In bold the names of gods that are treated in chapter 6. Redrawn from http://lostheroesrpg.com.

giants is the god Thor (see 6.5.3), who eternally fights against them. In the Jungian tradition, the giants are representatives of the collective unconscious, continuously invading the realm of the consciousness. Thor fights the chaos of the unconscious by applying his "lightning" of the conscious will.

In Germanic mythology, a dwarf (see 5.5) is a small, human-shaped being that dwells in mountains and in the earth, and is variously associated with wisdom, mining, melting and crafting (Fig. 20). After Christianization, tales of dwarfs continued to be told in the folklore of areas of Europe where Germanic languages were (and are) spoken (see 5.5).

## 6.5 Asgard and the Norse gods

In contrast to Greek and Roman gods, the Germanic gods have only partial control of the world and require additional insight from the underworld, which they visit to obtain wisdom and power. The gods do not only share power and influence with the giants; Asgard is unique because there is not only one group of gods present, but also two disparate groups: the patriarchal Aesir (the female Aesir are called *asynjur*, with Frigg being the most important [see 6.5.8]) and matricentric Vanir (the female Vanir are called *vanadis*). The Aesir are the gods of sovereignty and leadership. They govern in the heavens and move with various chariots or animals through the skies. They are thus always present when the Germanic tribes move (e.g., during the Indo-European pasturist invasion). The Vanir are older than the Aesir and represent local, sedentary agriculture and fertility gods. The patriarchal Aesir subjected the old matricentric Europe, dominated by fertility gods such as the Vanir. Ever since has the the world experienced generic patriarchal-matricentric conflicts. Woman's emancipation and gender balance in our times are expressions of this basic conflict. Gimbutas' term "Old Europe" comes to mind (see 2.2). As the coexistence of Aesir anf Vanir is a special characteristic of the Germanic tribes, a closer look at the ideas of Gimbautas seems appropriate.

Gimbutas articulated the differences between the Old European system, which she considered goddess- and woman-centred (gynocentric), and the Bronze Age Indo-European patriarchal (androcratic) culture that supplanted it[114]. According to her interpretations, gynocentric societies were peaceful, honored women, and espoused economic equality. In contrast, the androcratic, male-dominated Kurgan peoples imposed the hierarchical rule of male warriors upon its European natives. Gimbutas postulated that in Old Europe, the Aegean and the Near East, a great Triple Goddess was worshipped (see 6.3 and 6.5.4), predating what she considered as a patriarchal religion imported by the Kurgans. Skepticism regarding her goddess-centered Old Europe thesis is widespread within the academic community. Gimbutas' thinking may have been influenced by the zeitgeist of her times, to which belong a range of political and social movements and ideologies centered on feminism. These share a common goal: to define, establish, and achieve political, economic, personal, and social rights for women that are equal to those of men. Despite these arguments, the theories of Gimbutas are interesting and plausible in a Germanic mythology context: Balanced male and female mythological figures and contexts exist, unbiased gyno- and androcentric relation prevail (see Box XIV).

Special for the Germanic world is that peace between patriarchal and matricentric gods was settled due to the exchange of hostages, marriage, and partnerships. There is cooperation in Asgard, and a "balance" between patriarchal and matriarchal (female head of a family or tribal line) gods characterizes Germanic mythology[115]. As a result, the suppression by the patriarchal forces is not absolute. On the contrary, it paves the ground for a dualistic equilibrium (see Box XI). This is indeed reflected during the Norse times when the balance provides a fertile terrain for Germanic males and females, reflected in the Germanic partnership (Box XIV).

The coexistence of disparate gods such as the Vanir and Aesir did not come without conflict. The Aesir-Vanir war was a conflict between these two groups of deities that ultimately resulted in the unification of the Aesir and the Vanir into a single pantheon (Fig. 26). This war is an important and specific event in Norse mythology, and the implications are a matter of debate. Fragmented information about the war appears in surviving sources, including the Völuspa.

---

[114] Gimbutas, M. (1991).
[115] Metzner, R. (1994); Simek, R. (2004); Stockland, O. (1969).

125

Inside Asgard a plethora of Norse gods exists, and before we look closer into just seven of them, an overview of the gods' and goddesses' genealogy is presented (Fig. 26). The selected gods are indicated in bold and presented in greater detail in 6.5.1 to 6.5.7, and 6.6.1. Not only are some of the matricentric gods of Old Europe (Vanir) part of Asgard, but the number female gods in Germanic mythology outnumber the males by far. Among 48 gods listed, 25 are females[116]. If the names of 39 valkyries are added[117], then the male gods definitely become a minority. Is this characteristic for the Germanic worldview? However, much less is known about the female gods, and this may reflect patriarchate tradition in Christianity and that most written sources exist from times when Christianity already was a vital force. By marginalizing goddesses, the dominance of male gods in Germanic mythology became evident. Thanks to the strength of the patriarchate in recent centuries, male dominance among the Germanic gods became a self-fulfilling prophecy.

### 6.5.1 Odin/Wotan

Odin has been the main Germanic god since the times of written sources (earlier the main god was Tyr, see 6.6.1). Odin is a prominently mentioned god throughout the Germanic regions and tribal expansions of the Migration Period and Norse times. In modern times, Odin continued to be acknowledged in the rural folklore of Germanic Europe (see chapter 5).

In Norse mythology, from which stems most of our information about the god, Odin lives in Valhalla (from Old Norse Valhǫll [hall of the slain]), a majestic, enormous hall located in Asgard. He is the husband of Frigg (see 6.5.8; Fig. 26). In wider Germanic mythology and paganism, Odin was known in Old English as Woden, in Old Saxon as Wodan, and in Old High German as Wuotan or Wotan (Fig. 27). These terms all stem from the reconstructed Proto- Germanic root *wōđanaz (Old English woth [rage, related to German Wut]). Wuotan/Wotan can thus be

---

[116] Enoksen, L.M. (2008).
[117] https://en.wikipedia.org/wiki/List_of_valkyrie_names.

paraphrased with "lord of rage." In contrast, the name Odin derives from the complex, Old Norse term *odr* (ecstasy, divine madness, mind, soul or spirit) and stands for the inspiration, prophetic trance, rush, ecstasy, and divine madness associated with the god. These two names point at an ambivalence and a two-sidedness in the character of the god, in line with all collectively inherited unconscious ideas, pattern of thoughts, and images, i.e., the archetypes as Jung defined them. Through his name, Odin stands for inspiration, prophetic trance, rush, ecstasy and divine madness. Through his name Wotan, he stands for rage,

Fig. 27. Odin from Lejre is a small-cast silver figurine from approximately 900, depicting an individual on a throne wearing a floor-length dress, an apron, four bead necklaces, a neck ring, a cloak, and a rimless hat. Two birds are seated on the armrests, and the back of the throne features the heads of two animals. The identity of the figure depicted has been the subject of some dispute. The excavator interpreted it as the god Odin sitting on his throne Hlidskjalf, from which he sees into all the worlds. Lejre Museum, Denmark. Photo: Ole Malling

fury, wrath, and the wars and fights that are initiated by him. Like all recurring symbols or motifs of the deepest recess of the human psyche that make up the archetypes, the god reigns in contradicting but shimmering and opalescent ambiguity.

Odin/Wotan is the omnipresent wandering god that suddenly appears and vanishes. He is one-eyed (he sacrificed one eye), long-bearded, has a blue mantel, uses a stick (or a spear named Gungnir [Old Norse, swaying one]) and carries a slap hat. He rides through the skies on a horse with eight legs, Sleipner (Old Norse, the slipper)[118]. That the Germanic main god Odin rides a horse to travel in all realms

---

[118] Fathered by the god Loki (in the form of a mare, see 6.5.5) and the stallion Svadilfari (a disguised unnamed thurs; "the one that like to go where it is slippery").

Fig. 28. A plate from a Vendel era helmet featuring Odin riding a horse, holding a spear and shield, and confronted by a serpent. Is this the Midgard Serpent? For details, see Fig. 25. Wikimedia Commons.

Fig. 29. The Norse god Odin enthroned, flanked by his two wolves, Geri and Freki, and his two ravens, Huginn and Muninn, and holding his spear Gungnir. Engraving by Ludwig Pietsch (1824-1911). From Reusch, R. F. (1865). *Die nordischen Göttersagen.* Wikimedia Commons.

is not accidental (Fig. 28). The Indo-European pasturist invaders used horses and moved fast and widely westward through the immense sea of grass that stretched from Central Asia all the way to Europe[119]. In line with the god's character, the horse stands for power, grace, beauty, nobility, strength, and freedom.

Odin/Wotan is also associated with two additional types of animals, his "excursion souls." On his shoulders he has the "odinistic" ravens Huginn and Muninn (Old Norse [thought and memory/mind, respectively], Fig. 29). They fly all over the world and bring information to the god. He has also two animalistic embodiments of his "wotanic" lawlessness and his breaking of order: the wolves Geri and Freki (Old Norse [the ravenous or greedy one, respectively]). They may also be connected to beliefs surrounding the Germanic "wolf-warrior bands," the *ulfhethnar* (Fig. 25, see Box XIX). Both ravens and wolves are independent animals. The god's excursion souls fly where they wish or search vast territories.

---

[119] Anthony, D.W. (2007).

They represent the highest value of the Germanic tribes: freedom inside federalism. These animal types support Odin, they are his shamanistic, zoomorphic helping spirits[120].

Odin/Wotan is traditionally considered the god of warfare, but he probably started as the god of shamanism (which he acquired from the *vanir* Freyja, 6.5.2). He took over the warfare function from the earlier god of warfare, Tyr (see 6.6.1), at least in the regions covered by Tacitus (see 3.1). Odin/Wotan is the god of the wind, and through our breathing, we take part in the "word-giving" and the murmuring of secrets. He provides the language (wind, breath), i.e., the "logos" to his people. Odin/Wotan provided also the runes, which are the condensed secrets, the symbols of humans (see 4.1). This change in role is characteristic for Odin/Wotan. He is not a fixed god and develops over time (see Box XI).

## Box XI: From polytheism to monotheism: Odin and modernity

We argue that Germanic mythology does not represent a backward and outdated Europe, but rather prepares for modernity. This can be illustrated through the development of Odin over time. It is possible that the god Odin originated as a historical person, as stated by Snorri Sturlusson in the *Prose Edda* and Saxo Grammaticus in *Gesta Danorum* (see 3.2 and 3.3). This view finds support through the highly controversial book *Jakten på Odin* (*The Search for Odin*)[121]. It suggests that there is a distinct possibility that Odin was, in fact, a human chief of a people around the Sea of Azov (southwestern Russia/southeastern Ukraine), sometime between 100 and 300 B.C.E. As a result of Roman eastward expansion, Odin moved his people toward northern Germany, the Baltic Sea region, and Scandinavia. Through his charismatic leadership, he managed to get a reputation to be stemming from the gods. Odin became worshipped as a god in Northern Europe—thus founding the Aesir-faith, as we know it. Over time, Odin picked up more and more qualities that were originally

---

[120] Hedeager, L. (2011).
[121] Heyerdal, T., Lillieström, P. (2001).

found in separate gods and goddesses. He became the god of war (after Tyr), he adopted sorcery (which he learned from Freyja), and he developed his relationship with Loki (see Box XVI). This development reflects a movement from the polytheism of earlier days toward the more recent monotheism. Here, this development is interpreted as a move toward integration and merger of hitherto distinct psychological functions into self-awareness, autonomy, and modernity. Modernity refers to a period marked by cross-examination or rejection of tradition (reflected by fixed roles), for the benefit of prioritizing individualism, freedom, and subjective and existential experience (involving variable roles for each individual).

Both Jesus of Nazareth and Odin may have started as historic persons who attained divinity by hanging on the World Tree: the cross or Yggdrasil. Similar to Jesus of Nazareth, Odin progresses from the superego enforcement of the absolutistic patriarchate of the Old Testament, Jehovah[122], and its bondage-slaved ego (such as reflected by Moses on Mount Sinai, being subjected to the absoluteness of the 10 Commandments) to ego divinization and ego autonomy. Jesus is the empathic redeemer who provides humanity with the means to reunite with God (we ate from the tree of knowledge) through his self-sacrifice on the world tree/cross. Jesus is crucified by the will of his father. Paving the road of individuation, Odin sacrifices himself voluntarily on Yggdrasil (see Box XXI) and provides humanity access to the unconcious through the runes, the secrets of the world. By constantly breaking laws, he keeps the suffocation of the superego at bay, provides increased ego autonomy, and opens up for improved access to the collective unconsciousness (which he learned from the matricentric Vanir, see 6.5.2). Odin anticipates modern man: Hanging on Yggdrasil and wounded by his own spear (his consciousness?), he becomes the subject of his own experience (see Box XXI). He is not scarificed but does it himself to provide initiation and wisdom to his people. While Christ (the son), redeems our souls, Odin (the chief) proceeds from there and demonstrates ego autonomy, i.e., modernity. Here this implies that each person becomes more and more himself/herself by integrating various qualities (such as polytheism)

---

[122] He owns no empathy and says "I am who I am".

into one personality (monotheism). While Jesus of Nazareth was sacrificed by his father, Odin's self-sacrifice means that each person can obtain self-divination: through hanging himself on the world tree. This points at the advent of self-psychology[123].

The modernity of Odin is also reflected when we compare him with the god of the Old Testament, who is an indifferent, archaic absolutist that lacks the ability to experience empathy. As the worlds supreme megalomaniac, he can destroy city after city, man, woman, and child, down to the youngest baby. Odin killed only in combat against opponents of similar cal'iber and rank who had weapons. But the most important difference is that All-father Odin is not all-powerful and does not claim to be all-wise[124]. We can easily identify with a god that is like us. Through Christianization, and particularly Protestantism, Germanic tribes were forced to regress to Jehovah but could hope for Christ. In their hearts, the Norse kept the confidence that it was better to be the independent wolf of Odin than the slaughtered Lamb of God (or Jehovah). The Lamb of God becomes the victim to be sacrificed on the cross and dies, but Odin sacrifices himself, survives, thrives, and develops. The Germanic tribes, with their passion for autonomy, accepted rather the power of the wolf: instinct, intelligence, appetite for freedom, and awareness of the importance of social connections (e.g., family, clan, nation, *thing*). Jehovah represents the archaic times, and we may ask if Jung confused Wotan with Jehovah in his essay. With regard to man's future autonomy, the death and resurrection of Christ is humanity's turning point. Modern times commence with Odin, and he stands for the transgression of the ego: ego-automatization and the self.

---

[123] Self-psychology, a modern psychoanalytic theory and its clinical applications, was conceived by Heinz Kohut in Chicago in the 1960s, '70s, and '80s, and is still developing as a contemporary form of psychoanalytic treatment. In self-psychology, the effort is made to understand individuals from within their subjective experience via vicarious introspection, basing interpretations on the understanding of the self as the central agency of the human psyche. Essential to mirroring understanding self-psychology are the concepts of empathy, self-object, idealizing, and alter ego/twinship. Though self-psychology also recognizes certain drives, conflicts, and complexes present in Freudian psychodynamic theory, these are understood within a different framework. Self-psychology was seen as a major break from traditional psychoanalysis and is considered the beginnings of the relational approach to psychoanalysis.

[124] R. A. Heinlein (2004).

Odin/Wotan has numerous sexual relationships. With the goddess Jord (Old Norse [Earth)] he has the son Tor (see 6.5.3) and with Frigg, Balder (see 6.5.6). With Rind (Proto-Germanic *rind, bark, crust, described as a giantess goddess or a human princess from the east]) he has the son Vali (etymological origins unknown) and with the *jotun* woman Grid, he has the son Vidar (Old Norse [wide ruler]). With an unknown woman, he has the son Hodr, the blind god of darkness. He has a multitude of additional affairs. Odin/Wotan is thus potent, and this is reflected in what we today would call promiscuity, but what is actually the creative urge and the fathering of the Allfather (the father of all gods).

Odin/Wotan has a number of extrovert characteristics. Supported by the *valkyries* (see Box XII), he decides who will die in battle (Fig. 30). He receives the fallen warriors at his living place Valhalla. Here he gathers his elite troops, the *einherjar* (Old Norse [single, or once, fighters]), for the final battle against the enemies of the world, Ragnarök (see 6.7). He is visible at night in the skies with his tempestuous troops (see 5.6, Fig. 21). The god stands above all rules, he is transmoral as he excites to conflict and promotes the breaking of oaths. Odin/Wotan has also outspoken introvert characteristics. He takes care of the head of the decapitated giant Mimir (see 6.5.7; Fig. 39). Odin/Wotan is thus also the god of secrets, poetics, and sacred knowledge. He is the god of the initiated and the ultimate shaman.

## Box XII: Femme fatales and valkyries

In Norse mythology, a *valkyrie* (Old Norse *val-kyrja* [chooser of the slain]) is a female figure who decides who may die in battle and who survives (Figs. 21, 30). The *valkyries* bring their chosen to one of the two afterlife halls of the slain, Valhalla, ruled over by the god Odin (the other half goes to the goddess Freyja's afterlife field Folkvang). The warlike virgins mount horses and arm themselves with helmets and spears. They hover over the battlefield, like birds over their prey, to choose the warriors to their afterlife.

Toward the end of the 19th century greatly, exaggerated emphasis was offered to *valkyries* in music, paintings, and illustrations (e.g. Fig. 21). This is particularly true for their role in Richard Wagner's *Der Ring des Nibelungen* (*The Ring*), a cycle of four magnificent

German-language epic music dramas. Wagner wrote both libretto and music from 1848-1874. *Der Ring* plays an important role in the oeuvre of Wagner as a *Gesamtkunstwerk*[125].

Is the plethora of *valkyries* important elements in Germanic mythology? Superficially this is so (39 names of specific valkyries are mentioned). Like the berserkers, they represent just one of a plethora of figures and roles in the drama of Norse mythological accounts. The great attention toward the end of the 19th century probably reflects the monstrous zeitgeist obsession for femme fatales, a stereotypical character of a mysterious, seductive woman whose charms ensnare her lovers, often leading them into compromising, dangerous, and deadly situations. Their qualities can include promiscuity and the "rejection of motherhood." The latter is a most threatening quality since, by denying mans immortality and posterity (in the form of children, preferably a son), it leads to the ultimate destruction of the male[126]. Femmes fatale are typically villainous, morally ambiguous, and first of all frighteningly independent.

The fascination for femmes fatales in Western culture seems to reflect an unconscious reaction toward the advent of female emancipation and greater focus upon what Jung calls the anima[127] (Fig. 65). It is easy to find negative-loaded elements for projecting undesired or no unacceptable contents, e.g., man's traditionally suppressed female side (e.g., as reflected by the anima) upon contemporary women. The Wagnerian emphasis on *valkyries*, as part of a varied selection of female representations of unacceptable and dangerous femininity, is a true-born child of a patriarchate that is threatened to be relieved of its dominating position by gender equality. In essence, the previous emphasis on *valkyries* reflects the zeitgeist of the fin de siecle with its demands for more female emancipation, a veritable threat to the patriachate.

---

[125] A *Gesamtkunstwerk* is a work of art that makes use of all or many art forms or strives to do so.
[126] Walter, S. (2015).
[127] Coleman, W. (2012).

Fig. 30. A *valkyrie* figurine depicted from all sides. This unique silver *Valkyrie,* found in Denmark, holds a sword and a shield. Take note of the ornaments of her clothes and the elegant hair knot. Courtesy and photo: Asger Kjaergaard, Odense Bys Museer, Denmark.

Odin's essential act for humanity is his self-sacrifice on Yggdrasil (see Box XXI). Pretended hanging is an initiation procedure, a matter of worshipping the connection to the afterworld (see Box VIII). He is connected to death (dead warriors in Valhalla and the Wild Hunt; Fig. 21)) and is said to be present when people die: He wishes to obtain knowledge from the spirits of those transgressing to the other world. A second aspect of necromancy is that Odin/Wotan applies human skulls for divination. He drinks daily from Mimir's well with the purpose to foretell events or discover hidden knowledge. Odin/Wotan stands for the visionary extensions of the conscious: the god of ecstasy, the lord of runes and poetry. He knows shamanistic magic and can surface the unconscious, the Völva, one of the mothers of the underworld.

The true nature of Odin/Wotan

- Wandering and unrest. Odin is not: He becomes.
- Destructive and creative crossing of borders: He stands for growth and fathering.
- Breaking the rigid nature of normality through war, breaking of the law, ravaging, ecstasy, and magic.
- Providing language and symbolic magic.
- Creating space for the new, unheard, and unusual. His moving and changing brings modernity.
- He is a compound of fertility, death, and sexual power.
- The god of death: War is only one aspect of death and fate.
- Odin is fundamentally dualistic (see Box XIII).

In our daily life Odin/Wotan, stands for unrest and the crossing of borders. We owe him our language and the insight into secrets, the essence of what we call intellectuality and individuation. Odin personifies thus a central role in our lives.

## Box XIII: The Odin-Loki dualism

The gods Odin and Loki can be considered in a dualistic manner. Odin, the most powerful god in Asgard, cannot admit the adversary, shadow side of his character. Some of that is then realized by Loki. The role and psychology of Loki can be interpreted as the split-off personality of Odin. Both are gods that create change through a highly dynamic, dialectic discourse. Throughout Norse mythology Odin and Loki are the driving forces for change. This division finds analogs in several Indo-European groups, such as the old Iranian dualism, Zoroastrianism, which is one of the world's oldest religions, "combining a cosmogonic dualism and eschatological monotheism in a manner unique ... among the major religions of the world"[128].

---

[128] https://en.wikipedia.org/wiki/Zoroastrianism, Boyd, J. W. & Crosby D. A. (1979).

Ascribed to the teachings of the Iranian prophet Zoroaster (or Zarathustra), he exalted the deity of wisdom, Ahura Mazda (Wise Lord) as its supreme being. Ariman (destructive spirit) counteracts Ahura Mazda. Knowing the end of time, Odin and Loki act in order to promote the development of the world toward this goal. A Faustian dimension becomes visible. A pact is made with the "devil" to obtain knowledge, as reflected in the human dualism: "In me there are two souls, alas, and their division tears my life in two" [129].

The contrast between Odin and Loki does not stand for something out of the ordinary. It is part of the dialectic underlying forces that regulate the development of the world. This provocative duo stands for the vital idea of developmental dualism of Western civilization, in contrast to the cycling dualism of the East (i.e., yin and yang, wheel of rebirth). Developmental dualism is exemplified by various European religious and philosophical trends, such as Manichaeism[130], Catharism[131] and Anthroposophy[132]. In developmental dualism, both antagonists are mandatory for humans to find their pathway. Although Christianity (as we know it today) is based upon the fight between good and evil, it is not directly dualistic. Evil has to be overcome and excluded for good to reach paradise. The dialectic dualism that exists between the contrasting sides of each archetype suggests that analytical psychology also belongs to the developmental dualism direction.

### 6.5.2 Freyja

In Norse mythology, Freyja (from Old Norse fraujon [woman, lady]) is a goddess associated with love, sex, beauty, fertility, gold, *seidr* (see below), war, and death. Obviously, she is a goddess with contradictory qualities (Fig. 31). Freyja is the twin sister of Freyr, her brother. Freyr comes from *fraujaz* (Old Norse: who is ahead). Freyja and Freyr (Fig. 32) are Vanir,

---

[129] "Zwei Seelen wohnen, ach! in meiner Brust. Die eine will sich von der andern trennen." Goethe, J.W.v., Faust I, Scene 5: Outside the Town Wall.
[130] https://en.wikipedia.org/wiki/Manichaeism.
[131] https://en.wikipedia.org/wiki/Catharism.
[132] https://en.wikipedia.org/wiki/Anthroposophy.

and they have an incestuous relationship. They are twins out of the incestuous relationship between the old god Njord and his sister, Skadi (a *jötunn* and mountain goddess associated with bow hunting, skiing and winter). Njord is the god of the sea. When Skadi moved to her new husband's home near the sea, she missed her mountain home. She only spends half her time with her husband. When Skadi is away, Njord is sad, causing storms at the sea. Twin incest is a prominent feature in ancient Germanic mythology, including more modern manifestations, such as the relationship between Siegmund and Sieglinde in Richard Wagner's opera *Die Walküre*. In Norse mythology, marriage between brother and sister were common among the Vanir before their

Fig. 31. The goddess Freyia and her cat-drawn chariot. Engraving by Ludwig Pietsch (1824-1911). From Reusch, R. F. (1865). *Die nordischen Göttersagen.* Wikimedia Commons.

Fig. 32. Viking Age figurine, believed to depict Freya's brother, Frey, a widely attested god associated with sacral kingship, virility and prosperity, sunshine and fair weather. Freyr is pictured as a phallic fertility god in Norse mythology. Found in Rällinge, Sweden; Historiska Museet, Sweden. Wikimedia Commons.

alliance with the Aesir, which may be an older habit from times before the Indo-European invasion.

Although the Norse loved Thor, Freyja is probably the second-most significant god in Norse religion. Thus, she is presented right after Odin. Freyja loves jewelery and is the owner of the very attractive necklace Brisingamen, which was crafted by the dwarfs. In turn, she spent a night with them. Brisingamen makes her irresistible for both women and men. She lives at her hall Folkvang (Old Norse [people-field or army-field]) in Asgard, where she received half of the fallen warriors; the other half resides in Valhalla. This division reflects the peace and compromise that the Aesir and Vanir agreed upon after the Aesir-Vanir war (see 6.5.7). The generic impression that all the dead soldiers travel to Valhalla reflects the traditional dominance of the patriarchate that omits more balanced views of the Germanic times.

Freyja rides on a chariot through the skies that is pulled by cats (Fig. 31). Common characteristics of cats are that they are clever, secretive, mysterious, intelligent, intuitive, and, last nor least, independent (a true virtue of Freyja). At Folkvang, Freyja keeps the handsome boar Hildisvini by her side. She possesses a cloak of falcon feathers. Freyja assists other deities by allowing them to use her feathered cloak to reach widely into the world. She is invoked in matters of fertility and love, and is frequently sought after by powerful giants who wish to make her their wife.

Freyja has a close relationship with Odin. The Aesir, and in particular Odin, learned *seidr* from Freyja. *Seidr* is an Old Norse term for a type of sorcery and prophecy-making. Connected with Norse religion, its origins are largely unknown. It is likely that *seidr* (and *galdr* [Old Norse, spell, incantation]) is a form of shamanism that the invading Indo-European tribes picked up in central Asia on their trail westward. Following the Christianization of Scandinavia, *seidr* gradually eroded. Accounts of *seidr* made it into sagas and other literary sources. *Seidr* practitioners were of both genders, although females are more widely attested. Such sorceresses are being variously known as Völur (plural of Völva). There were also accounts of male practitioners, known as *seidmenn*. Within pre-Christian Norse mythology, *seidr* was associated with both the god Odin and the goddess Freyja. Odin's spiritual split character is thus directly connected to his interest in the Vanir and the

Völva and other female figures of the collective unconsciousness. To Odin's female qualities belongs his close relationship to Freyja and *seidr*.

Freyja is the personification of nature and creation, but also death and destruction. She has qualities that embody the bounty of the earth. Freyja reflects the unchallenged desire of expanding life, love and appetite, and desire for unfolding carnality of both women and men. Nature is sinful in the Christian tradition. To acknowledge human nature implies to recognize sin. To omit sin, control, and mastery of man's action is required. Nothing was more dangerous for Christianity than unfolding fertility and lust. Consequently, Freyja became and is the main target for Christian suppression of freedom and independence. Thus, the ambiguity of the Freyja archetype resulted in the splitting of woman into whore, nun into witch, spouse into mistress, and a clear distinction into women and men. Today we fight again for the peace, balance, and ambience that was created in Asgard between the Aesir and Vanir. Under the cover of female emancipation, we try to uncover the lost Germanic partnership (see Box XIV). The revival of Freyja and the overcoming of the patriarchate is thus of essential significance for modern man.

The true nature of Freyja
- The goddess is associated with love, sexuality, fertility, beauty, gold and sorcery.
- Straightforward in her affairs, but complex in her multilayered relationships.
- An independent, intense. and vehement woman.
- A reflection of our desire for unfolding life, beyond any etiquette.
- The main target for Christian suppression.

For the unfolding of our inner nature, drive, regenerative abilities, and enthusiasm for life, we need the goddess Freyja!

### 6.5.3 Thor

In Norse mythology, Thor is a hammer-wielding god associated with thunder, lightning, storms, oak trees, and strength. He acts for the protection of mankind. In wider Germanic mythology and paganism, he

Fig. 33. A reproduction in wood of an Icelandic original known as the Eyrarland statue depicting the Germanic war and thunder god, Thor. Displayed at the Swedish Armey Museum. Wikimedia Commons.

was known in Old English as *thunor* and in Old High German as Donar (from *\*thonaraz* [the thunderer]). He seems related to the Slavic god of thunder, Perun. Ultimately stemming from Proto-Indo-European religion, Thor is a prominently mentioned god throughout the recorded history of the Germanic peoples. Faced with Christianization in Scandinavia, emblems of his hammer, Mjölnir, were worn in defiance (Fig. 33). Norse pagan personal names containing the name of the god bear witness to his popularity (e.g., Torstein, Toralf, Torbjørn, etc.) into modern times. Thor continued to be acknowledged in rural folklore throughout Germanic regions.

Thor is the husband of the golden-haired goddess Sif, the lover of the *jötunn* Jarnsaxa (Old Norse [iron-sax]), and is generally described as fierce-eyed, red-haired and red-bearded. He is a muscleman, violent-tempered, noisy, hard-hitting, and tough (Fig. 34). He seems naive and simple-minded. He is a tremendous beer drinker and eater. His eternal mission is fighting the *jötnar, thurs* and trolls. Continuously, he is on his way into the stony, icy, and sterile deserts of Utgard to defend the gods from the constant attacks from the unconscious. With lightning force, he slays his enemies with his hammer Mjölnir. The name is derived from the Proto-Germanic root *\*malanan* (to grind)[133]. Mjölnir can thus be interpreted as "the grinder or crusher" (Fig. 18). He has also a belt of strength, *megingjörth* (Old Norse *gjörth* = belt). Thor has a hefty temper.

---

[133] This root is reflected in English/Scandinavian/German by meal/flour, mel and Mehl, respectively.

Fig. 34. *Tors strid med jättarna* (*Thor's Fight with the Giants*) by Eskil Winge Mårten (1825-1896; Nationalmuseum, Stockholm). Thor is depicted in a battle against the *jötunn*. The thunder god rides his chariot pulled by the goats Tanngrisnir and Tanngnjóstr, wears his belt Megingjörth, swings his hammer Mjölnir, and has obviously reached divine rage, *asmegin*. Wikimedia Commons.

It can flare up suddenly, and he can reach divine rage, *asmegin* (Old Norse "by the might of the aesir"). In this state of trance, his force multiplies, and his eyes send out flashes of lightning, and both friends and enemies are advised to stay away from the god.

Thor is tall and, as all Aesir, he drives through the skies with a cart, drawn by the goats Tanngrisnir and Tanngnjostr (Old Norse [teeth-barer and teeth grinder, respectively]). Thor cooks the goats for his meal; their flesh provides sustenance for the god, but the bones are not consumed. Thor brings the goats back to life with his magic hammer the next day. Sacrificial practice to save the bones of animals were common among Indo-European and Siberian tribes. Resurrection from death and taking care of the deceased bones (e.g., in a ossary, a container, or receptacle, such as an urn or a vault, for holding the bones of the dead) is a common idea in Europe. Taking care of bones is a ritual in preparation of resurrection.

The true nature of Thor
- He fights continuously with his divine range and enormous Aesir force.
- He is a naïve and well-meaning character, suffering from muscle mania.
- War tricks and deception are not the strategy of Thor.
- He fights constantly with lightning, smashing thoughts and actions of will so that our ego keeps control on the constant, osmotic invasion of the unconscious.

Our daily life depends on Thor. Without his constant guard and defense, we would be intervened and basically overran by the unconscious. No society, no culture could exist without Thor's protection.

### 6.5.4 Idun

Asynja Idun (ever young, rejuvenator) is a keeper of apples and granter of eternal youthfulness (Fig. 35). She keeps them in a casket that is big enough to contain a daily apple for each of the gods. She is the wife of

Fig. 35. Idun, Loki, Heimdall and Brage (left to right) by Lorenz Frølich (1820-1908). In Rydberg, V. (1906). *Teutonic Mythology Vol. I.* Frontispiece. Wikimedia Commons.

the *skaldic* god Bragi (excellent, outstanding). Bragi is renowned for wisdom and, most of all, for fluency of speech and skill with words; he knows most of *skaldship* (poetry), and after him *skaldship* is called *bragr* in Old Norse. Idun is a goddess associated with youth, spring, and rejuvenation. She is a precondition that the gods do not age and keep their immortality. In mythology, apples have various denotations, but in Norse mythology, the apple tree is a symbol of rejuvenation, rebirth, and beauty.

The *Prose Edda* tells that Loki (see 6.5.5) was once forced by the giant Tjatse (he is the father of Skadi, who was unhappily married to Njord) to lure Idun out of Asgard and into a wood, promising her interesting apples. Tjatse, in the form of an eagle, snatched Idun from the wood and took her to his home. Idun's absence caused the gods to grow old and become gray, and they realized that Loki is responsible for her disappearance. Loki promised to return her and, in the form of a falcon, found her alone at Tjatses home. He turned her into a nut and took her back to Asgard. After Tjatse found that Idun was gone, he turned into an eagle and furiously chased after Loki. The gods build a pyre in Asgard, and, after a sudden stop by Loki, Tjatse´s feathers caught fire, he fell, and the gods kill him. Thanks to Idun's return, the Germanic gods did not age.

A number of theories surround Idun, including potential links to fertility and the goddess Freyja and her potential origin in Proto-Indo-European religion.

The true nature of Idun
- She is the guardian of our youth.
- The goddess of our vitality, our inner core that does not age.
- She stands for eros (life energy and inner intellectual beauty).

In our daily life, Idun is a precondition of our liveliness, libido, rejuvenation, and life energy. Without Idun we die!

### 6.5.5 Loki

Loki is the god of mischief, guile, cunning, and trickery. He is also seen as the personification of chaos and evil as well as being the god of lies. He is full of contradictions: capricious, disrespectful, and completely untrustworthy. At one point in time, he was also known as being the god of fire. He is portrayed as a young, devious person who seemingly cares only for self-preservation and shallow pleasures. He is depicted as being playful, malicious, and at certain times even helpful, but he is always lacks respect, is nihilistic, and reckless. His name derives from Old Norse *luka* (to close, to finish), suggesting that he has the important role that will bring the gods to their end during Ragnarök. He is married to the goddess Sigyn (Old Norse [victorious girlfriend], Fig. 26). He brings the world to a close, and thus his major role is not to keep the universe functioning, but to provide the end of the world. He fulfils the Germanic god's destiny, which is death and downfall.

Loki is considered an Aesir (Fig. 35), but his father was a giant. He is thus a god and/or a *jötunn*. He is the trickster among the gods and the enforcer of the god's destiny. At Ragnarök, he is disloyal to the Aesir and fights on the side of giants toward the ending of the world. Loki gives advice to the gods that recurrently results in catastrophes. And then he has to help the gods to limit the fatal effect. Loki's has a "transgender" psychology. He has a gender/shape identity or expression, that differs from his assigned sex or shape. He eagerly takes women's clothes. Loki is a shapeshifter and in separate incidents he appears in the form of a salmon, a mare, a seal, or a fly. Converting into a mare, he gives birth to Odin's horse, Sleipner.

With the giant *jötunn* woman Angrboda (Old Norse [messenger of fear, the one who brings grief]), he fathers three monsters that control the world at Ragnarök: the Fenris Wolf, the Midgard Serpent, and Hel. The gods foresaw the tragedy these three monsters would bring. Through a deception, the gods fettered the Fenris Wolf (see 6.6.1). Thor threw the Midgard Serpent into the ocean. Here, she lingers and waits for the end of time. Hel is an all-black creature, half bones, half flesh, which the gods banned to Niflheim (Helheim). Her home becomes the kingdom of dead females and those males that did not die in battle. Christianity changed the character of Hel and provided her with an additional "l". Helheim resembles the sad and foggy Greek underworld and Christian limbo[134]. The torture for committed sins in hell is a non-Germanic matter.

Loki's worst accomplishment was the killing of the white god Balder, one of the most significant but mysterious gods in Germanic mythology (see 6.5.6). Loki got chained to a rock for this misdeed. Skadi was responsible for placing a serpent above him while he was bound (Fig. 36). The serpent dripped venom from above him that Sigyn collected into a bowl; however, she must empty the bowl when it is full, and the venom that dripped in the meantime causes Loki to writhe in pain, thereby causing earthquakes.

With the onset of Ragnarök, Loki and his broods will provide the downfall of the world, humans, and the gods. Loki slips free from his bonds and fights against the gods among the forces of the *jötnar*. He will encounter the god Heimdall, and the two will slay each other.

---

[134] In some Christian beliefs, the supposed abode of the souls of unbaptized infants and of the just who died before Christ's coming.

The true nature of Loki
- He challenges the existing and decided.
- He is the anti-god who becomes the motor of proceeding world history.
- He creates the fundamental new beginning.
- While Odin's transition of borders is always inventive, fertile, and creative, Loki's transitions tend always to catastrophes and destruction.
- He can be seen as the split-off personality of Odin (Box XIII).

Loki supports our daily life through defeats and destruction, the preconditions of the new beginning. He brings the old world to a close. Seemingly devastating to the world Loki is indispensable and prepares the development into the future.

Fig. 36. Loki gets chained to a rock for his misdeeds, by William Gershom Collingwood (1854-1932). The serpent drips venom from above him that his wife Sigyn collects into a bowl. From *The Elder or Poetic Edda*, illustrated by W.G. Collingwood (1908). Wikimedia Commons.

## 6.5.6 Balder

The god Balder is given a central but special role in Norse mythology. He is loved by the entire creation. His precise function is rather disputed. Balder is a light god and Odin's and Frigg's beloved son. He has a blind twin brother, Hodr. He is the most beautiful and best of all the Aesir. Balder also has a ship, which is the largest ship ever built, Hringhorni (Old Norse [ship with a circle on the stem]). His wife is Nana, and his hall is called Breidablik (Old Norse [broad-gleaming]). Balder is peaceful, and close to his home, Breidablik is the safest place in Asgard.

Balder has the gift of seeing the future and pays close attention to what he experiences in his dreams. Balder once had nightmares that he would be killed. His mother, Frigg, made all things on earth vow not to hurt him. The mistletoe did not vow, however, and Frigg considered it to be so unimportant that she thought nothing of it. The gods enjoyed quite a lot to shoot arrows, throw spears, or toss stones on Balder, and nothing could hurt him. Loki found out that the mistletoe had not vowed and thus made a spear out of mistletoe and tricked the blind Hodr into shooting at Balder. This killed him (Fig. 37). The death of Balder generated deep sorrow among the gods. Many gods and goddesses came to his magnificent funeral. His wife, Nana, died of grief and was placed in the funeral pyre with Balder (Fig. 38). His father, Odin, provided Balder his golden ring, Draupnir (Old Norse [the dripper])[135], but later Balder sent the ring back from Helheim. Upon Frigg's appeals, Hermod, Balder's brother, rode to Hel. Hel promised to release Balder from the underworld if all objects, alive and dead, would weep for him. And all did. However, the agreement fails due to sabotage. A *jötunn* woman in a cave named Thökk (Old Norse [thanks]), refused to mourn the slain god. Thus, Balder had to remain in the underworld. When the gods discovered that the giantess had been Loki in female disguise, they hunted him down, bound him to a rock (Fig. 36) and ensured his continued torment until his release at Ragnarök (see 6.5.5).

During Ragnarök (see 6.7), the barriers between Helheim and Asgard were destroyed, and Balder was able to escape from Hel while Loki used the open gates to lead his army of the dead against the gods. After

---

[135] The ring has the ability to multiply itself: Every ninth night, eight new rings "drip" from Draupnir.

Fig. 37. *Balder's død* (*The death of Balder*) by Christian Wilhelm Eckersbeg (1783-1853, Charlottenburg Palace, Denmark). Balder is lying in the foreground. He has just been hit by Hød's missile. Hød, Balder's blind brother, is standing on the left, stretching out his arms. On the very left, Loki tries to conceal his smile. Odin is sitting in the middle of the Aesir. Thor is on his left. Yggdrasil and the three *nornes* can be seen in the background. Wikimedia Commons.

Ragnarök (see 6.8), Balder and Hodr came back to the New Earth. Balder is best-known as the Norse god of spring and renewal, a youth whose goodness, purity and overall pleasant disposition made him nearly impossible to dislike. However, Balder's primary role in the Norse tradition results from the mythic circumstances surrounding his untimely death (and his prophesied return after the fires of Ragnarök have burned out).

The mythology surrounding Balder, with its strong themes of resentment, loss, and renewal, has resonances within several Indo-European contexts (such as the Greek god Adonis or the legendary musician, poet, and prophet Orpheus). Balder has also been linked to the resurrection of Jesus of Nazareth and the bright heavenly world that may follow after doomsday. The latter parallel is striking in the *Edda* text,

Fig. 38. *Balders bålfærd* (*The Funeral Pyre of Balder*) by Louis Moe (1857-1945). In Danmarks Historie i Billeder, 1898, Copenhagen, Denmark. Wikimedia Commons.

emerging right after the conversion of Iceland to Christianity. It may well have allowed Balder's character of the original Norse myth to lay him open to Christian influences. However, it may also be possible that behind the accounts of Jesus, Adonis, and Balder resides a common Indo-European mythologem that molds several European mythological accounts.

The true nature of Balder

- Balder demonstrates youth, beauty, and splendour: the bright world of gods.
- He becomes the god that returns to the New World, resurrected from death.
- He is the god of the new beginning, hope, peace, and the evergreen world of fertility and prosperity.

Our indispensable craving to believe in a bright and promising future, a better world beyond present darkness, suggests that Balder is a god that we cannot dismiss.

### 6.5.7. Mimir

Mimir (Old Norse rememberer, wise one) is an Aesir and figure in Norse mythology renowned for his knowledge and wisdom. He is the oracular, mysterious god that (for the sake of the significance of the collective consciousness in this book) is dealt with as one of the major Norse gods. He is mentioned a few times in various Norse writings, in particular in *Hávamál* (Old Norse [sayings of the high one, i.e., Odin]). *Hávamál* is presented as a single poem in the *Codex Regius* (see 3.3).

Mimir is mentioned in the *Ynglinga Saga*, as collected by Snorri in Heimskringla. Snorri presents an account of the world-threatening Aesir-Vanir war. The war reflects the colossal tensions that developed during the confrontations of patri- and matricentric cultures. Snorri states that both sides eventually understood the immense threat of the confrontation and agreed to establish a truce. Before the war turned the world into havoc, a—for the Germanic tribes typical—thoughtful and conscious compromise was negotiated: an exchange of hostages. Vanaheim sent to Asgard their best men: the wealthy Njord and his children Freyja and Freyr (see 6.5.2) in exchange for Asgard's Hønir (Old Norse [described here as large, handsome]). Balanced compromises between strongly opposing partners are not highly celebrated in our present culture, as we try to go for the one and only right solution and the "winner." And thus we hear little about the "impossible", the balanced relationshi between matricentric and patricentric cultures. This is to the detriment of modern societies that reluctantly have to find this balance.

Additionally, the Aesir send the wise Mimir in exchange for Kvasir, who Snorri describes as the wisest man of Vanaheim. Kvasir was born of the saliva of the Aesir and the Vanir. Extremely wise, Kvasir travelled far and wide, teaching and spreading knowledge. This continued until the dwarfs Fjalar and Galar killed Kvasir and drained him of his blood. Thus, the unconscious kills the wisdom. The two dwarfs mixed his blood with honey, resulting in the Mead of Poetry (also known as Mead of Suttungr). This is a mythical beverage that allows whoever drinks it to become a skald, or scholar, to recite any information and solve any question. Drinking this mead imbues the drinker with skaldship and wisdom. The drink is a vivid metaphor for poetic inspiration, often associated

Fig. 39. *Odin Mimir befragend* (*Odin asks Mimir*) by Carl Emil Doepler (1824–1905). Odin has close ties to the collective unconscious. He communicates daily with the head of Mimir at the well of remembrance. Here, he sacrificed one of his eyes to get insight into the world of the Völva. Mimir's head appears between the roots of Yggdrasil. Illustration from Doepler, D.J. & Ranisch, W. (1900). *Walhall. Die Götterwelt der Germanen.* Wikimedia Commons.

with Odin. The spread of this inspiration eventually resulted in the introduction of poetry to mankind. Scholars have connected Kvasir to methods of beverage production and peacemaking practices among ancient peoples[136].

Fearing trickery from the Aesir, the Vanir beheaded Mimir and returned his head to Asgard. In order to keep the wisdom of Mimir that he had picked up with the Vanir, Odin preserved his head with magic. Odin keeps Mimir's head at one of the roots of Yggdrasil, and here it recited secret knowledge and counsel to him (Fig. 39). Mimir continued to provide knowledge and be Odin's adviser (see Box XI). Mimir's name

---

[136] Kvass is a traditional Slavic and Baltic fermented beverage commonly made from rye bread.

appears in the names of the well Mimisbrunnr, the tree Mimameithr (a *kenning* of Yggdrasil), and the inner part of Yggdrasil, Hoddmimis holt (see 6.2). Odin´s desire to transgress the division between the conscious and unconscious and to integrate the wisdom of the Vanir becomes again visible.

When Odin, in his search for knowledge, arrived at Mimir's Well—which is surely none other than the Well of Urd (see 6.3)—Odin asked Mimir for a drink from the water. The well's guardian, knowing the value of such a draft, refused unless the seeker offered an eye in return. Odin gouged out one eye and dropped it into the well. The Austrian philosopher Rudolf Steiner (1861-1925) describes this sacrifice as a precondition for the development of the Germanic people[137]. Having made the necessary sacrifice, Mimir dipped his horn into the well and offered the now-one-eyed god a drink. For the purpose of divination (soothsaying, fortune saying, prophecy; see Boxes VIII, XI), Odin comes daily to the well of remembrance to obtain essential details from the world's collective memory. In addition, Odin, with trickery, got hold of the Mead of Suttungr. By combining the essence of the exchange of hostages Kvasir and Mimir, he is in control of knowledge and wisdom.

> The true nature of Mimir
> - Mimir is the divine animating force behind the wisdom of past tradition.
> - He is of indispensable value as a guide for present actions.
> - Mimir is the guardian that has access to the collective unconscious, the ultimate source of humanity's accumulated knowledge and wisdom.

Without abundant access to the wisdom of Mimir, the collective consciousness, we would resemble a plant without water or an animal without air to breathe. Deprived of access to Mimirbrunnr, or the Well of Remembrance (i.e., the collective unconscious), humanity could not exist.

---

[137] Steiner, R. (1974).

## 6.5.8 Frigg

In Germanic mythology, the *asynja* Frigg (Old Norse [own, dear, beloved]) is in nearly all sources described as the wife of Odin. In Old High German and Old Norse sources, she is also connected with the goddess Fulla (Old Norse [fulfilled]). Both *asynjur* are called upon in the second Merseburg Incantation to assist in healing (see text box 2), indicating that they may have been important throughout the Germanic world. Frigg is mentioned throughout the *Poetic Edda* and many other sources. Frigg is often associated with weaving, combining the aspects of a love and domestic goddess (Fig. 40). Frigg is also described as a goddess associated with foreknowledge and wisdom. Thus, both Frigg and Odin have the gift of prophecy. Despite the appearance that Freyja is the most important goddess, Frigg is the most distinguished and wisest of the *asynjur*. She knows the destiny of all people, but she does not communicate her knowledge. Frigg dwells in the wetland halls of Fensalir (Old Norse [Fen Halls]). She is ambiguously associated with the earth, otherwise personified as an apparently separate entity of Jord (Old Norse [arth]). The children of Frigg and Odin include the gleaming god Balder, and for

Fig. 40. *Frigg spinning the clouds* by John Charles Dollman (1851-1934). In Guerber, H. A. (1909) *Myths of the Norsemen from the Eddas and Sagas*. London: Harrap. Wikimedia Commons.

him in particular she plays a significant role in Norse mythology. She is also the mother of Balder's brother, Hermod. After Christianization, mention of Frigg continued to occur in Scandinavian folklore. In modern times, Frigg has appeared in modern popular culture and receives modern veneration in Germanic neopaganism.

Not so very much is written and known regarding Frigg. Some scholars hypothesize that both Frigg and Freyja may have their origin in a Common Germanic goddess. Together they represent the two aspects of the original Great Goddess, with Freyja serving as the maiden and Frigg as the wife/mother aspect. However, the lack of knowledge reflects also the times in which written accounts are available. The dominance of female goddesses in the Germanic world is not well-reflected in writing because written accounts became available during times of Christianity when males became increasingly dominant and the female world was obscured and demonized. The true nature of Frigg is thus not easily distinguished. Rather, a wide range of female characteristics is associated with her, as to other *asynjur*.

## 6.6 Germanic gods of continental Europe

Compared to Norse and, to a lesser extent, Anglo-Saxon mythology, examples of Continental Germanic paganism are extremely fragmentary (see chapters 3-5). Besides a handful of brief Elder Futhark inscriptions (see 4.1), the only genuinely pagan continental Germanic documents are the short Old High German Merseburg Incantations. However, pagan mythological elements seem to have been preserved in later literature, notably in Middle High German epic poetry (e.g., *Nibelungenlied*). In the Merseburg Incantations, Wodan and Frija are the cognates of Odin and Frigg (or Freyja). Phol is the *kenning* of Balder. Uolla has been linked to Fulla (Old Norse, possibly meaning bountiful), a minor goddess and a handmaid of Frigg. Sunna (the sun) in Norse mythology is Sol, though her sister Sinthgunt is otherwise unattested. Although the Merseburg Incantations suggest significant similarities between Norse and central Germanic mythology, one needs to be aware that there (may) exist differences. In order at least to indicate that Germanic mythology in central Europe may most likely have been different from that of Northern Europe, the reader is provided with a few established differences and additional gods of this basically unknown mythology.

### 6.6.1 Tyr/Ziu/Tiw

Tyr (Old Norse [literally god, plural *tivar*]) is a god associated with law and heroic glory in Norse mythology and is portrayed as one-handed. Corresponding names in other Germanic languages are Gothic Teiws, Old English Tiw and Old High German Ziu, all from Proto-Germanic *tīwaz*. In older Norwegian dialects, *tivar* means gods. Tyr is mentioned under the headline of Germanic gods of continental Europe because he is well-known under the synonyms of Ziu/Tiw in central Europe. Tyr was the god of war, and if a warrior carved the rune *tiw* (See Figure 1 vertical arrow) on his weapon, he would be dedicating it to Tyr, strengthening the odds that the outcome of a battle would be in his favor. This rune is increasingly used by neo-Nazi movements.

The origins of the god's name and his possible relationship to Tuisto (see *Germania* by Tacitus, 3.1) suggest he was once considered the father of the gods and head of the pantheon. His name is ultimately a cognate to that of *dyeus*, the reconstructed chief deity in Indo-European religion (see Latin deus). It is assumed that both Odin and Thor overtook the war role of Ziu/Tiw during the Migration Period. Odin shares his role as god of war with the original god Tyr (and other gods), i.e., he incorporates these qualities into his emerging character (see Box XI).

At one stage, the gods decided to shackle the Fenris Wolf, but the beast broke every chain they put upon him. Eventually, they had the dwarfs make them a magical ribbon called Gleipnir (Old Norse [open one]). It appeared to be only a silken ribbon but was made of six wondrous, seemingly unachievable, magical ingredients[138]. The Fenris Wolf sensed the gods' deceit and refused to be bound with it unless one of them guaranteed the plot by putting his arm in his mouth (Fig. 41). Tyr, known for his great wisdom and courage, agreed. After the gods had bound the Fenris Wolf, he struggled to try to break the rope. The Fenris Wolf could not break the ribbon and, enraged, bit Tyr's right hand off. When the gods saw that the Fenris wolf was bound, they all rejoiced, except Tyr. The Fenris Wolf remained bound until Ragnarök.

---

[138] the sound of a cat's footfall, the beard of a woman, the roots of a mountain, bear's sinews, fish's breath and bird's spittle.

Fig. 41. *The Tyr bracteate* from Trollhättan, Sweden. The bracteate shows the Norse god Tyr with the Fenris wolf biting his hand. The gold bracteate is dated to the Migration Period. Drawing by Gunnar Creutz. Wikimedia Commons.

Tyr is also the god of public meetings (the *thing*) and has thus the additional name *thingsaz* (the *thing* god). Therefore, he is the god of oath. Tyr is a moral god and he is, in contrast to Odin, reliable. He had probably a different and more central role among the Germanic tribes of central Europe.

### 6.6.2 Nerthus

In central European Germanic paganism, Nerthus is a goddess associated with fertility. The only place where Nerthus is attested, but at length, is in *Germania* by Tacitus. He records that the remote Suebi (a mobile tribe that is not reliant upon agriculture, first mentioned by Caesar) were united by their veneration of the goddess. They maintained a sacred grove on an unspecified island. A holy cart rests there draped with cloth, which only a priest may touch. With deep reverence, the priest attends the god's cart, which is drawn by young cows. Everywhere the goddess is met with celebration, hospitality, and peace. All iron objects are locked away, and no one will leave for war. When the goddess has had her fill, the priests return her to her temple. Tacitus adds that slaves then wash the cloth, the cart, and the goddess in a secluded lake, after which they were drowned.

The name Nerthus is generally held to be a Latinized form of Proto-Germanic *Nerþuz, a direct precursor to the Old Norse deity Njord, father of Freyja. While scholars have noted numerous parallels between the descriptions of the two figures, Njord is attested as a male deity. Various scholarly theories exist regarding the goddess and her potential later traces among the Germanic peoples, including that the figure may be identical to the unnamed sister-wife of Njord. She obviously belongs to the incestuous fertility gods, the Vanir.

### 6.6.3 Ostara

Eostre or Ostara (Old English Eastre; Old High German *Ôstara) is a Germanic goddess who provided a Germanic month her name: Ôstar-mânoth (Old High German, the month of Easter). This is the namesake of the festival of Easter. Pagan Anglo-Saxons held feasts in Eostre's honor, from which the celebration of the resurrection of Jesus Christ is still known as Easter.

By way of linguistic reconstruction, the goddess called *Austrō in Proto-Germanic has been connected to Ostara. Over 150 inscriptions referring to the *matronae Austriahenae* are known (see 6.6.4). Theories connecting Eostre with records of Germanic Easter customs, including hares, chicks, and eggs, have been proposed (see 5.4). She is the goddess of increasing light and spring, and love and carnal pleasure that lead to fecundity. Eostre and Ostara are venerated in some forms of Germanic neopaganism.

### 6.6.4 Matres and Matronae

The Matres (Latin mothers) and Matronae (Latin matrons) are female deities venerated in Northwestern Europe from the first to the fifth centuries. Most often they are depicted in groups of three. This Triple Goddess is portrayed on votive offerings and altars that bear images of goddesses. They feature inscriptions (about half are continental Celtic or Germanic names) that were venerated in regions occupied by the Roman army: Germania, Eastern Gaul, England, and northern Italy (Fig. 42). The Matres and Matronae are thus not well-defined Germanic goddesses, but rather a mixture of female goddesses venerated by

Fig. 42. Depiction of an altar dedicated to the Matronae Aufaniae (from Bonn, Germany). The Matrones Aufaniabus were local, Celtic-Roman mother deities. The text is translated to "Quintus Caldinius Celsus consecrates this alter to the aufanian matrones." Wikimedia Commons.

Roman soldiers that came from every corner of Europe. There is no intact surviving mythology and no information written by contemporary writers about them. Information about the religious practices surrounding the Matres is limited to stones on which their depictions and inscriptions are found (fewer than 1,100 surviving inscribed plaques, altars, statues, and temples). The Germanic Matres have been connected to the Germanic *dísir, valkyries* (see Fig. 42), and *nornes* (see 6.3). *Nutrices* is another term for them, being the protectors of maternity and motherhood.

In discussing examples of the Great Mother archetype, Erich Neumann (1905-1960) mentions the Fates as "the threefold form of the Great Mother."[139] The reason for their appearance in threes or nines is to be sought in the threefold articulation underlying all created things. Marija Gimbutas postulated that in Old Europe, the Aegean, and the Near East, a Triple Goddess was worshipped, predating what she deemed as a patriarchal religion imported by the Kurgan[140]. These interpretations have much in common with that of the *matres, matronae* and *nornes*, which may share a connection with the three world mothers in Greek mythology: Rhea, Demeter, and Persephone. In Norse mythology, the three *nornes* and their determination of fate (see 6.3) represent a parallel.

## 6.7 Ragnarök and the end of time

In Norse mythology, Ragnarök (from Old Norse *ragnarok* [End (or Fate) of the Gods] or Ragnarokr [reinterpreted as the Twilight of the Gods]) is a series of future events. They include a great battle, foretold to ultimately result in the death of a number of major gods (including Odin, Thor, Tyr, Freyr, Heimdall, and Loki), the occurrence of various natural disasters, and the subsequent submersion of the world in water (Fig. 43). Balder's death is believed to be the beginning of Ragnarök. Afterward, the world will resurface anew and fertile. The surviving and returning gods meet again, and two human survivors, Liv and Livtrasi, will repopulate the world (see 6.8). Ragnarök is an important event in the Norse canon. The event is attested primarily in the *Poetic Edda* and *Prose Edda*. Based on Karl Joseph Simrock's translation of the *Prose Edda* (where Snorri writes *ragnarokr*, not *ragnarok*) Richard Wagner selected the term "Twilight of the Gods" and made it popular. It became the title of the last opera of his *Der Ring des Nibelungen* quartet, *Götter-dämmerung* (1876). The fate of the gods and the twilight of gods seemingly have little in common. Twilight can hint at the evening (dusk,

---

[139] Neumann, E. (1974).
[140] Gimbutas, M. (1982).

Fig. 43. *Ragnarök* by Johannes Gehrts (1855-1921). Odin and Thor fighting with the Fenris wolf and the Midgard Serpent. The gods, the *einherjer* and the *valkyries* attack from the left, their enemies from the right. Xylograph after a painting/drawing. Wikimedia Commons.

the end of the world, and the fate of the gods) or the morning (dawn, the New Earth, and the return of [some of] the gods).

At the beginning of the final battle, the god Heimdall, who watches the bridge Bifröst, is poking his horn to alert the gods and the *einherjer*. The Völva proclaims the arrival of this time, for humans and Odin.

> *There crowed above the Aesir*
> *the roster Gullinkambi,*
> *who wakens the warriors*
> *at Herfather's;*
> *and another crows*
> *underneath the earth, a sooty-red rooster*
> *in the halls of Hel.*

A winter that lasts for three years starts, and there is no summer between. The sun provides no warmth, and it snows at all ends of the world. Icy coldness prevails, along with sharp frost and biting winds. It is Fimbulvinter, the great winter. It is part of the Great War that comes when humans forget the gods. Brothers will kill each other; sons will not spare their fathers. Girls will revile their mothers. The faithful will be called stupid, the honest a liar. No tribe, no country will be spared:

*Brothers shall fight and fell each other,*
*And sisters' sons*
*shall kinship stain;*
*Hard is it on earth,*
*with mighty whoredom;*
*Axe-time, sword-time[141],*
*shields are sundered,*
*Wind-time, wolf-time,*
*were the world falls;*
*Nor ever shall men*
*each other spare.*

All bands break, all support bursts. Loki breaks his ties, and the Fenris Wolf gets free. The time has come when the Fenris wolf swallows the sun. Never will humans suffer a greater loss. Blood gushes over the heavens. The stars fall, the earth trembles. Day and night are not different from each other. There is thunder and booming from the fallen mountains. Yggdrasil trembles down to the deepest roots, and the tree cannot stand upright anymore. In the ocean, the Midgard Serpent tosses and turns, and big waves fall over land (Fig. 44a). The Midgard Serpent curls onto land. Loki comes with an army of giants, and in front of them runs the Fenris Wolf (Fig. 44b). His mouth is so big that his upper jaw touches the skies while lower jaw scrapes the earth. Fire comes from his mouth and his eyes while the serpent spews venom that creates a fog all over the earth.

---

[141] Enjoy this unbeaten and frightening sequence of alliterations!

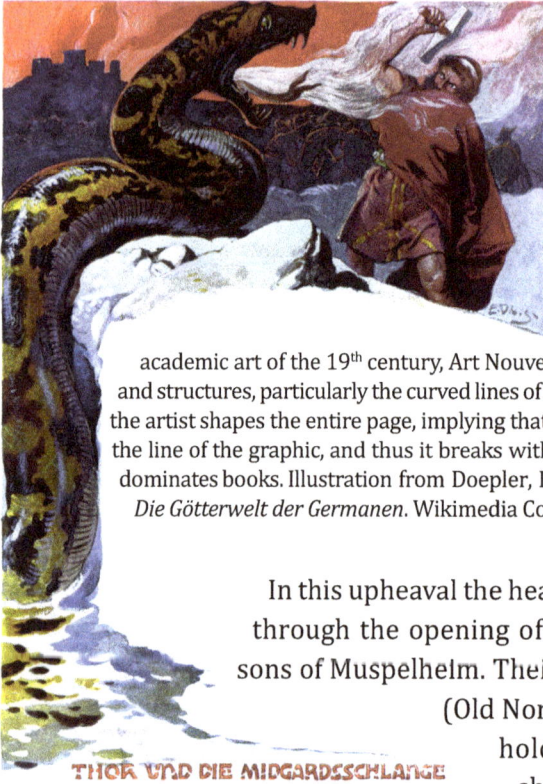

Fig. 44 a. *Thor und die Midgardsschlange* (*Thor's fight against the Midgard Serpent*) by Carl Emil Doepler (1824–1905). Thor in the decisive moment when he kills the serpent with his hammer, Mjölnir. The venom of the serpent hits Thor, and this kills the god. In the background, the fortress Asgard is already in flames. A reaction to the academic art of the 19th century, Art Nouveau was inspired by natural forms and structures, particularly the curved lines of plants and flowers. In this manner the artist shapes the entire page, implying that the text has to follow organically the line of the graphic, and thus it breaks with the perpendicular linearity that dominates books. Illustration from Doepler, D.J. & Ranisch, W. (1900). *Walhall. Die Götterwelt der Germanen.* Wikimedia Commons.

In this upheaval the heaven breaks into parts, and through the opening of fire and flames ride the sons of Muspelhelm. Their leader is the *jötunn* Surt (Old Norse black). In his hand he a holds a mighty sword that shines over the world. They ride over the bridge Bifröst, and it breaks under the hooves of the horses. The armies meet on the battlefield Vigrid (Old Norse, battle surge) that is the greatest battlefield ever.

Then the gods get ready for the battle. In their army fight also the *einherjer* from Valhalla. At the front rides Odin with his golden helmet and the spear in his hand (Fig. 44 b). He who has given the language and truth to the humans now meets the beast of lies, the Fenris Wolf. By the time of Ragnarök, all words will have lost their truth. And thus the wolf can open his mouth toward Odin.

Heimdall fights against his old enemy Loki, and both hurt each other to death, and Freyr fights with Surt, but he is defeated by Surt's sword of flames. They cannot support Thor in his distress with the Midgard Serpent. He raises his arm for a last strike, and the hammer does not miss its target. He smashes the head of the serpent (Fig. 44 a). While dying, she emits her venom, and Thor can only stride back nine steps before he is drawn in the venomous matter and dies. The Fenris Wolf swallows Odin, but the hour of Vidar, the silent god, has arrived. He places his right foot that is protected by a marvelous shoe into the gap of the animal. He takes the jaws of the animal and tears the gap into pieces. The wolf is annihilated.

Fig. 44 b. *Odin und Fenriswolf/Freys und Surt (Oding and the Fenris wolfe/Freyr and Surt)* by Carl Emil Doepler (1824–1905). Odin fights Fenris but gets killed by the wolf. Also the twin brother of Freya, the vane Freyr, is fighting against Surt, a major figure during the events of Ragnarök. Surt carries his bright sword, and afterward the flames that he brings forth will engulf the Earth. Illustration from Doepler, D.J. & Ranisch, W. (1900). *Walhall. Die Götterwelt der Germanen.* Wikimedia Commons.

In the fight that rages over the entire battlefield of Vigrid, almost everybody destroys one another. Only a few survive. At the end, Surt throws fire over the whole world and she burns down to ashes (Fig. 45). She disappears, covered by rubble and ash, into the sea.

*The Sun becomes dark. Earth sinks into the sea.*
*The shining star slip out of the sky.*
*Vapour and fire rage fiercely together.*
*Til the leaping flame licks heaven itself.*

Is this the end? "Now this is not the end. It is not even the beginning of the end. But it is, perhaps, the end of the beginning," exclaimed Winston Churchill during World War II, seemingly inspired by the Norse tradition. After the end (linear time) emerges the New Earth (cycling time).

Fig. 45. *Ragnarök* by Carl Emil Doepler (1824–1905). The fortress Asgard and the earth burn to ashes after which they sinks into the eternal ocean. The world has come to a prelimnary end, because in the circular-time view, new worlds arise after each downfall. Illustrations from Doepler, D.J. & Ranisch, W. (1900). *Walhall. Die Götterwelt der Germanen.* Wikimedia Commons.

## 6.8 The New Earth after Ragnarök

The Christian phrase in *saecula saeculorum* expresses the idea of eternity. Literally translated it means "in a century of centuries." It suggests sequences, cycles of times. The usual English, linear time translation is "for ever and ever," i.e., only one time, but one can also find "throughout all ages" (circular). Despite the present dominance of the linear time translation (that fits to our generic worldview) not only Christianity, but also Germanic mythology has not one time, but a sequence of time periods. The concept of cyclic time is prevalent in most Indo-European cultures. Germanic mythology combines both a linear (now) with a circular (future) time view. A new but qualitatively different world will resurface when the earth disappears at the end of one time.

Thus, after Ragnarök comes a new sequence of time, the New Earth. The world resurfaces from the sea anew, fertile, green, and beautiful

Fig. 46. *The New Earth* by Carl Emil Doepler (1824–1905). After Ragnarök, the new earth rises from the sea. It is fertile and green. The fields fertilize themselves, and food is abudnant. And the fish eagle flies to search prey. These are the words of the Volva. Illustrations from Doepler, D.J. & Ranisch, W. (1900) *Walhall. Die Götterwelt der Germanen.* Wikimedia Commons.

(Fig. 46). The surviving gods return and find the gold pieces of their previous games in the beautiful, green grass banks of Ithavoll (Old Norse, splendour-plain).

*The earth I see*
*Rising again, up*
*From the waters,*
*Growing with greenness,*
*Great torrents flowing.*
*High flies the eagle*
*Over the mountains,*
*Hunting for fish.*

The two humans, Liv and Livtrasi, who survived by the morning due in the innermost part of Yggdrasil, Hoddmimis Holt (see 6.2), become the new generation of humans. Some of the gods return to Ithavoll. Long do they talk about the happenings of the past. The fields are green and get ripe by themselves. Balder returns. He and his brother Hodr share the same house. A new, papradiselike stage of the world has arrived.

> *The fields will grow high,*
> *Without being sown;*
> *All harm will be healed,*
> *For Balder returns,*
> *Høđur and Balder*
> *In the halls of the High One.*
> *Do you know more?*

The Völuspa stops here abruptly and does not provide more evidence of the fate and destiny of the New Earth. We have to imagine how the New Earth develops or how it will develop, depending on our assumption if Ragnarök is behind (circular time) or in front of us (linear time). Do our current, seemingly dark times represent Ragnarök, or are we already in the phase of the New Earth?

## 6.9 Conclusion

The destiny of the gods and humans is the essential core of Ragnarök. The potential physical presence of the Germanic gods must have felt so dominating for the Germanic tribes that man's place on earth appeared bleak and remote[142]. In order to see a candle (here interpreted as man's awakening ego) in bright sunlight (the presence of gods), one needs darkness. The sun has to go down to ignite the inner light. Man had to forget the mighty gods in order to become himself. The Völva could see the coming dominance of (independent) humans, and thus she predicted the end of the world, the twilight (or dusk) of gods, darkness, and the Ragnarök. The gods had to fade to prepare the ground for the appearance

---

[142] Stockland, O. (1969).

of conscious man. Through Ragnarök, the gods in the outer world became inner beings (or psychological structures) in humans. The gods were internalized to form the psyche of man (see Box XI). Thus, Ragnarök may not be before us (as many fear), but already behind us. Or we are in the middle of it.

It is suggested that "the advent of the humans" seems to be the ultimate goal of the Germanic gods, the Ragnarök. The dusk of the gods is thus the dawn of modern and individual man. The destiny of the Germanic gods is individual human growth and development[143]. Today's reality is probably the long-winded version of Ragnarök. But with the sense for dramaturgy that is a distinctive trait of the original Germanic culture, Ragnarök had to take place abruptly after a long time of tension building, with drums beating and trumpets sounding.

If we adopt the above-mentioned interpretation, we may ask, what is so barbarous and primitive about Germanic mythology? When being in the vanguard of modernity, a thousand years before today, we may rightly question the cause for neglecting, demonizing, repulsing, and repressing the archetypical representations of the original Germanic culture (see e.g. Box XX). Why was Europe's unrecognized avant-garde suppressed by Christianity, which had a traditional, Roman worldview that does not support a strict individual, but rather patriarchal and collective worldview? Was Christian culture really so advanced and were the barbarians so barbarous? Tentative answers are provided in chapter 7.

---

[143] Lindholm, D. (1965).

*Livets dans* (*Dance of Life*) by Edvard Munch (1863-1944, National Gallery, Oslo). Life takes its circular pattern in the form of dancing couples. Life stages are presented on the fertile ground of the earth, in the glow of the midnight sun and adjacent to the expanse of the eternal sea (the premordial ocean?). Each culture can be young, naïve, lively, and full of expectations (like the white-dressed woman to the left) and feel sinister, old and isolated (the pale and drak-dressed woman to the right). The heydays of a culture could be interpreted as the magic meeting between two antagonistic, so far not combined qualities, as reflected through the intensity of desire of the couple in the center. Each culture can, mistreated and ravished, get detached and outsourced from the rejuvenating dance of life. The Germanic culture started very promisingly but has been neglected, demonized, repulsed, and repressed. Can it relearn dancing and enter the life-giving, never-ending round dance of life? Copyright: National Gallery of Norway, Oslo.

# 7. Germanic Culture and Mythology through Time: A Historic Overview

*What is most modern in our time frequently turns out to be the most archaic. The sculpture of Brancusi belongs to the art of the Cyclades in the ninth century BCE*

G. Davenport

*The sad truth is that most evil is done by people who never make up their minds to be good or evil.*

H. Arendt

After having presented some of the basic elements of Germanic mythology in chapter 6, we face finally the basic question of the book. How, where, and when were the representations of the original Germanic mythology neglected, demonized, repulsed, and repressed? What are the underlying causes for this cultural repression? How is the situation at present? And how much Germanic mythology is based upon facts or is fake[144]? To achieve answers, we deal first with the development of Germanic culture and mythology in this chapter, applying a bird's-eye perspective. A developmental line of 2,000 years will be presented with key events and important elements for the evolution of Germanic mythology and culture. In the chapter 8, we will focus upon the generic causes for cultural repression, i.e., we ask why. In both chapters it will be shown that neglecting, demonizing, repulsing, and repressing archetypical

---

[144] Brock, T. (2014).

representations of original Germanic culture is indeed a red thread and leitmotiv in European culture, in particular earlier on, but also today.

## 7.1 Arrival of Germanic tribes in central Europe, the Romans and Christianity

About 200 B.C.E., the Romans for the first time mention Germanic tribes. A multitude of tribes moved from southern Scandinavian and the Baltic shores to the northern regions of central Europe (Fig. 6). Confrontations with the Roman army were perpetual (Fig. 47). Fortified border defenses between the barbaric Germanic tribes in the north and the cultivated Romanized people in the south were erected: the Limes in today's central Germany and Hadrian's Wall in northern England.

From 372 and until about 800, the Migration of People initiated the collapse of the civilization of Western Rome. This period and earlier attempts were labeled the Barbarian Invasions, a term that obtained refreshed significance in post-Renaissance times (see 7.2). The Migration

Fig. 47. *Die Schlacht zwischen Germanen und Römern am Rhein* (*Battle of Germanic Forces with Romans at the Rhine*) by Friedrich Tüshaus (1832-1885; LWL-Museum für Kunst und Kultur, Münster). The painting has obvious nationalistic connotations. Strong and brave Germanic warriors defend victoriously a riverbank against the Roman army. The battle could also be the battle in the Teutoburg Forest, which during the rise of German Nationalism was celebrated as a feat and liberation from Roman yoke. The Rhine is a river that had symbolic character for Germany's independence. Take note of the winged helmets, cliché of the time. Wikimedia Commons.

of People gave rise to a significant spread of Germanic tribes throughout Europe and northern Africa. The Germanic tribes, by language and genes, have been a leading segment of the European population ever since.

Christianity became the state religion of the Roman Empire, adopted Roman culture and law, and it developed into its continuation. Roman culture and law became a dominating European force beyond Roman times. The Roman Catholic Church forcefully rejected Germanic culture, and as a consequence, the barbarians became even more barbarous. They were not only without culture, they were also pagan and heathens. The Romanization of the southern and western sections of Europe continued through Christianity. The subjugation of Saxons to the east of the Rhine by Charlemagne in 776 and onward resulted in an eradication of Germanic mythology and religion from Central Europe (Fig. 48). Scandinavia was far away from Rome, and therefore Norse religion and Christianity coexisted for hundreds of years in the north.

Christianity look down on nature (which is evil) and disproves the existence of ancestral and nature spirits. This resulted in a considerable loss of tolerance. Christianity's main impact on the Germanic culture was the split of the archetypes. The simultaneous balance between the positive and negative side that characterizes archetypes was torn apart. This resulted in saints and devils, nuns and witches, and heaven and hell. "But small is the gate and narrow the road that leads to life, and only a few find it"[145] reflects an important Christian attitude, but is the inverse of the Germanic universe, which is wide, open, and for all. Seen from a contemporary point of view, Roman law and Christianity deprived Europeans of essential modern values that had to be acquired anew (e.g., religious tolerance, individual rights, one-person one-vote, political independence through federalism).

When representing so much modernity, we may ask why the culture of the Germanic tribes so quickly disintegrated? The Germanic people were great individualists and federalists who lived in loose and steadily changing state structures. Confronted with the might of "Roman"-type empires, centralized kingdoms, and the highly hierarchical Roman Catholic Church, they had to succumb. They could not oppose the pressure against a crucial base of their culture: the federal nature of states, the *thing* (see Box VII), and

---

[145] Matthews 7:14.

Fig. 48. Karl der Große zerstört die Irminsäule (Charlemagne Destroys the Irminsul) by Hermann Wislicenus (1835-1902; Kaiserpfalz, Goslar, Germany). Inside the medieval building, the monumental, historicized murals by Wislicenus in the period 1879-97 testify to the national feeling of exuberance of that time. The convinced, imperial Charlemagne has just ordered the felling of the holy Irminsul, the symbol of the holy world tree of the Saxons. The Saxonian priests observe in disbelieve the result of Charlemagne's crushing of their holiest symbol. Take note of the national romantic elements that are fused into the mural, among them the inevitable winged helmets. Copyright: AKG Images GmbH.

the Germanic marriage/partnership (Box XIV). The latter is frequently epitomized by embracing couples on gold foils, interpreted as Freyr and Gerd (Old Norse, fenced-in), a Vanir, and a *jötunn* woman. These foils symbolize the intercourse between fertility and chaos as part of the sacred kinship (hieros gamos)[146] (see Fig. 49). By the end of the Middle Ages, the Germanic culture lay with a broken back throughout Europe: demonized, repressed, and repulsed. The gods withdrew into the woods and the unconsciousness, the culture went into internal exile. Some of the Germanic mythology persisted in the obscure configuration of festivals, names, myths, and fairy tales (see chapter 5). Deep down in the cultural pockmarks[147] of the Germanic people, a piping hot mess accumulated, sending at best streams of gas to the surface, but also building up a preparedness for eruption.

---

[146] Hedesager, L. (2015).

[147] Pockmarks are craters in the seabed caused by fluids (gas and liquids) erupting and streaming through the sediments.

## Box XIV: Germanic men and women: a threat to power execution

The union between a.) gods and giants and b.) fertility and chaos appears to have given Germanic marriage a cosmological legitimacy. Presentations like those in Fig. 49, in precious gold, were applied when building homes, the place for peace and friendship, guests and the basis for future generations. The depictions of the embrace of fertility and chaos were placed in the very center of the house: the four poles of the High Seat. There exists also a considerable earthly legitimacy for the Germanic marriage, but to provide a precise account of the role of women and men in the entire Germanic world is not possible. The sources for some regions are inadequate, and some information, e.g., through Tacitus, probably reflects first of all the author's wish to address the low moral standards of matrimony in Rome. Later sources on women and men in the Germanic world were clearly dominated by Christianity's assumption of the sinful nature of humans, in particular women. The only Germanic group for which we know about rights, limitations, and rules regarding men and women are the Norse people. The present account is thus based upon the roles and rights of women and men in the western Germanic culture toward the end of the pagan time.

In Germanic mythology, the Aesir and Vanir coexist in Asgard as equal and intermarried patriarchal and matricentric gods (see 6.5; Fig. 26). Because of the balanced situation between the Aesir and Vanir, the Norse tribes had unusual respect for their women. This provides the basis for genuine partnership. The rights of free women (they had slaves) in Norse times can be characterized by:

- Legal independence: They kept their own inheritance, which they would take with them in case of divorce; they kept their maiden name.
- They had access to divorce. The woman's wish was sufficient.
- Children inherited the bloodline of both father and mother.
- Alternative sexual partners were possible, and not a shame; these relationships could result in political complications between clans.
- Women had protection against sexual assault. Because honor was highly appreciated, her word was proof. The perpetrator could eventually face the death penalty.

- Women (and men) controlled fertility. Nine nights after birth, a child had to be recognized by the father of the household (when present). He placed the child on his knee while sitting in the high seat. Water was sprinkled on the child; it was named and thus admitted into the family. Newborns got humans rights after the "knee sitting" ceremony. Before that, they could be left to die in the wilderness.

These six aspects belong to the core of what we today call emancipation and women's right. For more than 100 years, arguments and fights have taken place (and still do so) to guarantee and establish these basic rights, creating the preconditions of a balanced partnership. The Norse world represent the backdrop of modern Scandinavia, and it is thus no surprise that a Scandinavian heralded women's liberation first[148]. Today's female rights are basically copies of female rights in Norse times. They may actually not be an innovation or new development. They had just been supressed by Christianity for a thousand years. This improved balance does, of course, also result in a crisis of the manliness as men's traditional roles become challenged[149].

The Germanic partnership (if it existed over the entire Germanic realm), endangered "Roman"-type power execution, which was vigorously patriarchal. Rome and the new state religion of the late Roman Empire, Christianity, with its strict line of command had to take decisive action against the federal Germanic culture and ideals of equal gender rights. To prevent the undermining of power, Rome and the Roman Catholic Church had to destroy Germanic matrimony. The Germanic husband became a patriarch. His wife became a servant and "brooding pouch" for his children[150]. Couple dialogues turned into male monologues or battlefields.

It is suggested that the greatest threat against those in power is a close and harmonious partnership. Real partners, i.e., those with equal rights but eventually different roles, have an open dialogue, exchange

---

[148] Henrick Ibsen's *Et dukkehjem* (*A Doll's House*) in 1879.
[149] Schnurbein, S. v. (2001).
[150] The homunculus sits in his sperm and thus the child is his.

ideas, and develop new ones in concert. By this, they become a cradle for opposition and resistance against any totalitarian regime. And thus the basic and balanced human partnership has been and still is a matter of immense resistance in many countries where the distribution of power is skewed toward the male side. Have those that resist real partnership considered that they may support political or religious totalitarianism? Why should people of Germanic orgin be associated with barbarism when they represented modernity a thousand years earlier and were prevented from becoming modern by those who considered them primitive, pagan, and the like?

Fig. 49. A *gullgubbe* (Scandinavian, little old man of gold), a small, thin gold object found in the longest Viking house found so far, at Borg in the Lofoten Islands, northern Norway (https://www.lofotr.no/en/. *Gullgubber* are art-objects, amulets, or offerings found in Scandinavia and dating to the Nordic Iron Age. They consist of thin pieces of beaten gold, usually between 1-2 square centimeters in size and stamped with a motif. Depicted are an embracing couple, probably the god Freyr (a *Vanir*) and the woman Gerd (a *jötunn*), symbolizing the intercourse between fertility and chaos as part of the sacred kinship or the empowerment of the divine of nature of marriage. *Gullgubber* are a Scandinavian tradition, connected to chieftain halls and centers of power and derive from the late migration to early Viking time. It has been suggested that the double figure foils were part of fertility rituals during the inauguration of chieftains. Or they may point at the divine or mythic origin of the chieftain's lineage. The foils of Freyr and Gerd point toward the importance of Germanic matrimony and the connection to the Old Europe and unconcious. Courtesy: Tromsø University Museum.

## 7.2 Renaissance and humanistic education

The Renaissance, from the 14th to the 17th centuries, became the cultural bridge connecting antiquity, the Middle Ages, and modern history. It started as a cultural movement in Italy in the late medieval period and later spread to the rest of Europe, marking the beginning of the Early Modern Age (Fig. 50). In a manner, the Renaissance started in 1439. A church meeting in Florence attempted to overcome the East-West schisms of Christianity that started in 1054 (and still prevails). The pressure of the Ottoman Empire on the Byzantine Empire resulted in an evacuation of all (in the west mostly unknown) antiquity manuscripts from Constantinople to Florence. Italy enjoyed the migration of highly educated Greek scholars following the fall of Constantinople to the Ottoman Turks. As a cultural movement, the Renaissance encompassed

Fig. 50. *La scuola di Athene* (*The School of Athens*) by Raffaello Sanzio da Urbino (known as Raphael, 1483-1520; Apostolic Palace, Vatican). This famous Renaissance fresco is part of Raphael's commission to decorate the rooms now known as the Raphael Rooms. It shows the philosophers of Athens and points at the cultural lineage between Greek antiquity and the culture of the Italian Renaissance. The insert exemplifies the central perspective (green lines), trueborn child of the Renaissance, that makes the ego of the spectator and the dialogue between Plato and Socrates to the center (of the universe). Wikimedia Commons.

the innovative flowering of Latin and vernacular literature, beginning with the 14th century resurgence of learning based on classical Greek sources. The availability of classic Greek originals to Latin gave rise to an earth-shattering impact on European culture. It was the start of the big role that antiquity played and plays in Western Europe: through its mythology, literature, terms, and imaginary.

The term Renaissance means rebirth in French and appeared in English as late as in the 1830s[151]. It was the 19th century glorification of the Renaissance that placed particular emphasis upon this period. It was argued that the "real" culture, that of the Greeks and Romans, was reborn during the Renaissance (after barbarism and medieval darkness destroyed classical Roman culture). Already in 1550, the historian Giorgio Vasari (1511-1574) laid the foundation for this view (see chapter 8). Thus, only a revival of Greek and in particular Roman art could compensate for the loss of a thousand years of culture.

To the intellectual basis of the Renaissance belongs the development of humanism, derived from the rediscovery of classical Greek philosophy. As an example, we can cite Protagoras (487-412 B.C.E.), who said that "man is the measure of all things." Humanism, turning away from medieval scholasticism, is a philosophical and ethical stance that emphasizes the value and agency of human beings, individually and collectively, and generally prefers critical thinking and evidence (rationalism, empiricism) to acceptance of dogma or superstition. This new thinking became manifest in art, architecture, politics, science, and literature. Is the Renaissance the rebirth of antiquity culture? Superficially, the answer may be yes, but in reality, the answer is a forceful no. The Renaissance is the birth of modernity and rationalism arising from the cultural modulations in postmedieval Europe, in the disguise of antiquity. It is inspired by the classical times, but modernity is, so to say, the inverse of the classical times. It is thus challenging that the Renaissance, seemingly the continuation of the classic, is in its core anticlassic.

The Renaissance implies a total change in perspective. Greeks experienced their gods as part of nature (Greek temples reflect the genius loci, i.e., the presence of a deity at a particular place of veneration).

---

[151] Before the period obviously had no specified name.

Greek architecture and its golden ratio[152] is thus observed and experienced from the outside: The emanation of architecture reflects nature through the genius loci. In contrast, Christianity looks at reality from the inside. Early Christian interior church architecture excludes the outside world and is particularly known for its amazing internalizing splendor of mosaics, colored glass windows, the mysticism of candles in the dark church naves, and captivating intoxication of incense. The inner experience of the one and only god became the human epicenter, preparing modern man who experiences himself neither as an integrated part of nature nor through the colorful translucence provided by Christian imagery. Modern man is an individualist who holds an ego at the center of his consciousness, providing him with a central perspective[153]. In contrast to antiquity, modern man understands himself not as a participating part of, but as the center of the world[154] (Fig. 50). The breakdown of the culture of antiquity and the individuality of the Germanic tribes provided the precondition for the Renaissance and modernity. Modernity does thus not start with the "classic" time, but with its defeat. In clear contrast to the 16th century personalities such as Vasari and 19th century Renaissance aficionados, modernity starts with the barbarian invasions. It is in particular shaped and inspired by the individualism and federalism of the Germanic tribes.

Renaissance enthusiasts such as Carl Jacob Christoph Burckhardt (1818–1897) seduced us into thinking that classical texts and philosophy make us cultivated[155]. The impact of the Renaissance upon our culture is immense, and it provided us with a suite of highly valued concepts, e.g., humanism. Moreover, it gave us great ideals on education, with strong ramifications into present time: classic texts (Latin, Greek, Hebrew) and natural science are believed to provide us a civilized world. The Renaissance is rarely suspected of having significant adverse effects. Some of the darkest moments of humanity are developed and executed

---

[152] The Golden Ratio is a mathematical ratio. It is commonly found in nature, and when used in design, it fosters organic and natural-looking compositions that are aesthetically pleasing to the eye.

[153] In about 1413, Filippo Brunelleschi demonstrated the geometrical method of perspective, used today by artists, by painting the outlines of various Florentine buildings onto a mirror.

[154] Normann Waage (2014).

[155] Burckhardt, C.J.C. (1878).

by and in the aftermath of the Renaissance. Witch burning, inquisition and the "barbarization" of cultures are trueborn children of the Renaissance. The Renaissance has, in the guise of culture not problematized, brought also immense suffering to the world. The founders of modernity did not recognize that the barbarians provided the basis for the innovation behind the Renaissance. Without the input of the Germanic individuation, the ideal separating political independence from central power execution and emphasis on federal structures, the Renaissance and the ultimate autonomization of the ego would not have been possible. Without the spirit of the Germanic tribes, the Renaissance and our independence from central powers would not exist as we know it. Much of what we today call freedom is launched in the Renaissance period, but the modulations that create the background for this period is fueled by Germanic barbarianism.

## 7.3 Romanticism

Humanism is criticized as being centered on the notion of the rational, autonomous self and ignoring the conditioned nature of the individual[156]. Thus after the of the baroque and rationalist periods, the idea of individuality and modernity accelerated through romanticism. Romanticism was an artistic, literary, musical, and intellectual movement that originated in Europe toward the end of the 18th century and, in most areas, was at its peak from about 1800-1850. Romanticism was partly a reaction to the Industrial Revolution, the social and political norms of the Age of Enlightenment, and the scientific rationalization of nature. The movement is characterized by its emphasis on emotion and individualism as well as glorification of the past and nature, preferring the medieval rather than the classical times. Romanticism provided a new change in perspective: that reality is found in man's interior and represented by the night (the day is an illusion) (Fig. 51). With a systematic discovery of the psyche and phenomena such as the night, dreams, fantasies, unconscious, madness, the doppelgänger, etc. (see 6.3), the psychodynamic tradition commences in these times. In contrast

---

[156] https://en.oxforddictionaries.com/definition/humanism.

Fig. 51. *Der Wanderer über dem Nebelmeer* (*The Wanderer Above a Sea of Fog*) by Caspar David Friedrich (1774-1840; Kunsthalle Hamburg) illustrates man's new, individual, and introverted perspective that was introduced by Romanticism. The wanderer in the center of the image exposes his back to the spectator, inviting the viewer contemplating the introspective view: a communion with outer (and inner) nature. The protagonist draws the viewer's awareness from the rocky sumit to the almost impenetrable sea of fog, alluding that life is a worrying voyage into the unknown. The right and left arms and legs point at the wanderer's active (conscious) and passive (unconscious) action. The spectator may experience a reunion with the spiritual self through the contemplation of nature. The image exposes the loneliness of individuation: Suspended over the fog that prevents observing the material reality, the thoughts of the protagonist hover through space and time (see also Fig. 61). Romanticism and this painting place Weltanschauung (worldview) in the center of humanity's self-conception. Wikimedia Commons.

to rationalism, romanticism discovered the psyche, mythology, (comparative) language, and national heritage already in the late 1700s.

Between 1780 and 1830, the tides of humanity changed, for good. The Romantic period had a significant and complex effect on politics and was associated with liberalism, radicalism, and internationalism. However, its long-term effect on the growth of nationalism was also significant (see 7.4). The continuity of history was discovered, and this resulted in thorough investigations of what was considered the dark times of the Migration Period and the Middle Ages. Foreign languages beyond French and Italian were discovered. For example, until then, William Shakespeare's oeuvre was, so to say, unknown in Central Europe. The relationship between languages was investigated. Sir William Jones (1746-1794) lectured on the striking similarities among three of the oldest languages known in his time: Latin, Greek, and Sanskrit, to which he tentatively added Gothic, Celtic, and Persian. Thomas Young (1773-1829) first used the term Indo-European in 1813, deriving from the geographical extremes of the language family: from Western Europe to northern India (Fig. 4). This led ultimately to the reconstruction of the Indo-European language and the discovery of the Indo-Europeans.

The Romantic period further uncovered the mythology of ethnic groups and sampled regional and national fairy tales. The Brothers Grimm (Jacob and Wilhelm) are an example. They were German academics, linguists, cultural researchers, lexicographers, and authors who together specialized in collecting and publishing German folklore during the early 19th century. Jacob Grimm was the founder of basic German(ic) antiquity and German philology (see chapter 3).

Thus Romanticism was a period of utmost significance in the rediscovery of the subdued Germanic culture and mythology and created the basis for psychology.

## 7.4 Searching for mythology, national self-esteem and the birth of nationalism

To investigate the sources of Germanic mythology and facts about the Indo-European people were a main aspiration during the Romantic period. While rich sources were found in Northwestern Europe, not much direct evidence was found in Central Europe (see 3.5). However, linguistic and grammar studies provided the reconstruction of the Indo-European language tree (Fig. 1).

In particular in Germany, the search for mythology and national identity was strong. Germany, being the very center of Europe since the times of Charlemagne, came under tremendous pressure during the Thirty Years' War (1618-1648), one of the longest and most destructive conflicts in European history. It was also the deadliest European religious war, resulting in 8 million casualties (40 percent and 33 percent of the German population in the countryside and cities, respectively). As a consequence, the Holy Roman Empire of the German Nation, for the most part today's Germany, got politically destabilized through a breakup into more than 30 feudal states. A fragmented Central Europe with weak cohesion created ideal possibilities for large nations on the periphery, such as England, France, Austria, and Spain to develop and flourish. A pauperized, feudal, and estranged Germany became the ideal projection screen for unfavourable qualities and terms (see chapter 9). The political conglomerate of Germany became envisioned as a nation with a medieval, uncivilized, and barbarian character. The region was con-sidered too dangerous to become powerful again.

To show the former might and power of Germany, ambitious Germans cultivated arts and science, the only manner to obtain world fame in a fractured political setting. The formally nonexistent but culturally highly present German nation launched challenging questions (Fig. 52). "What is genuine German? What is the mythology of the Germans? Should the German-speaking culture family, the German nation, have the privilege of residing in a united country?" These were highly controversial and politically worrisome questions. Most European countries supported their own national states by opposing the formation of a German national state.

Meanwhile, German scientists searched Europe high and low to find evidence for Germanic mythology and pre-Christian evidence of religious beliefs. They made an effort, if possible, to demonstrate that the German nation was ancient and based upon the cultural fusion of the Germanic tribes that formed the nation in the aftermath of the Migration Period. Some of them were influenced by German nationalism. In response to the invasion of Germany by the First French Empire, the German Campaign (Befreiungskriege) became a reality in 1813. This supported

German nationalism, which commenced with the birth of Romantic nationalism and the humiliation of the French occupation. As a consequence, it also supported Pan-Germanism (see Box II).

The researchers were faced with only a few, or a lack of, reliable sources (see 3.5). Influenced by the upcoming German nationalism, they did not wish to stay in such an indistinct state of affairs. Rather, they tried to raise German citizens by amalgamating a new "Germanity" through projecting the well-known Norse mythology (see chapter 3) into the

Fig. 52. *Erwachende Germania* (*Awakening Germania*) by Christian Köhler (1809-1861; New York Historical Society). The painting was executed under the influence of the 1848 revolution and the attempt to create a unified, democratic Germany. The German national colors (black, red, gold) were selected by the unsuccesful constitutional assembly in Frankfurt. The bear skin and the wreath of oak leaves refer to the old Germanic past, and weapons are ready to be used in the fight for the awakening of a new, democratic Germany. Germania reaches for the crown for the Holy Roman Empire of German Nations that had been removed by Napoleon. Despite the national-romantic, timely pathos, the painting debates positive values: It argues for a democratic Germany unified among other Europeans states. Wikimedia Commons.

Germanic world of central Europe. Blends of various sources were made to foster national feelings and promote German identity. The sagas of heroes such as Siegfried, Brühnhild, Attila, Dietrich von Bern were particularly supportive for national pride and a feeling of superiority. Questionable constructions, at the edge of forgeries and full of projections of an unbroken Germanic world, were launched (see Box XV). A seeming "Germanization" of the Germans was the consequence. Although much of the presented material in Jacob Grimm's epoch-making book derived from the Norse tradition sources, he titled the book *Deutsche Mythologie*[157], not Germanic Mythology. After the German Campaign, the intellect of Grimm (and many others) became over-shadowed by pride and nationalism. His wish to provide the German nation with an longed-for, missing mythology, got so strong that he committed a serious and consequence-rich faux pas.

## Box XV: Popular books on Germanic mythology and heroic epics

Nineteenth and 20th century books such as *Deutsche Heldensagen* or *Nordland Sagen* have been part of German standard literature. They were often read or provided to children in their early teens[158]. The original Norse literature, fused with local heroic literature, was revised and adapted for "the German house."[159] These books contain mainly stories for the Heroic Era, i.e., before the time of written accounts. The content is partly of a mythological, partly of historical nature. It contains first *Heldenlieder* (heroic songs), followed by *Heldenepen* (heroic epics). A Germanic hero is the protagonist and always a warrior, concerned both with his reputation and fame, and with his political responsibilities. The way in which he copes with fate is extremely important. His death usually brings destruction, not restoration, as in the classical Greek tragedy. His goal is frequently revenge for lost honor. To the figures

---

[157] Grimm, J. (1835).
[158] Engelmann, E. (1889, 1895); Weitbrecht, R. (no year); Eigel, K. (1953).
[159] Engelmann, E. (1889, 1895).

of the *Deutsche Heldensagen* belong courageous characters such as Dietrich von Bern, Siegfried, Gunther and Hagen[160].

A humble, critical and non-nationalistic interpretation was not a matter of priority when the German Nationalist movement attempted to provide the German nation (or the German house) anew with its lost mythology. The national heritage is reflected in how the *Deutsche Heldensagen* and *Nordland Sagen* were arranged and adapted into prose versions for young generations. It was important to foster the heroic nature of males, which is, of course, not peculiar to Germany, but the trend in many nations, particularly at the transition from the 19th to the 20th century. Through National Socialist organizations such as Hitlerjugend and Bund Deutscher Mädel, this trend continued with full strength in Germany during the 1930s and paved some of the way for the moral collapse of Germany.

Germanic culture was deliberately manipulated through adjustments and revisions of the Germanic literature from the heroic age, including the incorporation of material from the western Germanic into the central Germanic culture (see 3.7). Mythology was misused and doomed to serve narrow-minded political goals. With little respect for the original texts, a prose mixture was created and spread widely. We know that tomatoes are the main source of called ketchup. *Deutsche Heldensagen* is indeed based upon the original sagas and epics, but the prose translations, the removing of the "medieval and Christian varnish," the modification for the German house and the pompous illustrations and imaginary camouflage the substance. Instead of the original ingredients, Germans got addicted to the ketchup that was poured on top of every national meal.

Old High German literature sources, such as the *The Song of the Nibelungs* (see 3.5) were used for nationalist propaganda (Box XVIII). At the start of World War I, the catchphrase "Nibelungentreue" (literally "Nibelung loyalty") draws its essence through the absolute loyalty of Hagen for his Lord Gunther but now marked Germany's connection to

---

[160] Das Lied der Nibelungen (1833).

Austria-Hungary. In World War II, the term signified the bond to Hitler (expressing the concept of absolute, unquestioning, excessive, and potentially disastrous loyalty).

We cannot omit mention of Wagner's gigantic opera cycle *Der Ring des Nibelungen* and its influence upon Germany and Germanic culture. The quartet can be used to exemplify the strategy of the German nationalist movement. On the surface, the *Ring* is thematically inspired by Germanic mythology. Very often people think they know Germanic mythology by knowing the *Ring*, but this is based upon an unfortunate misconception. The *Ring* deals with greed, power, nihilism, and early capitalism. Wagner borrowed symbols, story fractions, and figures from Germanic mythology (based upon Karl Simrocks translation) to make the *Ring* fashionable, heroic, pathetic, and national, according to the taste of time (Fig. 53). Through Wagner's *Ring*, the German-National movement present how real Germanic people thought, acted, and looked

Fig. 53. Nibelheim (Nifelheim) by Josef Hoffman (1831–1904). This is one of 14 monochrome photographs taken of Hoffman's set designs for Wagner's opera *Der Ring des Nibelungen* in 1876. It illustrates the highly romantic opera scenery, including the costumes that obviously are inspired by D.J. Doepler. Wagner's *Ring*, in particular the outfits of the singers, contributed strongly to the notion of nationalism. The outfits have little, if anything, in common with a sober-minded understanding of the Germanic past. Wikimedia Commons.

like. Norse warriors, along with horned or winged helmets, became a clichéd signifier of the "barbarian" northern warrior (Figs. 47, 48, 57). The popular image dates to the 1800s, when the Swede Gustav Malmström (1829-1901) included the headgear in his portrayals of the Viking raiders. On this basis, Wagner's German costume designer, Carl Emil Doepler (1824-1905), created "Germanic" heroes on stage[161]. Germanic tribes used none of these outfits. An enduring stereotype falsification was born.

The *Ring* as a *Gesamtkunstwerk* has immense qualities in itself, but has also resulted in a perversion of Germanic mythology, thanks to the nationlistic movement. From a strict mythology point of view, the *Ring* is a fusion product where the original content has been manipulated to serve the authors'/composers' wishes and desires for his *Gesamtkunstwerk*. From a mythology point of view, the *Ring* is at the brink of forgery. When people, even the educated, think about Germanic mythology, they may imagine Doepler's scenography, blond beasts (an expression of F. Nietzsche), destructive nihilists (again under the influence of Nietzsche), and wars of the utmost destruction (Götterdämmerung = Armageddon). All of that is not reflected by what we really know from Germanic or Norse mythology.

An increasing schism opened up between the realistic and progressive intellectuals on one side and those who were in support of the National German state at any cost on the other side. Nationalism derailed the attempts to bring back an appraisal of Germanic culture and mythology.

## 7.5 The breakthrough of the primitive[162]

The stilted, stiffening, and nation-supporting development of culture was undermined by feelings of discomfort in culture and a disenchantment with the world[163] (see Box XVI). Into a setting of complete misjudgement of social circumstances and a sickly self-confident science around 1900, the neglected and suppressed primitive (aboriginal, basic, primordial, archaic) stepped suddenly onto the scene in the guise of primitivism.

---

[161] Langer, J. (2002).
[162] Here: belonging to the first or beginning; original, characteristic of an early state.
[163] Freud, S. (1930). Max Weber: Wissenschaft als Beruf, lecture 1922.

Primitivism had a profound impact on modern Western art. The discovery of African tribal art by Picasso around 1906 was an important influence on his painting in general and was a major factor in leading to cubism and expressionism. The upcoming modernity is characterized in visual art (e.g., Fauvism, Expressionism, Cubism, Suprematism, Surrealism, etc.), architecture (e.g., Bauhaus, etc.), music (e.g., late Romantic, expressionism, 12-note composition, etc.), literature (e.g., subjectivity, alienation, irrationality, symbolism, surrealism, etc.), and psychology (e.g., psychoanalysis, analytical psychology, etc.). The clash with the established society, characterized by nationalism, positivism, rationality, science, historicism, and Social Darwinism was momentous. The breakthrough of the primitive profoundly distressed the minds of the majority. The eyes of spectators were utterly challenged. The ears of music lovers were invaded by cacophony. The suppressed energies of the primitive broke into the European consciousness and reminded us that man had a primordial core. In analogy, the cortex is an ephemeral membrane that covers the main core of the brain, where the primordial core of our soul is situated. And woe betides us when forces of our inner brain surface and overwhelm the controlling cortex! It was a time for scandals, and the cultural crème de la crème shouted with immense dismay: The barbarians are back!

To the works of visual art that heralded barbarianism and the banned primitive were epigone examples of modern art such as *Scream* by Edward Munch (1893), *Adulthood* by Hilma af Klint (1906), *Les Demoiselles d'Avignon* by Pablo Picasso[164] (1907), *La Dance* by Henri Émile Benoît Matisse (1910), *Composition IV* by Wassily Wassilyevich Kandinsky (1911), *Amorpha, Fugue en deux couleurs* by František Kupka (1912) and *Black Square* by Kazimir Severinovich Malevich (1915). The attention that surrealism and many artists had for symbols and so-called primitive culture presents another modus of how archaic contents made it into the consciousness of modern man (see Fig. 54). These breakthroughs appeared to rejuvenate the stiff and fossilized culture, as defined and promoted by the ruling classes. Kandinsky characterized the extraordinary setting as the "Symphony of the 20th Century."[165] It was an extremely varied

---

[164] Pablo Diego José Francisco de Paula Juan Nepomuceno María de los Remedios Cipriano de la Santísima Trinidad Martyr Patricio Clito Ruiz y Picasso.
[165] Citation from a letter to Franz Marc, 1911.

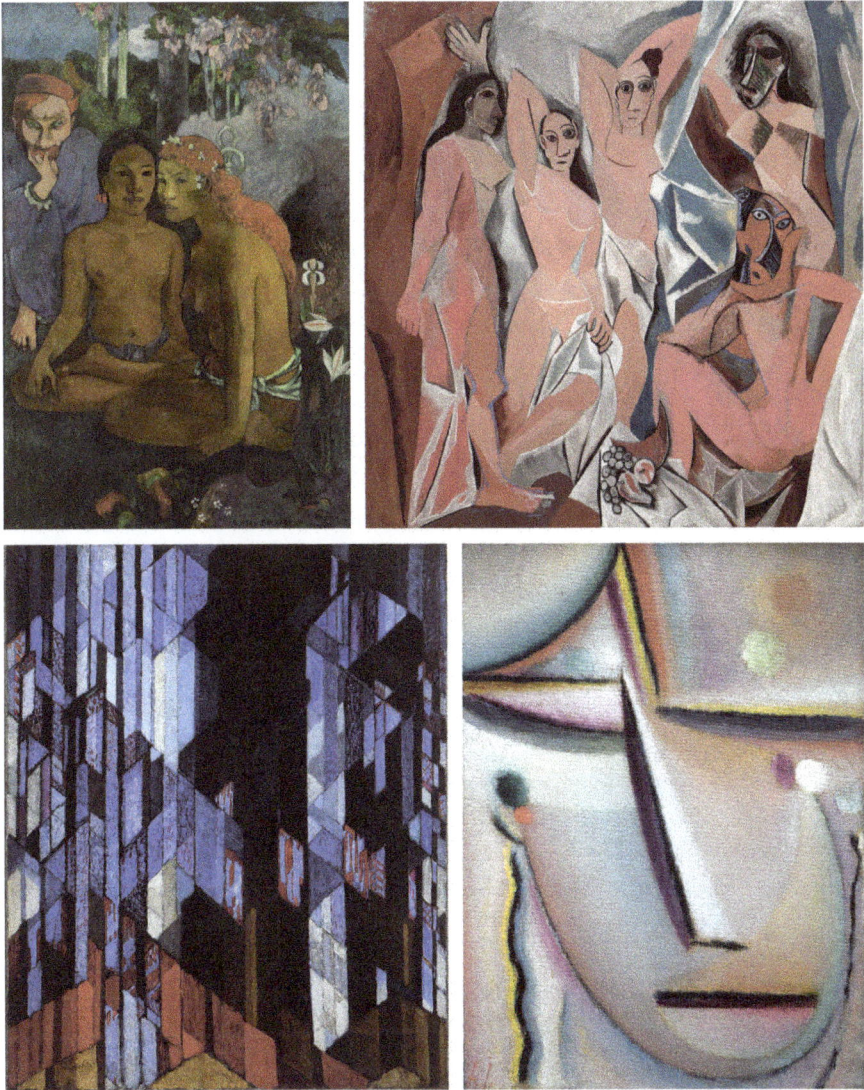

Fig. 54. Four prominent examples of the breakthrough of the primitive at the start of the 20th century. Upper left: *Contes barbares* (*Barbarian Tales*) by Paul Gauguin (1848-1903; Folkwang Museum, Essen); upper right: *Les Demoiselles d'Avignon* (*The Young Ladies of Avignon*, originally titled *The Brothel of Avignon*) by Pablo Picasso (1881-1973; Museum of Modern Art, New York); lower left: *Katedrála* (*Cathedral*) by František Kupka (1871-1957; Museum Kampa, Prague); lower right: *Meditation "Das Gebet"* (*Meditation "The Prayer"*) by Alexej Georgewitsch von Jawlensky (1864-1941; Lehnbachhaus, Munich). Wikimedia Commons.

orchestration that played tunes of the future, for those who had ears to listen and were mature for modernity. For the nationalistic blinded, it was not a "concord of sound" (symphonia) and "harmonious" (symphonous), but a disgrace of culture and the utmost decadence: barbarous.

The greatest scandal in the history of culture was the performance of *Le sacre du printemps* (*The Rite of Spring*, or short *Sacre*) by Igor Stravinsky (1882-1971) in Paris. The score was written for the 1913 Paris season of the Ballets Russes Company of the fabled stage director Sergei Diaghilev (1872-1929). The avant-garde nature of the music and choreography caused a sensation and a near-riot of the Belle Époque elegancy audience. The antagonizing concept behind Sacre, developed by the Russian painter and theosophist Nikolai Roerich (1874-1947), is suggested by its subtitle: *Pictures of Pagan Russia in Two Parts*. In the scenario, after various primitive rituals celebrating the advent of spring, a young girl is chosen as a sacrificial victim and dances herself to death. In addition to placing paganism and human sacrifice on stage, Stravinsky's score contained many novel features, including experiments in tonality, rhythm, instrumentation, and dissonance. The music has influenced many of the 20th century's leading composers and is one of the most recorded works in the classical repertoire. The cultural elite at the eve of World War I, where millions were brutally killed, full-throatily opposed ritual human self-sacrifice of primordial times. *Sacre* was considered too barbarous. In their elegant outfits, impeccable taste, and utmost elegance, they were unaware of how "primitive" civilized society had turned under the guise of culture. It allowed one of the most devastating episodes in human history. The most highly cultured were unable to imagine that they had promoted an arms race, but not an inner development and responsibility. It produced a human sacrifice of the 17 million casualties. They were unconscious that the old-fashioned, seemingly cultivated political situation allowed for barbarisms and cruelty of the worst sort. Stravinsky, Diaghilev, and Roerich placed a mirror in front of those who anticipated belonging to the cultural avant-garde. It is indeed difficult to face the confrontations of a mirror. The less we investigate our shadow, the less we will recognize that the terrible distortion in the mirror may not reflect the bad quality of the mirror, but our self.

Probably the strongest impact on modern man's consciousness was the revolutionary book *Die Traumdeutung* (*The Interpretations of Dreams*) by Sigmund Freud[166]. Right at the turn of the century, the book heralded a new time and a new manner of viewing human development, motivation, and action. This book and the subsequent development of psychoanalysis (including its many branches) changed the world entirely. It permeated entire societies to their remotest locations. Nevertheless, many in the leading classes, petrified by an outdated education, horrified by the personal challenges, and nurturing a narrow-minded view on culture, gender, and politics, were unable to perceive the leitmotif of modernity.

The breakthrough of the primitive was met with the fossilized mindset of the educated majority, limited in its attitude to foster nationalism at any costs and by the general inability to tackle its recuperative potential. The concurrent existence of the genres history painting and expressionism illustrate this incompatible dichotomy fully. The leading culture was static, old-fashioned, and much leaning toward the classical ideals of the assumed cultivated Roman and the Renaissance times. In Germany, modern art was repulsed. Parallel to this development, attempts were made to revive the long-suppressed Germanic mythology or religion. After World War I, paganist movements such as the German Faith Movement attempted to overcome what was considered the Central-Europe-alien Christianity, by reviving Germanic religion and anticipated rituals (see Box XVI). However, fascistic movements infiltrated and engulfed these circles and mindsets. The upcoming Third Reich utilized the inflation of the original Germanic archetypes by making the German-Nationalist/Wagnerian forgery of Germanic mythology shining. Further, they combined their endeavors with the repression of the primitive, the so-called degenerate art[167]. They used the psychological negative pressure of the neglected archetypes, frustration about Christianity, a national inferiority complex, and the unfair blame of Germany being responsible for World War I to created a superbomb.

Consequently, the advent of the rejuvenating and balancing primitive resulted in its utmost and reactionary suppression, leading to the world-shattering explosion of World War II and German moral collapse.

---

[166] Freud, S. (1900); Freud postponed it from 1899 to legendary 1900 to indicate the groundbreaking significance of his theory.
[167] Degenerate art (German: Entartete Kunst) was a term adopted in the 1920s by the Nazi Party in Germany to describe Modern art.

## Box XVI: Discomfort in culture and disenchantment of the world

Cultural and ideological confusion characterized the late 19th and early 20th centuries. Breakthroughs of modernity in the form of the invigorating, archaic, and primitive (see 7.5) were encapsulated or repelled by ignorant or ultraconservative surroundings. Cultural pessimism was widespread and arose from the conviction that the culture of modern civilizations, or humanity itself, was in a process of irreversible decline[168]. In a world that was increasingly dominated by science, technology, and pollution, one considered civilization in decline, caused by a loss of tradition, industrialization, proletarianization, and remoteness to nature.

Discomfort in culture (German: *Das Unbehagen in der Kultur*) and the disenchantment of the world (German: *Entzauberung der Welt*) were characteristic time views introduced by Sigmund Freud[169] and Max Weber (1864-1920)[170], respectively. The former phrase describes what Freud sees as the fundamental tensions between civilization and the individual. The primary friction, he asserts, stems from the individual's quest for instinctive freedom and civilization's contrary demand for conformity and repression of instincts. The latter describes the cultural rationalization and devaluation of mysticism apparent in modern society and the psychological vacuum that derives from it. Weber borrowed the concept of disenchantment from Friedrich Schiller to characterize a modernized, bureaucratic, secularized Western society, where scientific understanding is more highly valued than belief and where processes are oriented toward rational goals, as opposed to traditional society, where "the world remains a great enchanted garden."[171]

Obviously, the search for new, a more adequate worldview and the idea of an enchanted Garden of Eden haunted the minds and souls of many who were seeking for the meaning of life in the late 19th and early 20th centuries. Approaches to polytheistic or pantheistic nature-worshipping religions and tendencies to move away from Christianity were common. One of these that have a particular bearing on this book is *Deutsche*

---

[168] Bennet, O. (2001).
[169] Freud, S. (1930).
[170] Max Weber: Wissenschaft als Beruf, lecture 1922.
[171] Weber, M. (1920).

*Glaubensbewegung* (German Faith Movement). It started in the 1920s and grew strong in the 1930s, closely associated with the University of Tübingen professor, the Indiologist and religious studies writer Jakob Wilhelm Hauer (1881-1962). The movement sought to persuade Germany to abandon the alien religion Christianity that had been imposed upon the country and to advance toward a religion based on its original roots, Germanic paganism. It embraced early Nazi ideas, but the movement remained small. Following the Nazi accession to power, it obtained rights of civil tolerance but never the preferential treatment from the Nazi state for which Hauer campaigned. After the Nazi state attempted to obtain supporting relationships with the Roman Catholic Church, the Protestant *Landeskirche*, the owning classes, and industrial leaders, German Faith Movement became in fact outlawed.

The development of the German Faith Movement revolved around four main themes: a.) the propagation of the *Blut und Boden* (blood and soil) ideology, which refers to a belief that focuses on ethnicity based on two factors, decent blood (of a folk) and territory; b.) the replacement of Christian ceremonies by pagan equivalents; c.) the rejection of Christian ethics; and d.) the cult of Hitler's personality.

C.G. Jung considered symbols as a means for the numinous to return from the unconscious to the desacralized world. Because of the disenchantment when confronted with the modern world, Jung saw the recovery of myths as means to regain a sense of the wholeness they once provided. Already in 1917, Jung proposed that the time for Christianity was over[172]. In his essay *Wotan*, Jung characterizes the supporters of the German Faith Movement as "decent and well-meaning people who honestly admit their deep emotions (for the numinous)." He portrays Hauer's book *Deutsche Gottschau*[173] as an attempt "to build a bridge between the dark forces of life and the shining world of historical ideas." However, Jung did not comment upon the rejection of Christian ethics, the anti-Semitic character, and the cult of Hitler's personality by the German Faith Movement. He thus omitted or was unable to address the basis for what appears incomprehensible today: the movement's massive racist blind spot and belief in one Führer that became the basis for Germany's close to moral collapse.

---

[172] Dohe, C.B. (2016).
[173] Hauer, J.W. (1934).

## 7.6 The ultimate misuse of Germanic mythology and Germany's moral collapse

Europe's and Germany's nightmare started when a freely elected majority party, the NSDAP (National Sozialistische Deutsche Arbeiter Partei) took power in 1933. Already the acronym NSDAP signals fatal signs of incapability, as the terms in the party's names exclude each other. A socialist in these days was neither national nor German, and a nationalist party, for the most, was not a place for workers. Superficially, there was something for everybody in the term NSDAP. The term heralded the *Gleichschaltung* (coordination) and standardization of a diverse nation. Through calamity laws and the confidence of established parties, Hitler disabled the democratic constitution of the Weimar Republic. Communists, intellectuals, Jews, Gypsies, and homosexuals lost their jobs, were jailed or killed (see also Box I). Caught in a *perfide alieance* between medicine and the military, humans were tortured and humiliated (Fig. 55). Several hundred thousand of the intellectual crème-de-la-crème, emigrated. The remaining German avant-garde culture entered, for the most, the inner exile of the pleasant kingdom of Beethoven and Goethe. They were hiding there until they reappeared in 1945, asking how the almost total moral collapse could have happened in a nation of high cultural standing. Hanna Arendt and Ralph Metzner characterize this common attitude with utmost and sparkling clarity: The sad truth is that most evil is done by people who never make up their minds to be good or evil[174]; all that is necessarily for evil to flourish is for good people to stand by and do nothing[175].

The moral collapse of Germany came about through the combined force of composite factors and processes: a.) Christian demonization of the original Germanic culture; b.) mythological distortion and ideological perversion of imaginary (see Box XVIII); c.) nihilism; d.) white racism; e.) German-Nationalistic megalomania; and f.) classical education. For the intensity of these factors and processes, the educated and cultural elites of Germany bear significant responsibilities.

---

[174] Arendt, H. (1981).
[175] Metzner, R. (1994).

Fig. 55. *Ecce homo* by Lovis Corinth (1858-1925; Kunstmuseum Basel). The painting was sold by the Nazi regime as degenerate art to Switzerland. Painted at Easter, the painting is an act of meditation to mark the festival. It shows the moment where Pilate presents Christ to the hostile crowd, just before the crucifixion. Christ has been scourged, bound, and crowned with thorns, and Pilate's words "*Ecce homo*" are quoted from the Vulgate translation (behold, the man). Painted in 1925, Corinth seemingly foresees the devastating times for many individuals who were humiliated and massacred by the hostile brotherhood of oath-breaking doctors and brutal military recruits that so often accompany totalitarian regimes. The painting had to be removed from Germany: it placed a mirror in front of Nazi Germany. Wikimedia Commons.

195

It is widely accepted that Germany's civilization got to the edge of moral collapse because of emphasizing Germanic mythology and the barbaric forces that were set free through this pre-Christian lore. Consequently, it is too dangerous to deal with these evil forces, and thus we should stay with a worldview that rests upon the ideals of Christianity, Renaissance, and humanistic education. Nothing could be more incorrect. In reality, the Third Reich had, so to say, nothing in common with the original Germanic culture (see Box XVII).

## Box XVII: Is Nazi Germany reflecting Germanic values?

Hitler's Germany is frequently assumed as a manifestation of Germanic values. And thus a danger exists that dealing with Germanic mythology and German barbarism may support attitudes that make the world suffer again. This very plausible attitude provides a curse for those that have Germanic culture as their basis and do not support narrow-minded human suppression and racial supremacy goals. In order to improve peace and understanding, their mythology and ethnic heritage should stay neglected and suppressed, many may argue.

However, the assumption that Hitler's Germany is a manifestation of Germanic values is wrong. Hitler was not a new Germanic leader but acted rather like a late Roman emperor. The late Roman Empire was characterized by a number of features shared by Nazi Germany. It had one authoritarian leader (Caesar) and one religion (Christianity). It had a well-run administration, an outstanding infrastructure, and a well-armed and organized army. Like in Nazi Germany, the late Roman Empire had little respect for individual citizens and minorities. It had no political representation of single citizens and no freedom of speech. Nazi Germany offered a lot of entertainment (sport, film, shows, Olympics, etc.). The parallel to using arenas and bread and games of the Roman Empire becomes obvious. And the regime had, of course, no real partnership with women at the utmost periphery of society (*Kinder, Kirche, Küche*, an alliterative German slogan translated as "children, kitchen, church"). The Third Reich did not relate to the old Germanic culture but copied the totalitarian Roman Empire. It had one Führer, one religion, one army, and no respect for ethnic minorities, mental handicaps, and non-Aryans. Women had limited individual rights and became the ultimate birth machines for the new Germany. It mixed Wagnerian scenography and Nietzschian nihilisms and used basic Germanic symbols and terms as camouflage of its anti-Germanic, Roman base. Surprisingly, the Third Reich was the inverse of Germanic culture. Why then reject Germanic mythology because camouflaging symbols were applied by Hitler's Nazi regime? The real Germanic ideals were fanatically rejected because they threatened the Nazi power monopoly. The Germanic *thing*, federal structures, balanced partnerships, and respect for the freedom of thought were unbearable qualities that Nazi Germany supressed by all means. Unless seduced by the splendour of ephemeral decoration, where does the generic idea that Nazi Germany reflected Germanic values derive from? It must be based upon an understandable but highly superficial interpretation of Nazi propaganda. It is in line with the long tradition of rejecting so-called barbarism by Christianity and humanism.

Hitler turned the Ragnarök—in line with nihilism—from the rebirth of the new world into the ultimate downfall from which there is no return. In strict contradiction to the intentions, he interpreted Ragnaröck not as the decline of the old gods or the start of the New Earth, but the end of the world. Germany survived, but the country came very close to the utmost downfall. "When an inner situation is not made conscious, it appears outside as fate," says Jung[176]. Germany met its fate because it was unable to make its inner situation conscious. Following World War II, a culturally and morally raped Germany was left behind, where most mythological, symbolic, and folkloristic values were impossible to apply for decades. Fascist perversion even attacked the basic imaginary of the post-World War II generations (see Box XVIII). For them German mythology and tradition became disgusting and sickening.

With the moral collapse of Germany, the appreciation of the original Germanic culture and mythology hit rock bottom. How could Germans (and others) ever find their way back to their abused roots? How could they omit fate by making the ignored inner situation conscious?

---

[176] C.G. Jung Collected Work 9, 126.

## Box XVIII: Ideological perversion of imaginary

Ideologies are collections of beliefs held by an individual, group, or society considered correct by the majority. They can be described as a set of conscious and unconscious ideas that make up beliefs, goals, expectations, and motivations. Fascistic and communistic ideologies have shaped and influenced not only the 20th century, but also molded the mindset and opinions of those who were young at times when these ideologies were prominent. When these generations turned adult and times changed toward democracy, large portions or at least remnants of these ideologies radiated into the upbringing of forthcoming generations. The effects of communistic and fascistic ideology impose thus a long-lasting effect upon countless European descendants before they—if ever—ebb away.

In the storerooms of European art museums, entire sections are dedicated presently to more or less unacceptable fascist- or communist-influenced imaginary that waits to be displayed in the future. However, fascist posters that were used throughout Europe have already become public on websites[177]. These posters use traditional and archetypical imaginary such as the family, mother and child, St. George, and the virgin and the hero, but pervert them to serve fascist ideological goals. The (holy) family became a depiction of the racially pure, children-rich German family (healthy parents, healthy children). The eternal representations of mother and child (Mary and Jesus) became the blond, German mother with her even blonder child (in support of the National Socialist mother support organization). St. George fighting the dragon turned into an SS soldier killing the Bolshevik Moloch. The timeless hero with his open and fearless gaze became a torch- or (German hand grenade-) bearing young man, with his eyes firmly fixed at the horizon (where is the enemy?).

Exposed to such perverted symbolic settings, many of the younger generation rejected the entire suite of imagery that had influenced

---

[177] http://www.ideologicalart.com/fascism; http://fineartamerica.com/shop/posters/fascist.

their parent's generation, in particular in post-World War II Germany. Typically, they were reluctant to favor national/regional customs, the flag, folk songs, etc. In essence, neutral terms such as folk (*Volk*), homeland (*Heimat*), inferior (*minderwertig*) and leader (*Führer*) can be used in any other language, but not anymore in responsible post-World War II Germany. Thus, not only imagery but also words and terms became unacceptable, suppressed, or rejected. In the name of a better future, humanity, and peaceful international coexistence, parts of national, archetypical, and language background were neglected, demonized, and repressed. The repressive actions were often applauded by the German educated who arrogantly and cowardly went into internal exile in 1933 while a devastating ideology governed the streets for, thanks God, less than a thousand years.

Europeans with a strong fascistic and communistic history probably repress their misused archetypical imaginary. They may become double victims of a.) archetypical desertification that a Latin- and Greek-dominated humanistic education system imposed upon them, and b.) the ideological perversion of imaginary of the totalitarian regimes experienced by their parents and grandparents. Deprived of a harmonious contact with their cultural roots, they can easily be carried into various directions by the winds of the zeitgeist. How can nations overcome the consequences of misuse and forgery of archetypical imaginary for narrow-minded ideological purposes? The abuse endangers the foundation of our psychological and cultural wealth and richness. We should initiate and promote a constructive, more in-depth dialogue on the misuse of archetypical or ideological imaginary. The challenge is to return to an open-minded, fruitful dialogue and a stimulation of the positive, life-supporting aspect of all cultural imaginary.

## 7.7 Germany's post-World War II curse

The misuse during the Nazi regime increased the repression and demonization of Germanic mythology by the educated. The international and even the German cultural influential could triumphantly repeat their tribal shout, "Beware the barbarians!" and "As we said before, Germanic tribes and their mythology result in the downfall of the civilised world." Thus, Germanic mythology after 1945 was of strict academic interest. For the surviving generations, in particular the post-World War II generation and their children, a time of cultural lobotomy began, accompanied by a fundamental sense of shame for the abuse carried out in the name of the nation. Grandparents and parents provided younger generations with heavy, difficult-to-open backpacks of traumatic content that they had not caused but felt responsible for. The highly comprehensible consequence was that the national and Germanic background was at best ignored and most often suppressed. This points to the significance of forgetfulness and remembrance culture, i.e., behavioral configurations and socially approved or acquired manners of a society or group used to keep parts of the past in their consciousness and thus deliberately make it present[178].

National symbols such as today's German flag, reflecting the first democratic union in the St. Paul's church in Frankfurt (1848, see Fig. 52), was privately never flown by any postwar German. It took about 50 years after World War II before Germany had a major debate if that was an acceptable practice. Folk and traditional songs and dances were kept, if at all, alive inside the family, but rarely in public places (except for a few regions with strong traditions). The sagas of heroes and Germanic mythology were not any more the typical literature presented to the young. Even the language changed after the Nazi period. The adjective *völkisch* and arian titles such as Führer and the name Adolf were removed from everyday German life. The so-called 1968 generation unmistakably declared its anti-national attitude and sympathy for internationality. In order to avoid nationalistic pitfalls and favor tolerance and peaceful coexistence, many Germans still support supranational structures such as the United Nations, the European Union and NATO.

---

[178] Assmann, A. (2009).

It is essential to forget, but one needs also a remembrance culture. To forget the mythological basis of culture completely implies cultural lobotomy, with destructive and dangerous consequences. Germanic mythology was not only kept at bay from the public realm after World War II, but the ethnic background of an entire nation was also suppressed. This did not prevent subsequent misuse. To forget is natural (and maybe even necessary). In contrast, to remember demands attention and energy. When challenged with serious experience and assaults and attempts to overcome or live with challenges, a fruitful loop of remembrance and forgetfulness is mandatory, but painful.

## 7.8 Political reradicalization

Germanic-inspired neopagan movements, i.e., new religious movements influenced by or claiming to be derived from the various historical pagan beliefs of pre-modern Europe, have remained active in many countries after 1945[179]. In Germany some of them can be interpreted as a prolongation of the German Faith Movement (see Box XVI). These movements of Asatru followers, often termed Heathenry or Germanic Neopaganism, stayed, for the most, outside mainstream educational and social structures[180]. Lately and often combined with the mass spread of xenophobia, the world experienced anew an embrace of Germanic mythology, this time by pagan racists and Wotanists.

Wotanism is a form of *neo-völkisch* paganism. One branch was founded in the 1990s by David Lane (1938–2007) from the United Kingdom, founder of the white nationalist paramilitary group The Order. Wotanism heavily emphasizes Eurocentrism and National Socialism. We can also find the WOTAN movement, an acronym for Will of the Aryan Nation. Most Wotanists emphasize dualism and view the gods in manners as Jung defined archetypes. Wotanists consider *Hávamál* (Old Norse [sayings of the high one, i.e., Odin]) to be their holiest text (see 6.5.7). The poem, itself a combination of different poems, presents advice for living, proper conduct, and wisdom. In addition to *Hávamál*,

---

[179] Emberland, T. (2003).
[180] Schnurbein, S. v. (2018).

Wotanists and Neo-Nazi groups consider C.G. Jung's essay *Wotan*[181] as a most vital text for the movement. As an example, we mention a most controversial proponent in the Heathen and wider Pagan community, the American Stephen Anthony McNallen (born 1948), founder of the Viking Brotherhood and the Asatru Folk Assembly[182]. His advocacy of right-wing, ethno-nationalistic ideas and his insistence that Heathenry should be reserved for those of Northern European ancestry has resulted in controversy. He launched ideas of paganism, racism, and white supremacy, focussing on Wotan. The script of an influential, demagogic video follows in detail the arguments and elements that C.G. Jung applied in his essay *Wotan*.

There is a plethora of active or former paramilitary groups throughout the world that is inclined to Wotanism, such as Soldiers of Odin in Scandinavia (anti-immigrant street patrol). Among those who pray to Odin, the great father, is also the Norwegian mass murderer Anders Behring Breivik. Jung-inspired Wotanist and neopaganist groups can frequently be encountered in electronic media. They may highlight portraits of C.G. Jung and citations from *Wotan* on their places of honor. In recent decades, Jung's essay has thus become an important element of the reradicalization of racists. Jung (mainly though his essay *Wotan*) plays thus an important role inside these movements. What may be the reason for this?

## 7.9 Jung's ideas about Wotan in a historical perspective

Along with countless contemporaries, Jung felt a certain uneasiness with Christianity that he viewed as an alien cultural branch in Central Europe, grafted upon Germanic roots[183]. He looked out for religiosity that was in line with autochthonous archetypical representations, if acceptable by Christianity or not. Probably inspired by the German Faith Movement and his friend J.W. Hauer (see Box XVI), he seemingly interpreted the political and sociological circumstances in Germany in the 1930s as a

---

[181] Jung, C.G. (1936).
[182] https://en.wikipedia.org/wiki/Asatru_Folk_Assembly.
[183] Noll, R. (1996), Emberland, T. (2003).

new and alternative, collective psycho-spiritual attitude toward religion. He foresaw the birth of a new autochthonous, non-Christian religiosity that rested directly upon Germanic roots[184]. He explained the circumstances of moving people in Germany after World War I (Wandervogel[185], workers, paramilitary troops) as a "regression" toward the wandering and warlike aspect of Wotan. The "wandering" (exodus) of a hundred thousand of intellectuals, let alone Jews, who had understood what the new German era comprised remained uncommented upon in the essay. It was obviously not seen as an aspect of the wandering god. Jung points at that the awakening of Wotan in the 1930s is caused by an "over-civilized" German culture that became defenseless when confronted with ancient, repressed mythical images, the archetypes[186]. Jung not only looked upon the wild and destructive forces of Wotan as a revenge of the nonconscious aspect of a culture but also as an attempt by the culture to create an indispensable equilibrium and balance in reality orientation[187]. According to Jung, individuals, ethnic or religious groups, and nations can become victims for the forces that erupt due to neglected unconscious foundation.

The political realities soon indicated that Jung's vision must have been darkened by wishful thinking. Nazi Germany was not the birth of a new autochthonous, non-Christian religiosity that rested directly upon Germanic roots. As suggested in 7.6 and Box XVII, the Nazi regime represented actually the inverse of the original Germanic values. In Jung's 1945 essay *Nach der Katastrophe*, which had been very difficult for him to write, he dealt out seemingly little coordinated defensive blows into all directions[188]. The essay can be understood as an indirect confrontation with his personal involvement with Nazi Germany and his unwise interpretation of the German circumstances between World War I and World War II. It also launched the vividly discussed concept of German'y collective guilt. However, Jung did not admit explicitly that his

---

[184] Dohe, C.B. (2016).
[185] Wandervogel is the name adopted by a popular movement of German youth groups from 1896 onward; https://en.wikipedia.org/wiki/Wandervogel.
[186] Pollan, B. (2000); Stevens, A. (2012).
[187] Dohe, C.B. (2016).
[188] Jung, C.G. (1945).

wishful thinking regarding the birth of a new autochthonous, non-Christian religiosity had misled him to interpret the zeitgeist of post-World War I Germany. Had Jung had the courage and stamina to admit in public *"ich bin ausgerutscht"* (I slipped) as he admitted for Gershom Scholem,[189] much of the recent misuse of Jung by neopaganists would have been prevented. As a consequence, the essay *Wotan* (republished both in German and English after World War II and thus assumed of generic, everlasting significance) gleams in sparkling vagueness[190] and can still be fully applied and cited by neopaganist and fascists in support of their intolerant goals.

Thus, besides D. Lane and S. McNallen, C.G. Jung belongs surprisingly to the heroes of the Wotanist and many other movements of Germanic neopaganism with racial undercurrents. When one's focus is rather upon the world of classical culture and refinement, it is indeed easy to overlook how strongly Jung's essay *Wotan* supports today's neopaganism and fascism. However, a careful, updated, and dedicated observer cannot overlook the misuse of Jung's teachings and how he legitimated this misuse by republishing *Wotan* after World War II[191]. Without any prejudice, any modern education has to honor and reflect, support and amplify the cultural nature of all humans. Thus, illuminating our cultural shadow necessarily has to be a momentous element of education and in particular that of psychoanalytic self-analysis. Jungian education is in conspicuous contradiction of the application of Jung's essay by the neopaganists. This disagreement should be highlighted in Jungian institutions in order to make it perfectly clear that analytical psychology cannot be exploited for right-wing and white supremacy goals.

---

[189] Jaffé A. (1968).

[190] Rasche, J. (2012).

[191] In the English translation by his close collaborator Barbara Hannah, the central term and religious term *Ergriffenheit* is translated with the psychiatric term "being possessed." Spirit possession is a term for the belief that demons, gods, or spirits can take control of a human body (or a nation). In the English version of the essay and 10 years after publishing it for the first time, Jung changes a main point of the essay without any comment.

## 7.10 Conclusion

Since the arrival of the Germanic tribes in Central Europe, the representations of original Germanic mythology were first neglected, then demonised, and finally repulsed and repressed. Among the contemporaneous terms and ideas on Germanic culture and mythology, we find a multitude of ostracizing applications. For many, Odin/Wotan is only the ultimate and exclusive warlord. These are at best misconceptions but most likely straightforward blackmails of an entire sector of European culture. The attitude supports a cultural autocracy against assumed unfavorable cultures that characterized mainstream European culture from Roman and Christian times onward. The archetypical representations of original Germanic culture are in good company with the majority of European archetypical representations, such as the Slavic, Celtic, and Finno-Ugrian ones. The educated who consider themselves supporters of classical culture seemingly take the lead in this repressive and autocratic work. It is commonly assumed that repression causes mental illness in an individual. However, the same principle may also be applied to the repression of ethnic groups and cultures. In chapter 8, we investigate more closely the cause for this behavior, which continuously endangers peaceful co-existence.

*Stetind i tåke* (*Stedtind in Fog*) by Peder Balke (1804-1887, National Gallery, Oslo). Balke's oeuvre is today regarded as highly innovative, a forerunner of modernism. Brusque, confronting, and uninviting, the mountain surmounts its surrounding country. The repellent, towering and unattainable characteristics of the mountain can be seen as a symbol for cultural superiority and the ostracizing attitude that is the natural companion of human cultures. Shrouded by fog, we enjoy our self-imposed superiority and reject other haughty, assumed primitive, or even barbaric cultures. Could we define our culture as being more encompassing and having interactive manners? Copyright: National Gallery of Norway, Oslo.

# 8. Cultural Superiority by Ostracizing

*An individual's shadow is invariably bound up with the collective shadow of his group, and as he digests his own evil, a fragment of the collective evil is invariably co-digested at the same time.*

E. Neumann

*Freedom is what you do with what has been done to you.*

J.P. Satre

Ostracism (from Greek *ostrakismos*) was a procedure under the Athenian democracy in which any citizen could be expelled from the city-state of Athens. Ostracizing comprises any act or acts of ignoring and excluding an individual or groups. This could include social shunning, cultural sanctions, religious alienation and straightforward discrimination. Ostracizing is a convenient tool to claim or maintain cultural superiority and is executed by all nations and ethnic and religious groups. Here we focus primarily upon how the Germanic tribes and Germany were exposed to ostracizing, but the chapter also exemplifies the general principle of how to become seemingly culturally superior by ostracizing an assumed inferior culture. For simplicity, the chapter for the most part addresses the tradition of how Germanic people get ostracized. Obviously, also the opposite takes place.

## 8.1 Going berserk, vandalism and Vikings

The berserkers were not just seized and shape-shifting killers, but elite soldiers, similar to how they exist in any type of army (see Box XIX; Fig. 25). If so ordinary and universal, who then invented the widely used expression "to go berserk" (to erupt in furious rage, become crazily violent)? In modern times and to characterize persons who are destructively or frantically violent, the term berserker was first recorded in English literature in the early 19th century. However, erupting in furious rage is recurrent and widespread in humans. Why were the berserker war bands selected for this generic expression to erupt in furious rage? Why were not any other suitable, crazily violent groups selected? Any country has a suite of candidates. How was "going berserk" expressed in English before the 19th century?

## Box XIX: What is so special about the berserkers?

Berserkers (or berserks) were Norse warrier who are primarily reported in the Old Norse literature to have fought in a nearly uncontrollable, trancelike fury. This characteristic gave later support to the English expression to go berserk (see chapter 8.1). These champions would often go into battle without fighter's coats, wearing only animal skins (Fig. 25). The correct pronunciation of the term is *bér-serks*. It derives from *bérserkir* (Old Norse bear-shirts). During the Norse period "warrior-shamans" typically fell into two groups: *bérserkir* and *ulfhethnar* (Old Norse for wolf-hides). *Berserkers* and *ulfhethnars* are attested in numerous Old Norse and Anglo-Saxon sources. Some warriors also identified with boars (Fig. 25; see also the battle formation *svinfylking*)[192].

The phenomenon of *bérserkir* and *ulfhethnar* belongs to the concept of shape shifting (or metamorphosis), which is the ability of a being or creature to completely transform its physical form or shape (Fig.

---

[192] The *Svinfylking*, Old Norse for "swine array" or "boar snout," was a version of the wedge formation used in Iron Age Scandinavia by the Vikings. Its invention was attributed to the god Odin.

25). This is usually achieved through an inherent ability of a mythological creature, divine intervention, or the use of magic. The idea of shape shifting is present in the oldest forms of totemism and shamanism. The idea persisted through the Middle Ages, when the agency causing shape shifting was usually a sorcerer or witch, and into the modern period. Shape shifting remains a common trope in modern fantasy, children's literature, and works of popular culture. The most common form of shape-shifting myths is that of therianthropy (from Greek *theríon*, meaning wild animal [implicitly mammalian] and *anthrōpos*, meaning human being), which is the transformation of a human being into an animal or conversely, of an animal into human form (e.g., the werewolf [the first element has usually been identified with Old English *wer* = man] (see Scandinavian *verden* [world], i.e. man-wolf).

A most common form for all warriors to prepare for battle and survive is the attainment of ecstatic battle-fury. In the case of the Germanic tribes, this fury was closely linked to particular totem animals, usually a bear, a wolf, or a boar, and often occurring within the context of certain military groups. These groups were part of Germanic clan war bands and share much in common with the warlike shamanism of other circumpolar peoples.

A *berserk* in today's language is a person who is destructively or frenetically violent. But the real *berserks* were just Odin's elite soldiers who had trained their ecstatic battle-fury and who would, if dying in battle, become Odin's selected troops, the *einherjer* (Old Norse single fighters, those who fight alone). The *einherjer* are those who died in battle and were brought to Valhalla by *valkyries*. In Valhalla, the *einherjer* eat their fill of the nightly resurrecting hog Sæhrímnir ("sooty sea-beast") . The *valkyries* also bring their fill of mead (from the udder of the goat Heithrún). The *einherjer* prepare daily for the events of Ragnarök, when they will advance for an immense battle, which the *ein* (here meaning single-time) refers to. Berserkers are thus elite soldiers, as so many former (such as Roman soldiers, Crusaders, the famous Swiss mercenaries) and contemporary fighting clans (such as Japanese kamikaze, German Waffen SS, Russian Spetsnaz or British Special Air Service). Berserks play no major role in Norse mythology. In a standard Norwegian text on mythology, we find only one page out of 350 dedicated to berserks[193]. Many seem to be attracted/threatened by *berserks*, probably because of reading books such as *Wodan und der germanische Schicksals-glaube* by Martin Ninck[194]. Ninck focused strongly upon the ecstatic qualities of Wotan and thus provides a lot of space to the berserks. Ninck seems to be influenced by the demagogic spirit of the *völkisch* movement and a focus upon *Männerbünde*,[195] which haunted Germany in the 1930s (see Box VII). From a modern perspective Ninck's book and others reflect the unbalanced and tendentious spirit of the 1930s and should not be used anymore as a principal reference. In total, the emphasis that in some circles is provided to berserks appears to be so biased that the questions arises, Why this is so? Potential answers are provided in chapter 8.

Another negative term derived from the Germanic realm is the expression vandalism (the deliberate destruction of or damage to public or private property). The term is based upon the east Germanic tribe the Vandals (Fig. 56). The French bishop Henri-Baptiste Grégoire (1750-1831) introduced the term in 1794 to characterize the senseless destruction of art by radical Jacobins. Iconoclasm, an act performed by those who destroy religious images, is a universal phenomenon that can be identified in all countries. Grégoire could have selected the term "Jacobinism" in French but rather selected the name from a neighboring country. The Van dals did not execute more violence than other groups. How was vandalism expressed before the French Revolution?

In public opinion and literature, Vikings were Norse seafarers who raided and traded from their Northern European homelands across wide areas of Northern, Central, and Eastern Europe, during the late eighth to the late 11th centuries[196]. The term is also commonly extended in modern English and other vernaculars to the inhabitants of Viking home

---

[193] Steinsland, G. (2005).
[194] Ninck, M. (1935).
[195] An organization that requires its members to conceal certain activities, such as its rites of initiation, from outsiders, see *Hasenfratz*, H.-P. (1992).
[196] Winroth, A. (2012, 2014).

Fig. 56. *Sacking of Rome* by Karl Pavlovich Briullov (original name Charles Bruleau; 1799-1852; Tretyakov Gallery, Moscow). Between 390 and 1870 Rome, the cradle of modern culture, was sacked seven times by barbaric hordes. The term vandalism derives from the sack ordered by the Vandal leader Genseric in 455 (third sack on ancient Rome) who was then at war with the usurping Emperor Petronius Maximus. While Genseric kept his promise not to burn the city and slaughter its inhabitants, he did carry off some to be slaves. It is accepted that Genseric looted great amounts of treasure from the city, damaging objects of cultural significance, but he did nothing worse than other groups that sacked Rome. The Vandals did not bring the culture of Rome to an end. Wikimedia Commons.

communities during what has become known as the Viking Age. This period of Nordic military, mercantile, and demographic expansion constitutes an important element in the early medieval history of Scandinavia, Estonia, the British Isles, France, Sicily, Ukraine, and Russia.

In the written Norse sources, the word Viking is a.) neutral when it comes to ethnicity; b.) often used for non-Scandinavians; and c.) means pirate[197]. Scandinavians of these days did not consider themselves

---

[197] Winroth (2012).

Vikings. In fact, they fought against Vikings (pirates), alongside with other groups in Europe. The Norse verbal expression "to go in Viking," i.e. the endeavors of small fractions of the Norse population that carried out raids, means pirating. It was these scattered pirate groups, exaggerated by clergy reports, that provided the term for the so-called Viking time (see Box XX). This period was much more known for Norse cultural, mercantile, and demographic expansion than pirating. The term Viking is thus a xenonym for the Scandinavians during the age who have risen to the term Viking Age. It ostracizes an entire population that had pagan convictions as pirates. The term Viking Age obtains thus its essence from the pirating activity during these days that also included non-Scandinavians. It is not a balanced and representative term, a but deeply entrenched term. The term Viking stigmatizes the Norse populations, comprising the essence of northern barbarianism[198] (Fig. 57). The term Viking ostracizes the Norse population, provides arguments for Christianization and centralistic control through kingdoms. Consequently, in this book the term Viking is only rarely utilized. Rather the more appropriate term Norse or Norsemen is applied.

## Box XX: Two worldviews of the dragon

A dragon (from Latin *draco* and Greek *drákōn*, serpent of huge size, water snake) is a legendary creature. It features in the myths of many cultures around the world. It is typically scaled, fire spewing, and has serpentine, reptilian or avian traits. The European dragon derived from European folk traditions and is ultimately related to Western Asian mythologies. Most dragons are depicted as reptilian creatures with animal-level intelligence and are uniquely six-limbed (four legs and a separate set of wings). In the book *Norske natur-mytologier: fra Edda til økofilosofi* (*Norwegian Nature Mythologies: From the Eddas to Ecophilosophy*)[199] and inside the European

---

[198] Similarly, all Western and Central Europeans could be called Crusaders, based upon the various Crusades.
[199] Witoszek, N. (1998).

tradition, Nina Witoszek describes two different type of dragons: those of the Christian and the Norse tradition.

After the Fall of Man, nature became sinful. Nature's sinfulness became a bearing element of Christian belief. In the Revelation of John, the dragon, the epitome of Christianity's *bêtes noire*, represents the messenger of Satan. Or he is characterized as the devil at the ports of hell or the demon himself (demon derives from Greek *daimōn* [god, godlike, power, fate], implying that Christianity "demonized" the original term to an evil spirit or devil). More than 70 saints of the Roman Catholic Church have in one or other form won over the dragon with its animalistic power and the danger of sins. At times when the orginal Germanic culture was still prominent in Northern Europe and the advent of Christianity, this view was clearly reflected in the epos *Beowulf* (see 3.3) and stave churches (e.g. Fig. 9). Here the dragon pays a central role. For the monks and clergymen of the British Isles, the dragon represented the devil and approaching hell. And indeed, fire-spewing dragons flying through the skies and intimidating serpents undulating through the ocean were observed by them in abundance. When Beowulf defeats the dragon, culture wins over nature: Confronted with beastly powers, the Christian hero wins.

In the heroic poem *Favnesmal* of the *Elder Edda*, one of the sources of the Siegfried legend, a very different, almost opposite, view is presented. The dragon's blood contains unique powers, and he is greeted with respect. Siegfried obtains words of wisdom from the dragon before he eats its heart. In Wagner's opera *Siegfried*, the dragon's blood allows Siegfried to understand the language of the forest birds, i.e., he is initiated into nature's mysteries. The dragon opens thus a direct lineage to nature and its wisdom. The saga reflects a confrontation between equal entities; it is not about the conquering and subjection of evil nature. In the Norse world, the dragon is a highly respected animal that encompasses the rhythmic powers of nature and the cosmos.

When in 793 a Viking raid on Lindisfarne gave the starting signal for the Viking Age, one may imagine what impression the wildly fighting Norse using ships adorned with dragonheads imposed upon the monks when they came ashore. For the monks, the scenario resembled the arrival of hell's evil flocks en route to exterminate Christianity, i.e., culture. The raid on Lindisfarne and other attacks and sackings were a veritable shock for the monks and clergyman, but it actually represented the confrontation between Christianity's hatred and condemnation of nature versus people that felt they were part of nature and had a holistic nature view. The shocking confrontation has contributed to the strong repulsion of pagan Germanic culture by Christianity and nourished the prejudices against the Vikings that have radiated for more than 1,000 years into modern times.

The Norse people combined Christianity and Germanic paganism with effortless ease. Crosses and dragons, side by side, find their place jointly in ornaments and decoration of stave churches, some of them with mighty dragons looming into the skies and around ports (Fig. 9). Christian Norse churches blend sets of seemingly impossible domains that most Christians were unable to accept. Similar to the settlement between the traditionally incompatible gods such as the patriarchal Aesir and matricentric Vanir, the Norse world manages to combine Christianity with a holistic and mystic view on nature. The demons remained daimons, nature and nurture were not exclusive entities, and the old nature religion did not challenge a Christian worldview: cross and dragon in harmony. Despite the fact that Christianity has sucessfully preached the lore of Norse and Viking brutality and wildness, the leitmotif of these barbarians was peaceful coexistance and tolerance, qulities that had to be instilled by Europeans through vigorous struggles with Christianity and those that had power.

When we today turn our minds to a sustainable worldview, based upon our irrevocable knowledge of the limits of growth, ecophilosophy[200], which is a union of philosophy and ecology, may provide an answer. Arne Næss writes: "By an ecosophy I mean a philosophy of ecological harmony or equilibrium. ... Wisdom is policy wisdom, prescription, not only scientific description and prediction. The details of an ecosophy will show many variations due to significant differences concerning not only the 'facts' of pollution, resources, population, etc. but also value priorities."[201] Næss felt that philosophy would provide the wisdom to guide the actions necessary to prevent imminent ecological catastrophes. On this background we may also consider revising our vision of the Viking Age and Norse people. As mentioned before, the barbarian Norse people were modern and supported a balanced worldview but became overpowered by nature-despising Christianity. The Christian preoccupation regarding the sinfulness of nature has contributed significantly to man's devastating exploitation of nature and carries thus a significant responsibility for the gloomy prospects for man's ecological future. How can we overcome the subversive attitude regarding nature that Christianity imposed upon us in the name of civilization and culture, an attitude that threatens to break humanity's neck? Again, the despised and demonized barbarians may help to overcome today's suicidal culture. What is most modern in our time frequently turns out to be the most archaic, says G. Davenport. Are we able to take the consequences, or is our culture with its foundation in Christianity so entrenched that we would rather risk the sustainability of the world than accept the culture of the barbarians?

---

[200] Coined by the Norwegian father of deep ecology, Arne Næss, and French post-Marxist philosopher and psychoanalyst Félix Guattari.
[201] Drengson, A., Inoue, Y. (1995).

Fig. 57. Illustration of Vikings going ashore in North America by an unknown artist. It is found in *The Story of the United States* (1919) by Henrietta Elizabeth Marshall (1876-1941), a British author, particularly well-known for her works of popular national history for children. All the 18th century paraphernalia of a Viking are present. It looks as if Odin himself conquers the new continent, supported by a ship, his men, and accompanied by flocks of gulls. Wikimedia Commons.

Today, the term Viking is frequently applied casually to descendants and inhabitants of modern Scandinavia. Popular conceptions of the Vikings often differ strongly from the complex picture that emerges from archaeology and historical sources[202]. A romanticized picture of Vikings as noble savages began to emerge in the 18th century, developed and became widely propagated during the 19th century Viking revival (Fig. 57). Perceived views of the Vikings as alternatively violent, piratical heathens or as intrepid adventurers owe much to conflicting varieties of the modern Viking myth that had taken shape by the early 20th century. Current popular representations of the Vikings are typically based on cultural clichés and stereotypes, complicating modern appreciation of the Viking legacy (see the art of G. Malmström and C.E. Doeplers, see 7.4). The modern use of the term Viking is neither directly derogatory nor positive but rather a mixed blessing that throughout the world enjoys a compelling fascination. By applying the ostracizing terms berserk, vandalism, and Viking, the self-proclaimed civilized remain cultivated and do not have to confront themselves with negative aspects of their culture.

## 8.2 Gothic

An additional derogatory term associated with Germanic tribes is Gothic. Giorgio Vasari used the term "barbaric German style" in his famous book *Lives of the Artists*[203] to describe what is now (and only since the Renaissance) considered the Gothic style (Fig. 58). In the introduction to his famous book, he attributes various architectural features to the Goths, whom he holds responsible for destroying the ancient buildings after they conquered Rome. What is now termed Gothic script (also known as blackletter, Gothic minuscule, or Textura) was the universal, Latin-based script used throughout Western Europe from approximately 1150 to well into the 17th century. It continued to be used in German in various blackletter typefaces until the early 20th century. In line with the

---

[202] Langer (2002).
[203] Vasari, G. (1995).

Fig. 58. *Dom im Winter* (*Cathedral in Winter*) by Ernst Ferdinand Oehme (1797-1855; Gallerie Neue Meister, Dresden). Oehme was a German Romantic painter and illustrator who specialized in moody landscapes with architectural elements. Here he encapsulates the specific verticality and darker, solemn qualities of the Gothic style. Over time, God was experienced farther and farther away, leaving isolated humans on a frosty earth that had to strive more and more to achieve God's mercy. But in the inner world, light perpetually shines, and a candlelit altar awaits the believer on earth. The reality is not the outer, but the inner world. Wikimedia Commons.

Renaissance, the rest of Western Europe switched over to the "more civilized" Latin letters. As a consequence, older German books appear difficult to read, weird, and old-fashioned, but Gothic script is neither a particular Germanic nor German phenomenon. What might have been the reason to name black letters as Gothic script and connect them to the Goths (who had a completely different alphabet)?

In English, Gothic is a term generally used in relation to the macabre or other darker elements (Fig. 58). Gothic is the term for a movement in literature usually revolving around the darker elements of human nature. Today's term Gothic fiction began as a sophisticated joke. Horace Walpole (1717-1797) first applied the word "Gothic" to the novel *The Castle of Otranto* (1764), subtitled *A Gothic Story*. When Walpole used the word, it meant something like "barbarous," as well as "deriving from the Middle Ages." This tradition is continued in the popular genre of Gothic comics. The macabre or other darker elements are also a stereotype encompassing some of the younger generations who identify themselves by an immense use of black, vampires, blood, anarchy symbols, and heavy metal music (preferably with Norse gods and lyrics!). Today's application of the term Gothic has neither anything to do with the Gothic language nor the tribes of the Goths. Why were the Goths selected to express something dark and medieval? Were there no alternatives? Much of the application of the term Gothic is derogatory and ostracizing.

## 8.3 An odyssey of how Germany and Germans are named

Because of Germany's geographic position in the center of Europe, as well as its long history as a non united nation of distinct regions and smaller, feudalistic states, there exist many widely varying names of Germany and Germans. For example, in German, Scandinavian, Finnish, French, Spanish, Italian, Polish, and Dutch, the country is known as Deutschland, Tyskland, Saksa, Allemagne, Alemania, Germania, Niemcy, and Duitsland, respectively. The names Deutschland/Tyskland/Duitsland derive from Latin *theodiscus* or Old High German *diutisc* (which originally meant "popular, of the people," i.e., an expression of the mixture of tribes in Central Europe after the Migration Period). It is based upon a significant principle of the Germanic tribes: federalism. Germany comes from Latin *germania*. Allemagne and Alemania derive from the Alemann tribe[204]. Saksa is derived from the Saxon tribes. Niemcy (or Německo, nemetskiy, etc.) derives from the Protoslavic *\*nemc*. The Slavic *nemets* or *nemtsy* means "a foreigner." It literally means "a mute" but came to signify "those who can't speak like us."[205] According to a theory, early Slavs would call themselves the speaking people, as opposed to their Germanic neighbors, the "mutes." In Serbian/Croatian, a German can be called *Svabo/Svaba* (often with deprecatory connotations), derived from Swabian Balkan immigrants to Banat and Vojvodina. In Romanian, there exist the terms *Svabi* and *Germani basarabeni* for German immigrants to Transylvania and Bessarabia (Moldova), respectively.

In addition, a plethora of additional names for Germany/Germans exists. In the medieval Hebrew language, Germans could be called *Ashkenaz* (*Ashkenaz* is thought to be the ancestor of the Germans); in medieval Latin they could be called *Teutons* (*Teutonia, regnum Teutonicum*—after the Teutons); and in medieval Greek, they were *Frángoi* or *frangikós* (Germans, German)—after the Franks. In the Lower Sorbian language,[206] they could be called *bawory* (from the name of the Bavarian tribe). Finally, in Old Norse, Germany is called the clearly neutral *Suðrvegr* (literally "south way," opposite to *Norðrvegr,* "north way"). Obviously, the Germans invited characterization by xenonyms, some of them with tendentious adverse connotations.

Linguistic challenges exist in English when the terms Germanic tribes, Germany and German are applied. For example, it is not easy to apply an exact terminology in English when it comes to the Latin term *germania*, i.e., the region where the Germanic tribes lived (which includes most of today's Great Britain). The same is true for the Latin term *germani*, i.e., the various Germanic tribes (to which most of the British belong). In other languages this is uncomplicated and straightforward: They have a term for *germania* and *germani*, while

---

[204] The southern Germanic Alemanni are a Suebic tribe or confederation in today's Alsace, parts of Baden-Württemberg and Switzerland. Aleman means either "all men" or derives from Latin *alius* (the other).

[205] Take note of the similarities with the Greek term barbarous.

[206] The Sorbian languages are West Slavic languages spoken by the Sorbs, a West Slavic minority in the Lusatia region of eastern Germany.

English has changed these two terms to characterize Germany and its citizens. What was the reason that English reduced the encompassing Latin *germania* and *germani* to what is today called Germany and Germans? In the Middle Ages, the eastern region beyond the English Channel was called Dutchland, directly derived from *diutisc* and very close to Deutschland. After some time the term was reduced to what is now called The Netherlands and Flanders. The people living there were called Dutch[207]. The application of the terms *germani* and *germania* (the people and the region beyond Dutchland) reflects a trend that falls into the time when Great Britain ascended to become a world power, i.e., about 250 years ago. This is a period when Europe looked with apprehension at the post-Thirty Years' War setting in Central Europe and the endeavors of the divided German people to become unified into a national state. It is the first time the terms Germany and German obtained today's meaning in English. Before then, regional geographic and national terms were applied (e.g., Prussia, Bavaria, Hanover, Saxonia, Westphalia, etc). From 1871 and beyond, the original meaning of *germania* and *germani* was narrowed down to the people living in the new German national state. Germany also became the place where the Germanic barbarians were to be found. Due to this linguistic maneuver, the British acquitted themselves from their barbarian Germanic past. Were the terms Germany and Germans used to ostracize and to make sure that the inhabitants of Great Britain, strongly dominated by Germanic roots (Angles, Jutes, Saxons, Scots, Danelaw), could be considered more civilized than their ethnic relatives on the continent?

English literature often wrongly translates the term Germanic with Teutonic. For example, Grimm's and other epochal works are not translated German, but Teutonic, mythology[208]. Could this be due to a mix-up of the term Teuton with Deutsch? Deutsch (see above) derives from the Germanic word *diutisc* (belonging to the people) and *thioda* (Volk). The Teutons (Latin: Teutones, Teutoni) were either a Germanic or Celtic tribe. Teutonic mythology does not signify the mythology of the Teutons, which we do not know and which may not even be a Germanic

---

[207] Janson, T. (2017).
[208] Grimm, J. (1835); New Larousse Encyclopaedia of Mythology (1959).

tribe. Compared to Germanic, the term Teutonic may sound more barbaric, and that may be part of the reason for the mix-up of terms.

## 8.4 Conclusion

The leitmotif for the applications of unfavourable expressions and terms for ethnicity appears to be the desire to support or prove cultural superiority. The generic technique applied is ostracizing. Keeping nondesirable qualities at bay may be the reason that terms from the original Germanic culture were selected to describe destructive behavior, blind violence, and assumed (medieval) darkness. "It is they, not us that have barbarian qualities" could be the motivation for applying negative terms and expression involving disliked ethnicities. Those who consider themselves culturally superior banish undesirable features to cover up for their own flaws and cultural inadequacies.

The demonization of Germanic tribes, their mythology, and qualities creates challenges for Germanic descendants: Who wants to be embedded in a culture impacted by a primitive background? As a response, both nations of Germanic origin (or with a strong Germanic influence) and in particular German citizens may feel alienated and disassociated from their historic heritage. In psychology, the term dissociation describes a wide array of experiences, from mild detachment from the immediate surroundings to more severe disengagement from physical and emotional experience. The generic characteristic of alienation and dissociation phenomena involves an uncoupling from reality. Any alienation and disassociation will provide psychological challenges on a personal, national, and cultural level. It prevents the integration of the shadow and opens the door for unconscious constructs that darken our times.

In general, ostracism is the widespread activity of social and cultural rejection. We feel better when those who have attitudes or cultural traditions that challenge our self-image get ostracized and thus expelled from our good company. We all are familiar with a technique that has been applied for thousands of years[209]. In times of large-scale migration, worldwide traveling,

---

[209] "Why do you look at the speck of sawdust in your brother's eye and pay no attention to the plank in your own eye?" Matthew 7:3.

and global economy, it may be appropriate to focus increasingly upon this technique. Can we disperse these prejudices in order to promote a peaceful and inspiring coexistence of cultures and nations? To be seen as an individual and with a specific ethnic background is a precondition for any fruitful conversation. This is even more important for a client in analysis. To really know and accept one's cultural background and to limit ostracizing associations are essential elements of security and respect that each human may claim. Believing in freedom requires an open mind. One has also to tolerate and pardon the unfortunate ostracizing that nations and ethnic groups commit: Retaliation should be omitted. Freedom is what you do with what has been done to you, i.e., that you forgive and excuse.

*Blick auf Schloss Pillnitz* (*View of Pillnitz Castle*) by Johann Christian Clausen Dahl (1788-1857, Folkwang Museum, Essen). The imaginative window prospect, looking onto the castle outside, is from the painters studio (or his inner self?). The expansive landscape gets mirrored in the glass of the panes inside his studio (and our memory). If we wish to study the unknown world outside, we have to frame, open the psychological windows and the world is immediately reflected in the panes of our soul. We obtain a view, a perspective. Achieving a relationship to our Germanic archetypes starts by opening up our inner windows, study the reflections in ourselves and then reaching out. All cultures need visions of unknown territories and fresh air. Copyright: Museum Folkwang Essen/ARTOTHEK.

# 9. How can we Reach an Adequate and Recuperative Relationship to Germanic Archetypes?

*True ignorance is not the absence of knowledge, but the refusal to acquire it.*

K. Popper

*The reason for evil in the world is that people are not able to tell their stories.*

C.G. Jung

The lack of congruence between our ideal and realized self creates complications for those majority Europeans who do not enjoy the approval of their ethnic and cultural background by the cultural influencers. The dearth of supportive and constructive relationships regarding Germanic archetypes may give rise to weakened identities and possibilities to get overwhelmed by suppressed elements from the unconscious. Can we overcome the negative aspects of Roman-Christian culture and humanistic education and relieve the discomfort of Germanic cultural self-amputation? Many have, without being aware of it, voluntarily imposed cultural suppression upon themselves and others. Who has no opinion about barbarian conduct, but maybe it is only barbarian because we decided so? For a debate of the clash between Christian culture and Germanic barbarism and the underlying dynamics, see Box XX.

Fig. 59. Through the nightly skies of our dreams, an entire plethora of stars shines upon humanity. These stars and star signs resemble humanity's archetypes. They tell us stories we call dreams. Can we decipher the star signs of archetypes of the various cultures and do we understand the stories they tell us? Our recognition of humanity's culture heritage and the atmosphere of "being at home" depends upon literacy, the ability to recognize the shadows of the ideas, the archetypes. Photography: Rudi Caeyers/UiT The Arctic University of Norway.

Various forms of cultural lobotomy may result in cultural and political malfunction, complications, and harmful recoils and knock-backs. Once we comprehend that cultural suppression of a European majority is rather a curse than a blessing, we can take steps to reverse the development and relieve the suppressed. We may tell our stories and prevent the spread of evil. We can let the archetypical material work for us personally, and the cure and development of our ethnic group and nation. By selecting a dynamic and inviting attitude to cultural arche-types, whatever they may be, we support self-realization. Inspired by humanity′s archetypical fixed stars, the psyche acquires images and stories while we dream. By recognizing the archetypical fixed stars of Germanic mythology across the expanse of the nightly dream sky (Fig. 59) and by understanding more of the narratives, we will improve our psychological orientation, feel more "at home" in the world. We then need less impetus to ostracize other cultures, we may open our door for the world outside (see page 224) and welcome the dawn of a new time (Fig. 65).

## 9.1 European cultural literacy

A balanced evaluation of the various European culture branches may be a first step to improve our cultural literacy (see the Indo-European language tree, Fig. 1). To get acquainted with the original Germanic culture and mythology, we could start to read the *Edda* and some of the sagas. That may already lift some of the fog of our self-imposed ignorance and repression. Indeed, both *Eddas* ought to find a natural place in a set of basic books that should be found on the shelves of those who wish to know what the term European culture truly comprises. If we neither find nor read basic books of the Slavic, Germanic, Celtic, and Finno-Ugric "bedrock" knowledge, we neglect the existence of a majority of the European cultural heritage and we are thus culturally not true Europeans (see chapter 1). The definition European and European values may have to be revised in view of large-scale cultural suppression.

Some, if not the majority, may mention that what is not based upon Roman, Greek, Christian, or humanistic culture is primitive and archaic. This is a self-fulfilling prophecy of Europe's intellectual gentry that makes us drift toward ostracism, cultural conservatisms, and away from an open society and modernity. What is most modern in our time frequently turns out to be the most archaic[210] (see page 52). To be really modern implies that we ramp up our cultural knowledge with the suppressed archaic. The primitive and the archaic may scare us, but both provide essential realism to our souls. They are the indispensable nourishment for our individuation voyage. Individuation is not a smooth pathway with elite-approved literature, remote religions that do not interfere with our daily lives, dreams, and fascinating symbols, but often a brutal exposure to local forces and demons in our psyche. It is a fearful thing to fall into the hands of a (the) living God[211]. Our lack of training in encountering the plethora of unknown and demonized European gods and goddesses increases our fears. We should have full empathy for those who get exposed to the archaic and experience of god(s).

---

[210] Davenport, G. (1981).
[211] Hebrews 10:31.

We may accuse Roman-, Greek-, or Christian-based culture and humanistic education for disregarding Germanic mythology, but, according to Karl Popper (1902-1994), true ignorance is the refusal of knowledge. Living in freedom, as most of us do in Europe, we must ask if the suppression of the Germanic (or any other suppressed) archaic is unavoidable or actively pursued by us? Most of us contribute daily to the suppression processes that banned Germanic mythology into the psychological dungeons of the sub- and unconsciousness. We are actively refusing knowledge because we consider it dangerous and barbarous. Europe's recent history supports this process. The historic development took place and was shaped with the acceptance, tolerance and/or ignorance of fascist and communistic states by many of the educated. Current education and culture only partly supports our individuation journey. Both may continue to alienate us from our roots. They prevent us to get acquainted with our primordial core. They contribute to and may increase the darkness of our shadow. European literacy is far more limited compared to what it could and should be.

## 9.2 The shadow of European culture and education

We have to address a most significant concept of analytical psychology, the concept of the shadow[212]. Whenever light shines upon us, we cast a shadow. According to Jung, the shadow is the unknown, dark side of our personality. In Jungian psychology, the shadow may refer to an unconscious aspect of the personality that the conscious ego does not identify. Because one tends to reject or remain ignorant of the least desirable aspects of one's personality, the shadow is largely negative. The shadow may also refer to the entirety of the unconscious, i.e., everything of which a person is not fully conscious. "Everyone carries a shadow," Jung wrote, "and the less it is embodied in the individual's conscious life, the blacker and denser it is."[213] According to Jung, the shadow, being instinctive and irrational, is prone to psychological projection, in which

---

[212] E.g. Casement, A. (2012).
[213] Jung, C.G. (1938). "Psychology and Religion" In CW 11: Psychology and Religion: West and East. p. 131.

a perceived personal inferiority is recognized as a perceived moral deficiency in someone else. These projections isolate and harm individuals by acting as a constantly thickening veil of illusion between the ego and the real world. Our inferiority complex regarding the archaic nature of the majority of European cultures may be reflected in projections that are perceived as moral deficiencies these cultures. This reasoning suggests that ostracism may be a projection of the shadow.

Jung also believed that "in spite of its function as a reservoir for human darkness—or perhaps because of this—the shadow is the seat of creativity."[214] The shadow may be the dark and sinister side of our being, but it may also represent a true spirit of life (see the painting opening the prologue). Dealing with the shadow thus implies two basically opposite processes. We may either get exposed to a merger with our shadow that consequently overwhelms us. Or we may accept our shadow and continuously watch out for its assimilation. The latter should be the *ora et labora*[215] of our daily life. 'The integration of the shadow, or the realisation of the personal unconscious, marks the first stage of the analytic process," writes Jung[216] (Fig. 60). And we may add that this seems not only to be valid for individuals, but also for ethnic and religious groups and the nation each individual belongs to.

For many Europeans, the neglect, demonization, and repression of original Germanic mythology contributes a major fraction of the shadow that they cast, either as a person, a group, or society. A merger with the shadow is what we should be or are afraid of. An acceptance of the shadow and continuously watch out for it is our constructive alternative. The ostracizing terms "barbarians," "vandalism," "Gothic," the expression "to go berserk" or even the terms "Germany" and "Germans" (see chapter 8) may be interpreted and analyzed as an expression of a shadow of those who apply the terms. These terms and a plethora of others are part of the reservoir of man's darkness that haunts humanity and a peaceful future. It is the ostracizing attitude that makes so many of us culture promoters and thus, indirectly, advocates of a merger with the shadow.

---

[214] Cited in Kauffmann, C. (2007).
[215] Christian monastic practice of working and praying.
[216] Jung, C. G. (1959).

Fig. 60. *Perro semihundido (The Dog)* by Francisco Goya Lucientes (1746-1828; Museo del Prado, Madrid). Being part of Goya's Black Paintings, it exposes the head of a small dog gazing upward at a structureless object. The dog itself is almost lost in the vastness of the rest of the image, which is empty except for a dark sloping area near the bottom of the picture. Numerous interpretations have been provided. Here we focus upon how the earthly pigmented dog of the underworld (the guardian of Hel [*Garm*] or Cerberus in Germanic and Greek mythology, respectively) carefully brings some knowledge into a dark and seemingly open and unstructured reality. Access to and incorporation of unconscious material provides our life with inevitable substance, but the advent of the material in our consciousness may involve frightening encounters. Wikimedia Commons.

To watch out for our cultural shadow and to pay attention to life-giving breakthroughs of the primitive and archaic could become the sustainable strategy that may convey us constructively into a fruitful future. The dark side of our being, our sinister shadow, is not only a threat but represents also the seat of creativity that will support our endeavors to become what is our ultimate goal, i.e., fully human. This is the opposite of what the educated, for the most, are now: They may rather represent more sectarian than open-minded individuals. Our shadow is also our best friend, but only if we try to accept, observe, and integrate it.

The author's emphasis on the shadow of the European educated, tendentiously titled the cultural elite, should not give rise to misunderstandings. The author is also part of this group. He is exposed to the same cultural shadows as everybody else. Loving Greek and Latin culture, and enthusiastically taking care of what we were entrusted with, should admit that Greek and Roman mythology and humanistic education are not sufficient for our European reality. It is an important, but only one, sector of European culture and mythology. Our cultural setting resembles a parliament where the majority of the representatives and parties have either their mouth taped by some superordinate authority or verbalize only what the ruling minority faction determines. We are culturally and voluntary lobotomized.

## 9.3 Cultural security of the individual

Archetype illiteracy and extensive ostracizing may not only give rise to serious political but also personal complications. For example, can any psychodynamic professional act reliably while working with clients who come from different culture groups when his/her basic attitude is characterized by ignorance, arrogance, exclusion, and repression? Let's assume that archaic Germanic or Slavic material (63 percent of the Europeans speak Germanic or Slavic languages) surfaces in a client's dream. What impact will archetype illiteracy and cultural prejudice have upon the therapist-client relationship? Will the therapist be educated enough to interpret the elements for what they are, and, if so, will he/she be able to provide the client a fair treatment when the dream elements are unknown or considered barbarian/primitive? Does it not imply that the therapist may be biased and commit the fundamental mistake of ostracizing the world that may have shaped the challenges that bring clients to therapy? Lacking archetype literacy introduces serious challenges for the transference[217]/countertranference[218] in the analytical process. There is, of course, always the general danger that our cultural shadow may be projected upon our contemporaries. However, when we deal with the 70 percent or so of the mythology of Europeans (see 1.1) that is neglected, demonized, and repressed, and little emphasis is provided to alter this fact, then the situation may be grave.

What might happen when Germanic mythology elements (e.g., the world tree, the different manifestations of Odin/Wotan, the three *nornes*, the well of remembrance, Mimir's skull) appear in the dreams of clients and are not understood by the analytical therapist? The representations will probably be subjected to generic amplification (with material from the Greek, Roman, Egyptian cultures or from the extensive quarry of fairy tales). The author is convinced that the realities behind a dream will become manifest, but lacking archetypic literacy will slow down progress. We are only able to decipher a small fraction of archetypes because most of humanity's stars and star signs on the nightly dream sky have been assumed irrelevant (Fig. 59).

Archetype illiteracy is worth a thorough investigation because the cultural security of each individual needs to be ensured. Our cultural shadow needs to be illuminated and analyzed. Just like the self-sacrifice of Odin on Yggdrasil, each of us, and the therapist in particular, has to pick up the runes (see Box XXI). All humans wish and actually have a right to be adequately perceived. Our cultural background (or indoctrination) should not prevent us from taking care of an individual's wholeness.

---

[217] The redirection to a substitute, usually a therapist, of emotions (that were originally felt in childhood).
[218] Countertransference is defined as redirection of a psychotherapist's feelings toward a client—or, more generally, as a therapist's emotional entanglement with a client.

**Box XXI: A Germanic mythology portrait illuminating the archetypical circumstances of analytical psychologists**

In a condensed and symbolic manner, some of the most significant stanzas in *Hávamál* in the *Poetic Edda* portray the generic challenge that humans and particularly psychodynamic psychologists experience. In *Hávamál* 138-141, the most central and metaphysical aspect of Odin, the self-imposed hanging of the god on the world tree Yggdrasil, is portrayed[219].

*I know that I hung on a windy tree*
*nine long nights,*
*wounded with a spear, dedicated to Odin,*
*I myself to myself,*
*on that tree of which no man knows*
*from where its roots run.*

*No bread did they give me nor a drink from the horn,*
*downwards I peered;*
*I took up the runes, screaming I took them,*
*then I fell back from there.*

*Nine mighty spells I learned from the famous son*
*of Bolthor, Bestla´s father[220],*
*and I got a drink of the precious mead,*
*poured from Odrerir[221]*

*Then I began to quicken and be wise,*
*and to grow and prosper,*
*one word found another word for me,*
*one deed found another deed for me.*
*The runes you must find and the meaningful letter,*
*a very great letter,*
*A very powerful letter.........*

---

[219] Translation into English by Larrington, C. (1999).
[220] His mother's uncle, i.e., the collective unconscious.
[221] The vessel with the mead of wisdom and poetry.

The verses reflect, in the author's opinion, the basic situation and fundamental position of analytical and other psychoanalytical-oriented therapists. This is the background for the following paraphrase of the above cited text.

Through self-analysis and daily therapy work, an analyst gets exposed to the universal difficulties, despair, and suffering of clients and humanity. This is analagous to hanging on the world tree, which has roots deep in the collective unconscious and is exposed to the ambience of life and fate (e.g., wind, sun, and rain). This is the momentous scope in which the therapists carry out their daily work. It is a sacred, nocturnal setting, characterized by the holy number of Germanic mythology: nine. The nights indicate that we deal with the dark side of our psyche, our unconscious side. The nights further point at the daunting nature of an intrapsychic, depth-psychological journey often referred to as "The Night Sea Journey."[222]

The analyst has not been placed there. He/she[223] voluntarily chose the profession, and thus the analyst hangs there for himself. The spear of the personal consciousness is directed toward the analyst, it has wounded him, and this causes him to suffer, bleed. The psychologically significant terms "I", "Odin", "I myself" and "myself" are mentioned directly after each other. *Hávamál* 138-141 separates between a.) the ego, b.) the persona, c.) the conscious (I myself), and d.) unconscious self (myself): I..., dedicated to Odin, I myself to myself. The hanging god is thus dedicated to his ego (I), his persona (name), and carries out a dialogue between the personal, conscious sector of the self and the unconscious self. This suggests that Odin reflects an intricate, multi-layered dialogue between intrapsychic instances, as reflected by modern theories of self-psychology[224]. The uppermost god of the Germanic tribes, hanging voluntarily on Yggdrasil, used his already available autonomization of the ego (see Box VII) to provide access

---

[222] Sünner, R. (2011); https://doi.org/10.1080/19409052.2013.822691.

[223] For simplicity I use the masculine form, well knowing that both genders act as therapists.

[224] Self-psychology is a modern psychoanalytic theory and its clinical applications. It was conceived by Heinz Kohut in Chicago in the 1960s and onward and is still developing as a contemporary form of psychoanalytic treatment. For the cultural history of the individual, see Normann Waage (2014).

to the unconscious and the self. All that is condensed into four, short lines.

The analyst cannot share the difficulties, the despair, and the suffering of clients with others because of mandatory confidentiality. He is alone, hungry, and thirsty in a figurative meaning. The analyst experiences fully the hardship and loneliness of individuation (Fig. 61). With one eye open (the extrovert side) and the other closed (the introvert side, which has become available through self-analysis [losing an eye to get access to the well of remembrance]) the analyst simultaneously looks inward and outward as well as upward and downward. The professional insight (obtaining knowledge) is based upon sacrifice: the self-analysis, exposure to man's suffering, deprivation, loneliness.

The analyst hangs painfully on the tree until he understands some of the meaning of fate and life. That happens when he finally can decipher the concepts, secrets and symbols of life, the runes, on the mold below the world tree: toward the end of the self-analysis and analytical training. The integration of the concepts, secrets, and symbols of life is agonizing. When this is achieved, the initiation has come to a temporary and preliminary end. The analyst falls to the terra firma, the realm of the unconscious upon which all is based. The detected runes become more and more assimilated and integrated into the psyche and worldview of the therapist.

The analyst releases secrets out of the firm grip of the unconscious: He takes a sip from Odrerir, the vessel with the mead of wisdom and poetry or Mimir's well, the well of remembrance (Fig. 39). The analyst shares the wisdom with the clients and feels better and becomes wise. One single word turns into sequences of words, meaningful sentences. From a single accomplishment many others develop. The improved client-analyst relationship supports the healing process in the client. Simultaneously, it provides more autonomy to the analyst.

*Hávamál* 138-141 with its hanging, bleeding, and suffering god that provides the runes is a veritable embodiment for Jung's term, the wounded healer (Fig. 62), which can be elucidated in two ways. Frist, the analyst is consciously aware of his own personal wounds. These wounds may be activated in certain situations, especially if the client's wounds are similar (or contrary) to his own. Second, the client's wounds affect the less-known wounds of the analyst. "The wounded healer is the archetype of the Self and is at the bottom of all genuine healing procedures,"[225] says M.L.v. Franz (1915-1998). The analyzed's and analyst's projections become an important part of the self-awareness and represent a dialogue between various psychic entities, as hinted at in Fig. 62.

The interpreting paraphrase uncovers and suggests that *Hávamál* 138-141 encapsulates the essence of the reality experienced by psychoanalysts. In the European world, Odin exemplifies the wounded healer par excellence. The hanging god Odin and his initiation are the archetypical settings of the emergence of the Self. Consequently, we question why the self-sacrifice of Odin seemingly has not become a significant part of the portfolio of Jungian analyst education, Is the resistance against the barbarian tradition so strong that even the analytical psychologists are unable to detect the fundamental archetypical connotation of *Hávamál* 138-141 for their profession?

There is a world between the spiritual Odin (from *odr* [ecstasy, divine madness, mind, soul, or spirit] as compared to the wandering warmonger and warlord Wotan [Lord of the *woth* (rage, fury, wrath)]). Odin stands for the magic of the therapeutic relationship, and analytical psychology cultivates and nourishes the archetypical realm around the hanging god Odin. There is substantially more essence in the Odin/Wotan archetype than war, wandering, confusion, uproar, and rootlessness. It is suggested that Odin is one of the closest friends of analytical psychologists. His self-sacrificial initiation on the world tree is his contribution to humanity and modernity: self-realization.

---

[225] Levy, P. http://www.awakeninthedream.com/the-wounded-healer-part-1/.

## 9.4 Conclusion

Without any prejudice, forward-looking education has to honor and reflect, support and amplify the cultural nature of all humans. Thus, our cultural shadow necessarily has to be a momentous element of our national and self-analysis. We need to be prepared to endure the challenges of our self-realization, a demanding and lonely exposure to the world (Fig. 61). Projecting prejudices and inadequate cultural literacy, i.e., staying firmly and unprepared in the realm of one's inherited shadow, can ultimately result in misjudgment, encroachment, and cultural harassment.

Fig. 61. *Der Mönch am Meer* (*The Monk by the Sea*) by Caspar David Friedrich (1774-1840; Alte Nationalgallery, Berlin). The broad expanses of sea and sky emphasize the meager figure of the monk, standing before the vastness of nature. The monk is cut off from us spatially and existentially, and there are no traditional landscape elements that might soften the effect. There is only a cold sky and a flat foreground, void of greenery, and a dark sea on which no vessels sail. Friedrich in a manner anticipates what today is called abstract: in thought or as an idea and not having a physical or concrete existence. Abstract as many of the constructs that we use to understand the psyche. Friedrichs transfers his experience of solitude and lostness in a pantheistic world to the viewer, addressing our deep-rooted anxiety for the loneliness of the individuation pathway. The monk addresses the individual core in us and our ultimate solitude flanked by nature and eternity. Wikimedia Commons.

Fig. 62. *Haavoittunut enkeli* (*The Wounded Angel*) by Hugo Simberg (1873-1917, Atheneum, Helsinki). The angelic figure with her bandaged forehead and bloodied wing is central, framed by her two youthful bearers in somber clothing. She clutches a bunch of snowdrops, symbolic of healing and rebirth. The introverted attitude of the left-hand and the direct gaze of the right-hand figure touches the viewer. It reflects how we take care of our wounds: Most of the time we deal with them in an introverted and uncommunicative manner like the left-hand figure. Being more mature and conscious, we may hope to sort out our wounds as the communicative right-hand person. There are as many interpretations as there are viewers. Here we assume that the picture portrays different aspects of our psyche. Our injured soul is guided by our introverted or extroverted attitudes to handle situations. To heal our existentialist wounds, we need to care about our "angelic" soul and the flowers of healing and rebirth. And we should not forget that "operational" units are required, like the two brave, dedicated, and recuperative boys who make sure that their angelic friend will be healed, by carrying on along our pathway and supported by (inner) constructs (stretcher). Wikimedia Commons.

When will, for a start, the cultural avant-garde also embrace the Germanic primitive and promote drinking from Mimir's well, which is so essential for many Europeans? Can, for example, Jungian psychology make a prominent contribution to fight archetype lobotomy, cultural desertification, and the plague of cultural elite conduct? And can it thus support one of its main goals: lighten up our shadow and promote the realization of the self? We reach an adequate and recuperative relationship with Germanic archetypes by a.) recognizing their existence; b.) being sufficiently open-minded to detect them; and c.) lightening up our cultural shadow. Along with the plethora of humanity's archetypes, we should let the Germanic archetypes do their work for the best of humanity in our part of the world.

It is important to acknowledge that we encompass an over-abundance of psychic entities that are less or not fully developed. Because of this inadequacy, we will be injured by the times and the cultural environment in which we live (Fig. 62). By recognizing the state of these internal entities and by accepting that we are wounded, we create the preconditions for healing our injuries. Admitting our deficiencies and psychological wounds is the start of a recuperative process, which simultaneously provides the competence to heal the wounds of our contemporaneous compatriots.

*Solen* (*The Sun*) by Edvard Munch (1863-1944; University of Oslo, Faculty of Law, Grand Hall of the University of Oslo). Rising from the coastline of Norway's south coast at the end of January, the image of the blazing sun sends its rays to dispel winter darkness. After a severe winter, the prospects of increased light drives away the shivering icy coldness and prospects of warmth and budding life warms our soul. The painting anchors the theme "enlightenment," transforming the central task of any place of learning into a majestic, abstract image. We all can let the sun rise to fight darkness, ignorance, and carelessness. By being unbiased and honestly accepting all the rising suns from the mythologies of the human race, we could form a true avant-garde of future, all-encompassing humanism and a road map to peace. Wikimedia Commons.

# 10. Epilogue: Can Global Archetype Literacy Become a Road Map to Peace?

*Knowing your own darkness is the best method of dealing with the darkness of other people.*

C.G. Jung

*I am not what happened to me. I am what I chose to become.*

C.G. Jung

The night sky of dreams embodies a universal setting for humans, wherever they live, whatever culture they come from, whatever nation may empower them, and whatever local culture and offshoots of humanity they belong to (Fig. 59). It is universal for all humans: At night we are all equal. And for millenia, humanity has gazed into the vault of stars at night before electricity deprived us of the fundamental experience of a nocturnal numinous. During our dreams the signatures of humanity's collective memory glare down upon us in the form a plethora of fixed stars and star signs, but we recognize only a few of them. To become really human implies also to become a world citizen, and, in order to become one, we have to make every effort to move toward global cultural literacy. We have to learn to decipher the various languages of humanity's archetypes, as reflected here in the form of fixed stars and star signs. All learning is remembering, says Socrates (470-399 B.C.E.) through his disciple Plato (424-348 B.C.E.). According to Socrates,

241

we lose the conscious memory of humanity's collective knowledge during birth. But as our archetypical legacy, according to Jung, is phylogenetically acquired, we all may recognize humanity's mythological heritage at the depths of our souls: in the collective unconscious (Fig. 1). Thus, all cognition is recognition. We have not only to recognize but also learn to remember and to sip from the well of remembrance. And thus, according to Plato's cave allegory and tied to the stool of our earthly existence, the recognition of our own or other cultures' archetypes demands recognizing the shadows of the ideas, which are the archetypes. They cast a silhouette onto the screen of our psychological recognition where we can identify them as the ideas.

Within current education, the majority of archetype shadows deriving from European cultures can hardly be deciphered, except for those of the classical Greek and Roman culture that traditionally have been brought to our attention[226]. These should continuously belong to our education and cultural portfolio, but they comprise only a fraction of the bewildering multitudes of uncommented, "wordless" European archetypes that, harmless, may haunt our subconscious and unconscious. Every now and then, subconscious material permeates our conscious-ness, and because the content is unknown and new to us, it frequently manifests itself in the form of a frightening visions (Fig. 60, page 8).

## 10.1 Archetype illiteracy and education

Can we accept and live with the impending perils of archetypal illiteracy? The current answer is that this is what we do, the fundamental answer is a sound no! To continue our lobotonomic ignorance like now is far too dangerous. Our perspective should be transcultural because of the fundamental assumption that people, deep down in their souls, share similar experiences, independent of their culture, ethnicity, and religion. After all, biologically we all belong to the one and only human race[227]. At the surface obviously different, we have increasingly similar cultural and

---

[226] In Scandinavia and the Nordic countries, the Germanic archetypes are more easily accessible.

[227] https://www.nationalgeographic.com/magazine/2018/04/race-genetics-science-africa/.

religious experiences as we go back in humanity's evolutionary time toward the collective consciousness (Fig. 1). Those who consider world citizenship and a universal attitude as their highest priority cannot exclude any culture, ethnicity, or religion. However, is this unbiased and unconditional universality reflected in the core presented by teaching institutions or generally in the mindsets of intellectuals, politicians, and artists? Don't we live in times where man's cultural and historical development is paid much attention? Don't we travel as tourists extensively through the world and learn about cultural diversity without major prejudices? Despite of all this, seemingly numerous branches of Indo-European culture are overlooked or ignored. Jungians often proceed from the cultural expressions of the here-and-now directly to the very base of the human development tree with its universal archetypes (see Fig. 1). In this manner, the layering of human cultural evolution is ignored. And the confrontation with the bothersome and disgusting barbarian cultures of our ancestors and disagreeable ethnic-specific imaginary can be elegantly omitted. This shortcut leaves the descendants of disagreeable cultures "homeless," disregarded, and abandoned. It also prevents from learning about humanity's archetype evolution. We became "historyless." History is written by the victors, says Winston Churchill, and who are the ignored cultural losers in Europe is by now well-described. With a twist of the original citation,[228] we could mention that "nothing in humans makes sense except in the light of cultural evolution." However, are the educated Europeans really interested in cultural evolution? How can we realize our European self when large sectors of our archetypical nature and human cultural evolution are disregarded and left abandoned? We are welcome to the shining elevation of the culture elite, but a majority has to ignore where they come from and what their heritage is. This is an act of self-contempt.

This book is a small contribution in living up to the goals of making education universal and philanthropic in the very meaning of the term.

---

[228] "Nothing in Biology Makes Sense Except in the Light of Evolution" is a 1973 essay by the evolutionary biologist and Eastern Orthodox Christian Theodosius Dobzhansky, criticising anti-evolution creationism and espousing theistic evolution. The essay was first published in American Biology Teacher in 1973.

It tries to enlighten the reader about Germanic mythology, which appears by and large, at best marginalized, but for the most part repressed and neglected. At times, the repressed and neglected stretch into our subconscious, and we may get scared (Fig. 60). The general idea embedded in this book is to endorse generic mythology literacy. Our knowledge about European culture should be congruent with the multi ethnic audiences of institutes, high schools, universities, and learning institutions. These intentions involve ultimately the entire human mythology, which is certainly a formidable but inevitable task for any truly universal and philanthropic movement. We deserve training that meets—culturally speaking—all of humanity[229], not only trendy cultural subsets. As suggested by Plato's cave allegory, real recognition depends on adequate explanations of the shadows and of becoming conscious of what we already know, but have forgotten.

## 10.2 Cultural landscape restoration

In his essay *Wotan*, C.G. Jung formulated three key sentences that are fundamental for the purpose of this book[230]. "An archetype is like an old watercourse along which the water of life has flowed for centuries, digging a deep channel for itself. Archetypes are like riverbeds that dry up when the water deserts them, but which it can find again at any time. The longer it has flowed in this channel the more likely it is that sooner or later the water will return to its old bed." The Germanic culture topography, characterized by archetypical riverbeds and a rich hinterland, was purposely denudated to become a "cultivated" part of the world. The science of ecology shows that most types of landscape manipulation result in a loss of biodiversity, fertility, resilience, and sustainability. From a systemic point of view, this must also be true for human culture. So far, humanity has not paid sufficient attention to the dynamics of what could be termed "human system ecology."

---

[229] For an example of the world of Indo-European mythology see Leeming, D. (2003); Kisak, P.F. (2016).
[230] Jung, C.G. Collected Works 10, Wotan (1936), page 371-399.

Desertification of the lush and fertile mythological landscapes that badly affected the Germanic tribes by the late Middle Ages had their cultural heritage eradicated by the Roman Catholic Church and the Holy Roman Empire of the German Nation. This cultural extermination prevented humidity from accumulating, which in turn resulted in a lack of rain. A devastated, vegetation-poor and desertlike cultural landscape—seemingly a no-man's-land—remained. The fertile Germanic archetypical river valleys (see 5.10) turned into wadis[231]. Under irregular "meteorological", e.g., political, circumstances, original Germanic archetype valleys that had turned into dry wadis accumulate tremendous amounts of water (accumulation of psychic energy through nonrealized archetypes) that rush to the ocean with uncontrolled, tremendous devastation. Clearly, events during Germany's Nazi era and World War II comprise examples for such devastating flood episodes. Such episodes can happen again if the desertification of major sectors of the European culture persists. They just depend on the large-scale weather pattern, i.e., the general political climate.

We suggest that sociological and political floods are not only caused by irregularities in "weather" but also by changes in (cultural) land use and human-induced vegetation. As an analogue, we could imagine the forceful and deliberate denundation of the "savage" archetype landscapes. The denudation and aridification was and is carried out by either power-hungry individuals or highly educated, well-meaning people who think they know what a brighter future implies. Like Christianity, they dislike nature but love culture. A cultural marshland is only "good" when it is drained, a primordial wood is only "profitable" when it is planted and logged, and the ocean is only "useful" when it is fished. These people, i.e., us, are suffering from the unrecognized arrogance of a cultural elite. They are not aware of how they harm their fellow humans and human heritage, and thus themselves. Ecological theory suggests that any type of biodiversity and biotope loss gives rise to negative, ecological consequences, particularly in the long run. There is no reason that this should be different for human culture.

---

[231] A dry (ephemeral) riverbed that contains water only during times of exceptional, but heavy rain.

Humanity is pursued by "apocalyptic riders" in the form of lacking attention to the dynamics of defense mechanisms (such as neglect, demonization, repulsion, and repression). While these mechanisms reduce anxiety and fear arising from unacceptable or potentially harmful stimuli (here barbaric cultures), they not only have short-term healthy but also long-term unhealthy consequences. The apocalyptic riders cause the denudation of nonacceptable, barbarian and foreign culture landscapes and thus detrimental archetypal lobotomy. Human biodiversity changes create a source of unrest and potentially even tragedies in Europe. Surprisingly, our celebrated mainstream culture and humanistic education creates the precondition for the cultural deforestation and desertification of originally fertile cultural landscapes. And thus culture and education may contribute to devastating flooding. One does not become enlightened by figures of light, but by making the darkness conscious. The latter procedure, however, is unpleasant and therefore unpopular. As a consequence, the contrary took place, and the lights were directed toward the Roman-Christian-Renaissance culture while the shadow of the original Germanic culture darkened. Based upon the nonacceptable ambivalence of any archetype, Christianity attacked life by brightening the image of Christ/God, and as a result its shadow darkened, i.e., the devil. Christianity became unilateral by splitting the archetypes. The more we long for God, the greater the impact of the dark forces. The more we wish to be civilized and cultural (i.e., according to Greek, Roman, and Renaissance ideals and patterns), the more barbaric and primitive the majority of the Europeans may become. It started with the conversion of the pagans, but the mission to make the Europeans cultivated and civilized has not ended. We not only became more enlightened, but also darkened (Fig. 63).

Jung attempts to uncover that the horror that haunted the world during the World War II period found a psychological base in culture. The wild destruction of Wotan's force became the revenge of the lack of awareness of the nonconscious aspects of civilization, here the original Germanic culture. The eruption of violence and the breakdown of morality also can simultaneously be seen in a systematic manner: as an attempt of nations to create an adequate equilibrium, an improved balance in reality orientation. Jung warns that such episodes may happen anew anytime. Both persons and nations can become the victims of

Fig. 63. *Krasnyy zakat na Dnepre* (*Red Sunset on the Dnieper*) by Arkhip Ivanovich Kuindzhi (1842–1910; Metropolitan Museum of Art, New York). After a hot day, a bloodshot sun descends through the afterglow toward the encroaching darkness of the night. Letting darkness reign the scene fills us with anxiety, and with passionate sentiments and yearning we cling to our colorful emotions while losing control. The night and the unconcious are our enemies as long as we neglect, repulse, and repress them, our unconcious, but they can be our supportive partner when we let them influence our lives. Darkness does not hide danger for those who apply a permeable, psychological diaphragma and who are able to listen to the inner language. To expand our current culture with the neglected, demonized, repulsed, and repressed archetypical representations of original Germanic and other "barbaric" cultures will support the dawn of a brighter human future (page 240, Fig. 65). This painting is typical of Kuindzhi's later days. Known for his large, nearly empty landscapes, the scene shows a sunset over the banks of the Dnieper, the great river that was the main connection for Norse people funding the Rus kingdom in Kiev. Wikimedia Commons.

neglected, unconscious forces. This is a danger that cannot be over-looked. What humanity needs is not more enlightenment by the traditional culture elite, but an age of human culture systemics[232] that puts today's monoculture in place. We could start to study human and cultural systems in a systemic manner.

---

[232] https://en.wikipedia.org/wiki/Systems_theory#Systems_psychology.

This book intends not to focus upon the entire expanse of today's archetypical deserts. It tries to take a step in a direction that makes the neglected and unconscious forces of Germanic origin that threaten our civilization accessible. It attempts to shed light upon a fraction of European darkness. It wishes to portray the apocalyptic riders that keep the realm of the original Germanic archetype landscape at bay. The book attempts to show what this Germanic landscape actually looked like before the "fall of grace": essentially fertile, pleasant, green, and experiencing seasons, rain, and sunshine.

Some readers may point out that the demonic forces of the neglected Germanic archetypes had their reappearance in recent years. Eurocentric racism and white supremacy (with Germanic connotations) show their ugly face again, at times under the mask of Allfather/ Odin/Wotan. Some other readers may recognize deep down in their preconscious or unconscious the roots of their subdued, original culture. They may even enjoy taking a deep breath of relief as they experience Ergiffenheit (sensu Rudolf Otto)[233]. They may recognize a feeling of coming home to a long-yearned-for land of origin, a Garden of Eden from which they were expelled by furious angels with flaming swords. Some others may experience how long-deserted vistas in their souls green again. Could this book make a small contribution to the reforestation that would green Europe's archetype deserts, make the rain fall, the rivers flow softly, stimulate plant growth, and prevent unprecedented floods? Could an adequate phylogenetic, evolution-orientated culture education make Jungian psychology and other forms of education to a road map toward human understanding, which ultimately implies peaceful coexistence?

## 10.3 Road map to peace?

Some readers may object and state that we already walk the road of peace since World War II. Are not many of us tolerant and interested in human culture? Have we not managed to keep extensive nationalism and wars to a minimum in Europe? Are our transcultural approaches not

---

[233] Dohe, C.B. (2011).

fundamentally based upon the assumption that people have similar basic experiences, independent of their culture, ethnicity, and religion? This has been the case in post-World War II Europe, but these ideals are currently on the decline. Unfortunately, few appear unconditionally interested in generic human culture. Our frequent voyages to foreign countries do not resemble genuine culture encounters, but we are surfing our own cultural waves at great speed, sharpened by a few foreign spices. The most popular movies rarely provide insight into cultural diversity, but are rather monocultural. A dwindling number of correspondents report from foreign countries to explain, every now and then, why this or that country responded unexpectedly. Introductory courses in philosophy, psychology, and history were removed from the portfolio of universities in order to streamline education and to focus upon what really matters: reason and rationality.

Political movements are on the rise that argue against the ethnicities and religions that potentially may challenge the homogeneity and self-conception of countries[234], if that homogeneity ever existed. Like most of us, these organizations distinguish between the desirable high and unpleasant and dangerous low cultures. After all, who wishes to be characterized as barbaric or primitive or interested in a takeover of the refined Occident? Every day newspapers, journals, media debates or demonstrations convey to us that the world is threatened by seemingly inferior, wretched cultures that need to be kept at bay. Fences are raised, and camps are erected. Many countries engirdle themselves physically and literally by fences and barbed wire. Refugee homes are set alight. On the surface, we support education and peaceful coexistence, but ostracize quickly to clearly distinguish between what we think supports or attacks our civilization (see chapter 8). Is this a road map to peace? In our static perspective, we forget that today's nations are all based upon the immigration of inferior cultures that challenged identities.

Humanism should affirm our ability and responsibility to have meaningful, ethical lives, capable of adding to the greater good of

---

[234] E.g. Patriotic Europeans Against the Islamisation of the West (Occident) (Pegida), a German nationalist, anti-Islam, far-right political movement, or Mc Nallens Viking Brother-hood and Asatru Folk Assembly.

humanity[235], but is this really the case? Our highly appreciated humanistic education and culture appear at times a matter of border-setting between the small territory of culture and the vaste expanses that, by definition, are uncultivated. We prefer rather to live inside our civilization (with hostile trenches, walls and barricades directed against the barbarians outside) than in humanity's open field of encompassing cooperation and give-and-take. It has always demanded courage to step outside the protection of a woods or a cave to enter an open landscape. Humanity dared to do so, and that shaped its progress. To step back into the protection of the woods or cave may be necessary or wise at times, but in the long run, it represents regression that cripples development.

The Western, humanistic-educated and Christianity-impacted cultural privileged pay little attention to regressive aspects, such as culture suppression and ostracizing. Our proud cultural background and ethnicity may have, literarily and physically, engirdled us with barbed wire. Education and our definition of what culture is may not exclusively be our friend, but also one of humanity's enemies. Current education appears to alienate us to variable degrees from our "inferior" and "barbarian" roots (Fig. 64). Surprisingly, there is only a small footstep between "Entartede Kunst" (degenerate art[236]) and degenerate culture and civilization. Ostracizing "hostile" cultures prevents us from getting acquainted with our primordial core and inhibits awareness of our cultural shadow. If the most modern turns out to be the most archaic[237], then our dominant culture prevents modernity. We should vigilantly take care of the remnants of utensils from humanity's African "archaicum" that are left in our soul and not isolate and reject them (Figs. 64). Humanism may be so rational and focused upon science that the conditioned nature of the individual, born in a variety of cultures and ethnicities, is ignored for the benefit of one generic worldview. The Universal Declaration of Human Rights states that we are all equal and enjoy equal rights, but could it be that these praiseworthy principles are those of an elite that has constructed an unbroken line from the Greek-Roman and Renaissance culture into modern times? Is this the essence

---

[235] https://americanhumanist.org/what-is-humanism/definition-of-humanism/.
[236] https://en.wikipedia.org/wiki/Degenerate_art.
[237] Davenport, G. (1981).

Fig. 64. *Afrikanska kulturföremål* (*Objects from African Culture*) by Gustav Ludwig Heinrich Mützel (1839-93). The African origin of modern humans, also called the "Out of Africa" theory, dominates modern paleoanthropological thinking. That implies that modern man has a primordial memory that was formed in Africa, reflected in archetypes and mythologems. Like all parts of our primitive and archaic core, this nucleus frightens us when we get in touch with it. But similar to the sunset of the consciousness and appearing inner darkness in our current lives (see Fig. 63), the prehistoric darkness in our psyche is our friend, despite its occasional terrifying apparition. The memory of humanity's fertile African mold comprises be the foundation out of which our conscious life germinates. The various African artifacts are supposed to remind us that we, at the depth our soul, are all out of Africa and that we should admit our dark, aboriginal heritage. By admitting them we will experience a new sunrise (Fig. 65). Published in *Nordisk familiebok* (1904), Vol. 1 *Afrika, Nordisk familjeboks förlags aktiebolag, Nordisk familjeboks tryckeri*, Stockholm. Wikimedia Commons.

251

of what is called equal rights for all humans? Do equal rights exist for those who do not obey the ideals of a Western-centered elite? George Orwell's words come to mind: "All animals are equal, but some animals are more equal than others."[238]

Hastily, the author wishes to state that he grew up with the Greek and Latin fraction of Europe's rich cultural landscape and is impacted by the strength and greatness of these essential European cultures. But this cultural knowledge may not necessarily be sufficient to create lasting harmony and peace for all humanity. It may be sufficient as long as the dominating culture does not feel threatened. As long as the inter-pretation of non-Greek, non-Roman and nonhumanistic knowledge is characterized by prejudice, exclusion, demonization, and repression, there is a need to truly open up for the majority of the European cultures that do not belong to the canon of declared culture. In order to make the world really a peaceful and fruitful place, we have to overcome the "iron curtain" that education and dominant culture have erected to keep the supposedly evil empire of barbarism at bay.

## 10.4 Future humanism

Cosmopolitan and all-encompassing movements such as Jungian psychology or organizations such as the West-Eastern Divan Orchestra[239], to mention two, can make a contribution to fighting archetype lobotomy, cultural desertification, and the plague of elite conduct, and thus support some of humanity's main goals: peaceful coexistence, cultural develop-ment, and understanding. The individual precondition for this is to lighten up our shadow and contribute to the realization of the self. In concert with other movements, we could make the deserted archetypical riverbeds carefully flow again and support the advance of human conditions. Many art projects actually promote such visions by challenging present-day culture. We can indeed reforest the deserts created by

---

[238] Animal Farm: A Fairy Story (1945).
[239] A youth orchestra based in Seville, Spain, consisting of musicians from countries in the Middle East (Egypt, Iran, Israel, Jordan, Lebanon, Palestine, and Spain); founded in 1999 by the conductor Daniel Barenboim and academic Edward Said. It is named after a collection of lyrical poems by the German poet J.W.v. Goethe, who was inspired by the Persian poet Hafez.

today's dominant culture if we really wish and develop an unprejudiced integration of humanity's many facets. We could start with scrutinizing ourselves! What are our actual roots, and do we stand up wholeheartedly and with a humble mind for all fractions of our ethnic and cultural heritage? And should we be in doubt, will any commercially available genetic tests provide us with a stratigraphy of a multitude of inheritance layers. We are not fully uniform and solid, but are layered, a composite, like plywood. We hold the entire human development inside us.

Ultimately, we can reach a human culture ecology for which the first step is a systematic ecological[240] integration of humanity. What is needed is not more traditional humanism, but a holistic approach to studying human (eco)systems, an approach that keeps the arrogance and supremacy of humanism at bay. Genuine education, i.e., one that takes care of humanity in the most comprehensive meaning of the term, may contribute to the prevention of horrendous flooding events that repressed archetypes bring over us. We involuntarily promote flood events when we distance ourselves from undesired cultures, as defined by a self-appointed culture clique.

Humanism is seemingly generous, tolerant, empathetic, and wishes not to discriminate, but hides antibarbarianism and nontolerant rationalism, our civilization's Trojan Horse, behind the scenes. The definition and execution of today's humanism is based upon the underlying assumption that only one "civilized" cultural line stretches into our current era and the future: that of the Roman, Christian, and Renaissance, ending up in secularized societies, the declaration of human rights, etc. Most of humanity is asked to break over the ties to (or even the backbone) their original culture in order to enjoy the splendor of today's humanism. Resistance against this development is often interpreted as regression. But humanity needs not today's, but a new, more open-minded, all-encompassing humanism that reflects and balances humanity, i.e., that of all cultures and archetypes. Future humanism (if that will be the preferred term) will ask for the integration of the entire world. It must not only rest upon the culture of the fraction

---

[240] Systems ecology is an interdisciplinary field of ecology, a subset of Earth system science that takes a holistic approach to the study of ecological systems, especially ecosystems.

Fig. 65. *Frau in der Morgensonne (Woman in Morning Sun)* by Caspar David Friedrich (1774-1840; Folkwang Museum, Essen). During recent centuries, the dawn of modernity is accompanied by a weakening of the patriachate and more balanced scenarios between men and women. In the male unconscious, a balancing archetype finds expression as a feminine inner personality: the guiding anima ("the eternal feminine, draws us upward," see 6.3). In the late 19th and early 20th centuries, female emancipation, a society characterized by more equal rights, and the introduction of psychoanalysis resulted in a plethora of paintings depicting idealized, demonized, or glorified female figures. Friedrichs points at an awakening of the anima and the advent of a new age when humans become more closely connected to the archetypes beyond the reign of the fading patriarchate. It is dawn time, and a new gender-balanced age is on the verge of becoming a reality: The anima is awakening. Wikimedia Commons.

that has arrogantly annexed the power of defining what genuine human culture and equal rights are. Humanity needs a united nation of archetypes, its all-encompassing heritage. A look at the stars at night illustrates this complex view (Fig. 59), and most of the stars may have been ignited in Africa (Fig. 64). This brings us back to the quotation of Terence: "Nothing human is alien to me." Will we ever be able to achieve this ultimate of all ambitions?

Man lives a truly human life thanks to culture—not the culture of a self-appointed, cultural theocracy, but man's all-encompassing culture. We are not only what has happened to us, but what we choose to become. By actively, unbiasedly, and honestly accepting all mythologies, we could form a true avant-garde of future, all-encompassing humanism and a road map to peace. This could represent a new beginning, a dawn that could find its foundation in a new and more balanced understanding of our psyche (Fig. 65). I am not what happened to me. I am what I chose to become.

What is culture and what is not will always be a matter of opinion and discussion. The process of productive questioning is what we should pursue to make progress. Who does not answer the questions has passed the test, says Franz Kafka[241]. We will not be judged by finite answers, but by our inquisitive accomplishments along a curve toward an asymptote toward infinity. Our ordeal is not to answer questions, but to question, over and again.

---

[241] Kafka, F. (1920). Die Prüfung.

*Vinter ved Sognefjorden* (*Winter at the Sognefjord*) by Johan Christian Clausen Dahl (1788-1857, National Museum of Art, Architecture and Design, Oslo). The archetypes of the original Germanic culture tower, like stately and menhir-like monoliths, project into our present-day cultural landscapes. Their tacit weightiness is connected to subdued memories of the crypts of our souls and the primordial times of our cultures. Like a silent, threatening cry, they loom in a frostbitten, wintery landscape. Humanity would benefit from understanding and relating to the silent, archetypical expressions of our bygone days. Copyright: National Gallery of Norway, Oslo.

# Author biography

Paul Wassmann was born in Germany, but spend his adult life in northern Norway. He is a professor in marine ecology at UiT The Arctic University of Norway in Tromsø, Norway. He has extensively worked with ecosystem functioning in all European seas, but particularly in the ice-covered waters in the European Arctic, focusing upon the consequences of climate warming. Wassmann has been leading a range of research projects, a PhD school, various national and international networks and contributed to an integrative understanding of Arctic marine ecosystems. He studied also basic psychology and has frequently attended lectures at C. G. Jung Institute in Küsnacht, Switzerland. Based upon analytical psychology and cultural history he frequently lectured about Germanic mythology. Photography: Rudi Caeyers/UiT The Arctic University of Norway.

# 11. References

Anthony, D.W. (2007). The Horse, the Wheel and Language: How Bronze-Age Riders from the Eurasian Steppes Shaped the Modern World. Princeton University Press.

Arendt, H. (1981). The Life of the Mind. A Harvest Book, Harcourt, Inc. San Diego, New York, London.

Ascherson, N. (2007). Black Sea: The Birthplace of Civilisation and Barbarism. Vintage Books, London.

Assmann, A. (2009). Erinnerungsräume: Formen und Wandlungen des kulturellen Gedächtnisses, C.H.Beck, München.

Bæksted, A. (2001). Nordiske guder og helter. Aschehoug & Co., Oslo.

Barber, E. W. (1999). The Mummies of Ürümchi. Macmillan Publishers, Ltd, London.

Bennett, O. (2001). Cultural Pessimism: Narratives of Decline in the Postmodern World. Edinburgh University Press.

Beowulf: Verse Translation (Penguin Classics) Paperback (2003).

Bodkin, M. (1934). Archetypal Patterns in Poetry, London: Oxford University Press.

Boyd, J.W., Crosby D.A. (1979). Is Zoroastrianism Dualistic or Monotheistic? Journal of the American Academy of Religion, Volume XLVII, Number 4, 557–588.

Brock, T. (2014). Alles Mythos. 20 populäre Irrtümer über die Germanen. Konrad Theiss Verlag, Stuttgart.

Brown, N.M. (2012). Songs of the Vikings. Snorri and the Making of Norse Myths. Palgrave, Macmillan, USA.

Burckhardt, C.J.C. (1878). The Civilization of the Renaissance in Italy. The Middlemore translation of the 1860 German original. Penguin Classics (1990).

Burri, M. (1982). Germanische Mythologie. Zwischen Verdrängung und Verfälschung. Schweizer Spiegel Verlag, Zürich.

Campbell, J. (1949). Hero with a Thousand Faces. Pantheon Books.

Campbell, J. (1974). The Mythic Image, Princeton: Princeton University Press.

Campbell, J. (1988). The Power of Myth, Doubleday and Co.

Campbell, J. (1991). Occidental Mythology: The Mask of God. Penguin.

Casement, A. (2012). The Shadow. Chapter 4 in: The Handbook of Jungian Psychology: Theory, Practice and Applications, Papadopoulos, R.K. (editor), Routledge.

Coleman, W. (2012). Anima/Animus. Chapter 6 in: The Handbook of Jungian Psychology: Theory, Practice and Applications, Papadopoulos, R.K. (editor), Routledge.

Davenport, G. (1981). The Geography of the Imagination. David R. Godine Publisher.

Davidson, H.R.E. (1964). Gods and Myths of Northern Europe. Penguin Books.

Drengson, A., Inoue, Y. (Editors) (1995). The Deep Ecology Movement: An Introductory Anthology. Berkeley, North Atlantic Publishers.

Emberland, T. (2003). Religion og rase. Humanist Forlag Oslo.

Das Lied der Nibelungen (1833).

Doepler, D.J., Ranisch, W. (1900). Walhall. Die Götterwelt der Germanen. Edition Offizin, Koblenz.

Dohe, C.B. (2011). Wotan and the 'archetypal Ergriffenheit': Mystical union, national spiritual rebirth and culture-creating capacity in C. G. Jung's 'Wotan' essay. History of European Ideas 37: 344-356.

Dohe, C.B. (2016). Jung's Wandering Archetype: Race and Religion in Analytical Psychology. Routledge, Taylor & Francis, London.

Eggertsson, J.M. (2015). Sorcerer's Screed: The Icelandic Book of Magic Spells. Lesstofan, Reykjavik.

Egerkrans, J. (2016). Norrønne Guder. Spartacus Forlag AS, Oslo.

Eifel, K. (1953). Deutsche Götter und Heldensagen. Verlag Kremayr & Scherian, Wien.

Eliade, M. (1957). Das Heilige und das Profane. Rowohlts Taschenbuch Verlag GmbH, Hamburg.

Eliade, M. (1961). Images and Symbols: Studies in Religious Symbolism. Princeton University Press.

Eliade, M. (1964). Shamanism: Archaic techniques of ecstasy. Princeton University Press.

Eliade, M. (1968). Myths, Dreams and Mysteries: The Encounter Between Contemporary Faiths and Archaic Reality. Collins, London.

Eliade, M. (1963). Myth and Reality. New York: Harper & Row.

Eliade, M. (1978). The Forge and the Crucible: The Origins and Structures of Alchemy. Chicago: University of Chicago Press.

Engelmann, E. (1889). Germania's Sagenborn: Mären und Sagen für das deutsche Haus bearbeitet. Paul Neff Verlag, Stuttgart.

Engelmann, E. (1895). Nordland Sagen. Nordisch-Germanische Lieder und Mären für das deutsche Haus bearbeitet. Paul Neff Verlag, Stuttgart.

Enoksen, L.M. (2008). Norrønne guder og gudinner. Schibsted Forlag, Oslo.

Fehr, H., Rummel, P.v. (2011). Die Völkerwanderungen. Konrad Theiss Verlag, Stuttgart.

Feist J., Feist G.J. (2009). Theories of Personality. New York, New York; McGraw-Hill.

Frazer, J.G. (1922). The Golden Bough: A Study in Magic and Religion. MacMillan, New York.

Freud, S. (1900). Die Traumdeutung. Leipzig und Wien, Franz Deuticke.

Freud, S. (1930). Das Unbehagen in der Kultur. Internationaler Psychoanalytischer Verlag, Wien.

Frog (2018). Myth. Humanities 7, 14. Doi:10.3390/h7010014.

Gimbutas, M. (1982). The Goddesses and Gods of Old Europe: Myths and Cult Images. London, Thames and Hudson.

Gimbutas, M. (1991). The Civilization of the Goddess: The World of Old Europe. San Francisco: Harper.

Golther, W. (1895). Handbuch der Germanischen Mythologie. Neu gesetzt für Marix Verlag GmbH Wiesbaden (2004).

Grimm, J. (1835). Deutsche Mythologie. Göttingen.

Gudmundsson, O. (2011). Snorri Sturluson. Homer des Nordens. Böhlau Verlag, GmbH & Cie, Köln, Weimar, Wien.

Haarmann, H. (2016). Auf den Spuren der Indoeuropäer. Von den neolithischen Steppennomaden bis zu den frühen Hochkulturen. C.H. Beck, München.

Hallberg, P. (1962). Old Icelandic Poetry: Eddic Lay and Skaldic Verse (Lincoln: Univ. Nebraska Press, p.136.

Hasenfratz, H.-P. (1992). Die Germanen. Religion, Magie, Kult, Mythus. Verlag Hohe GmbH, Erdstadt.

Hasenfratz, H.-P. (2011). Barbarian Rites: The Spiritual World of the Vikings and the Germanic Tribes. Inner Traditions, Rochester.

Hauer, J.W. (1934). Deutsche Gottschau: Grundzüge eines deutschen Glaubens. Stuttgart, K. Gutbrod.

Hedeager, L. (2011). Iron Age myth and Materiality: An Archaeology of Scandinavia, A.D. 400-1000. Routledge, New York.

Hedeager, L. (2015). For the Blind Eye Only? Scandinavian Gold Foils and the Power of Small Things. Norwegian Archeological Review 48 (2): 129-151.

Heinlein, R.A. (1984). Job: A Comedy of Justice. Ballantine Books/ Del Rey, New York.

Herrmann, P. (1898). Deutsche Mythologie in gemeinverständlicher Darstellung. Aufbau Verlag GmbH & Co, Berlin (1991).

Herrmann, P. (1903). Nordische Mythologie in gemeinverständlicher Darstellung. Aufbau Verlag GmbH & Co, Berlin (1991).

Heyerdahl, T., Lillieström, P. (2001). Jakten på Odin. På sporet av vår fortid. Oslo, Stenersens forlag.

Jacoby, E. (2011). 50 Klassiker. Mythen und Sagen des Nordens. Gerstenberg.

Jaffé A. (1968). Aus Leben und Werkstatt von C. G. Jung. Rascher Verlag, Zürich und Stuttgart.

Janson, T. (2017). Germanerne. Mytene, historien og språket. Pax Forlag A/S Oslo.

Jung, C.G. (1936). Wotan, in Neue Schweizer Rundschau: Wissen und Leben (March 1936), 663. GW 10.

Jung, C.G. (1938). Psychology and Religion. In CW 11: Psychology and Religion: West and East. p. 131.

Jung, C.G. (1945). Nach der Katastrophe, in: C.G. Jung – Aufsätze zur Zeitgeschichte. Zürich, Rascher, 1946, pp 73–117. GW 10.

Jung, C.G (1945). The Philosophical Tree, W 13, Alchemical Studies.

Jung, C.G. (1983). Memories, Dreams, Reflections, London.

Jung, C.G., M.-L. von Franz, Joseph L. Henderson, Jolande Jacobi, Aniela Jaffe' (1964). Man and His Symbols. Anchor Press Doubleday, New York London Toronto Sydney Auckland.

Kaufmann, C. (2007). Three-Dimensional Villains - Finding Your Character's Shadow. http://ezinearticles.com/?Three-Dimensional-Villains—-Finding-Your-Characters-Shadow&id=428279.

Kisak, P.F. (editor) (2016). Cultural Mythology. The Similarities of Mythology Across Cultures. Amazon.

Koestler, A. (1977). Introduction to Fred Uhlmans book Reunion. William Collins Sons & Co., Ltd.

Langer, J. (2002). The Origins of the Imaginary Viking. Viking Heritage Magazine, Gotland University/Centre for Baltic Studies. Visby (Sweden), n. 4.

Larrington, C. (1992). Egill's Longer Poems: Arinbjarnarkviða and Sonatorrek, an Introductory Essays on Egils saga and Njáls saga, pp. 49–63.

Larrington, C. (Trans.) (1999). The Poetic Edda, Oxford World's Classics.

Leeming, D. (2003). From Olympus to Camelot. Oxford University Press.

Lindholm, D. (1965). Götter-Schicksal Menschen-Werden. Verlag Freies Geistesleben GmbH, Stuttgart.

List, G.v. (1914). Das Geheimniss der Runen (The Secrets of the Runes). http://www.othroerirkindred.com/resources/Secret-of-the-Runes.pdf.

Maier, B. (2003). Die Religion der Germanen. Verlag C.H. Beck, München.

Metzner, R. (1994). The well of remembrance. Shambhala Publications, USA.

Murphy, G.R. (2013). Tree of Salvation: Yggdrasil and the Cross in the North. Oxford University Press.

Nemenyi, G.v. (2003). Heilige Runen. Zauberzeichen des Nordens. Ullstein Heyne List Verlag GmbH & Co KG, München.

Nemenyi, G.v. (2004). Götter, Mythen, Jahresfeste, Heidnische Naturreligion. Kersken-Canbaz Verlag. Holdenstedt.

Neumann, E. (1974). Die Große Mutter. Die weibliche Gestaltungen des Unterbewussten. Walter Verlag, Olten.

New Larousse Encyclopedia of Mythology (1959). The Hamlyn Publishing Group Limited, London/New York, Sydney, Toronto.

Nietzsche, F. (1882). Die fröhliche Wissenschaft.

Ninck, M. (1935). Wodan und der germanische Schicksalsglaube. Eugen Diederichs Verlag, Jena.

Noll, R. (1996). The Jung Cult: Origins of a Charismatic Movement. Fontana Press, London.

Normann Waage, P. (2014). Ich – Eine Kulturgeschichte des Individuums. Urachhaus, Stuttgart.

Olden-Jørgensen, S. (2001). Til Kilderne: Introduktion til Historisk Kildekritik. København. Gads Forlag.

Papadopoulos, R.K. (editor) (2012). The Handbook of Jungian Psychology: Theory, Practice and Applications. Routledge, London.

Pötzl, N.F., Saltzwedel, J. (2013). Die Germanen. Geschichte und Mythos. Deutsche Verlags Anstalt, München.

Pollan, B. (2000). Carl Gustav Jung, in Symbolene og det ubevisste. Gyldendal, Oslo.

Rasche, J. (2012). C.G. Jung in the 1930s: Not to Idealize, Neither to Diminish. Jung Journal: Culture & Psyche, 6, 54-73.

Rydberg, V. (1889). Teutonic Mythology, translated by Rasmus B. Anderson.

Rydberg, V. (2004). Investigations into Germanic Mythology, Volume 2, Parts 1 & 2, translated by William P. Reaves.

Schnurbein, S.v. (2001). Krisen der Männlichkeit. Schreiben und Geschlechterdiskurs in den Skandinavischen Romanen seit 1890. Wallstein Verlag, Göttingen.

Schnurbein, S.v. (2018). Norse Revival. Transformation of Germanic neopaganism. Haymarket Books, Chicago.

Sedgwick, D. (2002). Answer to Job Revisited: Jung on the Problem of Evil. San Francisco Jung Institute Library Journal 21, no. 3, 521.

Simek, R. (1998). Die Wikinger. Verlag C.H. Beck, München.

Simek, R. (2004). Götter und Kulte der Germanen. Verlag C.H. Beck, München.

Simek, R. (2006). Lexikon der germanischen Mythologie. Alfred Körner Verlag, Stutgart.

Skogemann, P. (1986). Arketyper. Lindhardt og Ringhof Forlag, Copenhagen.

Smith, R.J. (2008). Fathoming the Cosmos and Ordering the World: The Yijing (I Ching, or Classic of Changes) and its Evolution in China. Charlottesville, University of Virginia Press.

Steiner, R. (1974). Die Mission einzelner Volksseelen im Zusammenhang mit der germanisch-nordischen Mythologie. Rudolf Steiner Verlag, Dornach/ Schweiz.

Steinsland, G. (2005). Norrøn religion. Myter, riter, samfunn. Pax Forlag A/S, Oslo.

Stevens, A. (1994). Jung: A Brief Insight, Oxford University Press.

Stevens, A. (2012). The Archetypes. Chapter 3 in: The Handbook of Jungian Psychology: Theory, Practice and Applications, Papadopoulos, R.K. (editor), Routledge.

Stockland, O. (1969). Av Norges indre historie. Antropos, Forlag, Oslo.

Sturlason, S. (1970). Kongesagaer. Gyldendal Norsk Forlag, Oslo.

Sturluson, S. (2005). The prose Edda. Penguin Classics.

Sünner, R. (2011). Nachtmeerfahrten – Eine Reise in die Psychologie von C. G. Jung. DVD. Atalante Film, 2011, chapter Wotan's Nacht.

The Poetic Edda (1936). Translated by H. A. Bellow. Princeton University Press.

The Poetic Edda (1996). A new translation by C. Larrington. Oxford World´s Classics.

The Elder Edda: A book of Viking Lore (2011). Translated and edited by Andy Orchard. Penguin Classics.

Thurén, T. (1997). Källkritik. Stockholm: Almqvist & Wiksell.

Tjelle, I. (2015). Sterke krefter. Om blodstoppelse, lesere og hjelpere. Calliid Lagadus – Forfatternes Forlag, Karasjok.

Tolkien, J.R.R. (1937). The Hobbitt.

Tolkien, J.R.R. (1955). The Lord of the Rings.

Vasari, G. (1995). The Lives of Three Renaissance Artists. Penguin Books Ltd.

Wagner, W. (1901). Unsere Vorzeit. I. Nordisch-Germanische Götter und Helden. Verlag Otto Spamer, Leipzig.

Walter, S. (2015). Images of the Femme Fatale in Two Short Stories by Emilia Pardo Bazan. Romance Notes. Volume 55, Number 2, 177-189.

Weber, M. (1920). Gesammelte Aufsätze zur Religionssoziologie.

Weitbrecht, R. (no year). Deutsche Heldensagen. Union Deutsche Verlagsgesellschaft Stuttgart/Berlin/Leipzig.

Winroth, A. (2012). The Conversion of Scandinavia: Vikings, Merchants and Missionaries in the Remaking of Northern Europe. Yale University Press.

Winroth, A. (2014). Die Wikinger. Das Zeitalter des Nordens. Klett-Cotta.

Witoszek, N. (1998). Norske naturmysterier. Pax Forlag, Oslo.

Wolfram, H. (1995). Die Germanen. Verlag C.H. Beck, München.

Ystad, A. (2016). Frimurerne i vikingtiden. Pax Forlag, Oslo.

www.ingramcontent.com/pod-product-compliance
Lightning Source LLC
Chambersburg PA
CBHW050804270326
41926CB00025B/4536